Globalization and Human Rights in the Developing World

Global Ethics Series

Series Editor: Christien van den Anker, Reader, Department of Politics, University of the West of England, UK

Global Ethics as a field builds on longer traditions of ethical reflection about (global) society and discusses ethical approaches to global issues. These include but are not limited to issues highlighted by the process of globalization (in the widest sense) and increasing multiculturalism. They also engage with migration, the environment, poverty and inequality, peace and conflict, human rights, global citizenship, social movements, and global governance. Despite fluid boundaries between fields, Global Ethics can be clearly marked out by its multidisciplinary approach, its interest in a strong link between theory, policy, and practice and its inclusion of a range of work from the strictly normative to the more empirical.

Books in the series provide a specific normative approach, taxonomy, or an ethical position on a specific issue in Global Ethics through empirical work. They explicitly engage with Global Ethics as a field and position themselves in regard to existing debates even when outlining more local approaches or issues. The *Global Ethics Series* has been designed to reach beyond a liberal cosmopolitan agenda and engage with contextualism as well as structural analyses of injustice in current global politics and its disciplining discourses.

Titles include:

Carlos R. Cordourier-Real
TRANSNATIONAL SOCIAL JUSTICE

Anna Grear
REDIRECTING HUMAN RIGHTS
Facing the Challenge of Corporate Legal Humanity

Shahram Khosravi
'ILLEGAL' TRAVELLER
An Auto-Ethnography of Borders

Ivan Manokha (*editor*)
THE POLITICAL ECONOMY OF HUMAN RIGHTS ENFORCEMENT

Darrel Moellendorf
GLOBAL INEQUALITY MATTERS

Derrick M. Nault and Shawn L. England (*editors*)
GLOBALIZATION AND HUMAN RIGHTS IN THE DEVELOPING WORLD

Global Ethics Series
Series Standing Order ISBN 978–0–230–01958–4
(*outside North America only*)

You can receive future titles in this series as they are published by placing a standing order. Please contact your bookseller or, in case of difficulty, write to us at the address below with your name and address, the title of the series and the ISBN quoted above.

Customer Services Department, Macmillan Distribution Ltd, Houndmills, Basingstoke, Hampshire RG21 6XS, England

Globalization and Human Rights in the Developing World

Edited by

Derrick M. Nault
Instructor, University of Calgary, Canada

Shawn L. England
Assistant Professor, Mount Royal University, Canada

First published 2011 by
PALGRAVE MACMILLAN

Palgrave Macmillan in the UK is an imprint of Macmillan Publishers Limited, registered in England, company number 785998, of Houndmills, Basingstoke, Hampshire RG21 6XS.

Palgrave Macmillan in the US is a division of St Martin's Press LLC, 175 Fifth Avenue, New York, NY 10010.

Palgrave Macmillan is the global academic imprint of the above companies and has companies and representatives throughout the world.

Palgrave® and Macmillan® are registered trademarks in the United States, the United Kingdom, Europe and other countries.

ISBN 978–0–230–29220–8 hardback

This book is printed on paper suitable for recycling and made from fully managed and sustained forest sources. Logging, pulping and manufacturing processes are expected to conform to the environmental regulations of the country of origin.

A catalogue record for this book is available from the British Library.

Library of Congress Cataloging-in-Publication Data
Globalization and human rights in the developing world / edited by
  Derrick M. Nault, Shawn L. England.
     p. cm.
  Includes bibliographical references and index.
  ISBN 978–0–230–29220–8 (alk. paper)
   1. Human rights—Developing countries. 2. Globalization—
  Developing countries. 3. Human rights and globalization—
  Developing countries. I. Nault, Derrick M. II. England, Shawn L.
  JC599.D44G56 2011
  323.09172′4—dc22   2011012071

10   9   8   7   6   5   4   3   2   1
20 19 18 17 16 15 14 13 12 11

Printed and bound in Great Britain by
CPI Antony Rowe, Chippenham and Eastbourne

Contents

List of Tables

Preface

This volume is the product of a conference entitled *Globalization and Human Rights in the Developing World* that was held at the University of Calgary in Calgary, Alberta, Canada, on March 21–22, 2009. Organized under the auspices of the Asia Association for Global Studies (AAGS), a scholarly association based in Osaka, Japan, the event saw scholars from 21 nations present papers on a wide range of themes related to the impact and significance of globalization for the human rights of peoples in Asia, Africa, the Middle East, and Latin America.

The event and this resulting book were made possible through the combined efforts of many people. Dr. Tamara Seiler, former Head of the Department of Communication and Culture, was instrumental in securing much-needed financial support as well as helping publicize the conference. Dr. Aradhana Parmar, on behalf of the Development Studies Program at the University of Calgary, also helped locate funding and provided much-appreciated moral support. Janet Keeping, of the Sheldon Chumir Foundation, delivered a thought-provoking keynote speech that set the tone for the gathering. Dr. Denise Brown, coordinator of the Latin American Studies Program at the University of Calgary, welcomed delegates with warmth and enthusiasm to the university while also arranging for a contingent of Latin American specialists to present papers. Also helping to make the event a success were Bibiana Cala, Erwin Blanco, Brenda McDermott, Hans Peter Liederbach, and Keiji Fujimura. Finally, the paper presenters and attendees at the conference deserve special thanks, particularly for braving inclement weather in the form of an unexpected snowstorm on the second day of the gathering.

Derrick M. Nault
Shawn L. England

Notes on Contributors

Bei Dawei has doctorates in comparative religion from the California Institute of Integral Studies (CIIS) and philosophy from the University of South Africa (UNISA). An assistant professor in the foreign language department of Hsuan Chuang University in Hsinchu, Taiwan, he is interested in such subjects as Western esoteric traditions, new religious movements, Central Asia and Tibet, artificial languages, linguistic human rights, Western/Eastern cultural interactions, and alternate history.

Shawn L. England specializes in Latin American political history. His research, based on archival investigations in Mexico City, analyzes the complexities underlying the military professionalization that developed concurrent with the solidification of Mexico's revolutionary state in the years 1920–1940. His interest in Mexico's civil-military relations is intimately connected to his concern regarding militarization more generally, and the dire threat this process often poses to human rights throughout the world. In addition to his work on military rule in Mexico, Dr. England has also investigated the area of federal policy concerning indigenous peoples in both the United States and Canada. He has taught Latin American history and international relations at the University of Calgary in Calgary, Canada and was recently appointed as an assistant professor in the Department of History at Mount Royal University, also in Calgary.

Maureen S. Hiebert is Assistant Professor of Political Science and Law and Society at the University of Calgary, Calgary, Alberta, Canada. She currently teaches courses in comparative politics (Asia) and socio-legal studies. Her research interests include comparative genocide theory and methodology, the Holocaust, the Cambodian genocide, comparative politics, processes of elite decision-making, international humanitarian law, and international criminal law. Recent publications include: "The Three 'Switches' of Identity Construction in Genocide: The Nazi Final Solution and the Cambodian Killing Fields," *Genocide Studies and Prevention* (2008); "Theorizing Destruction: Reflections on the State of Comparative Genocide Theory," *Genocide Studies and Prevention* (2008);

and "Genocide in Chile? An Assessment" (co-authored with Pablo Policzer), in *State Violence and Genocide in Latin America: The Cold War Years* (2010).

Adugna Lemi is an Assistant Professor of Economics at the University of Massachusetts Boston. He currently teaches courses in economic development, international trade, and international political economy, both at the graduate and undergraduate levels. His publications mainly focus on the determinants of US FDI in Africa, the role of economic and political volatility, the role of taxation in intra-firm trade, and poverty in Africa in general and in Ethiopia in particular. His works have appeared in the *African Finance Journal, International Trade Journal, Journal of Economic Development, Eastern Economic Journal, Journal of Global Awareness,* and *Journal of Agricultural Economics.* He is currently researching the issue of poverty dynamics in Africa as well as the impact of capital flows on governance in Africa.

Derrick M. Nault is a former visiting professor of Seoul National University, Korea and Kwansei Gakuin University, Japan. The founder and former president of the Asia Association for Global Studies (AAGS), a scholarly organization based in Japan, Dr. Nault is currently its Director as well as the Editor in Chief of the *Asia Journal of Global Studies* (AJGS), the association's official journal. In addition to assuming these duties, Dr. Nault lectures in world history and development studies at the University of Calgary in Calgary, Canada. His research interests include globalization, development, and human rights from a historical perspective, particularly with regard to nations of the Global South.

Browne Onuoha is an Associate Professor of Political Science at the University of Lagos in Lagos, Nigeria. His areas of specialization are comparative politics, public policy, and political economy. His latest publication is *Transition Politics in Nigeria, 1979–1999* (2002) (co-edited with Dr M. M. Fadakite). Currently, he is conducting research on policy reforms in Africa and security concerns in the Gulf of Guinea in West Africa.

Onyeka Osuji is a lecturer in Law at the University of Exeter, Cornwall Campus, United Kingdom. He has published numerous articles and book chapters. His published articles have been on the subjects of corporate social responsibility, non-financial reporting, transnational corporations, and globalization. He has published in such journals as the *Journal of Business Ethics* and the *Journal of Knowledge Globalization.*

Rab Paterson is a lecturer at the International Christian University in Tokyo and a part-time lecturer at Dokkyo University's Faculty of International Liberal Arts where he teaches courses on international affairs, globalization, and media studies. He is also in the final stages of his PhD at Waseda University's Graduate School for Asia Pacific Studies where his research focuses on missile defense and its role in US foreign policy in Asia. His publications and presentations have been on subjects such as US foreign policy, missile defense, globalization, media studies, and direct democracy. He is currently researching the spread of direct democracy in the developing world as a challenge to US economic and political hegemony.

Patrick Strefford is a lecturer in International Relations at Kyoto Sangyo University, Japan. Since graduating in political science from the Graduate School of International Cooperation Studies, Kobe University, Patrick has published articles on the humanitarian crisis in Myanmar, on international assistance to Myanmar, and on Japanese ODA to Myanmar/Burma. His research interests include foreign aid and development, Japanese ODA, and economic and political development in Myanmar. He is currently working on a survey of Japanese government-financed foreign students in Japan.

Evangelos Voulgarakis specializes in symbols of national and religious heritage in contemporary times. He has examined modern interpretations of ancient Greek democracy and drama for the purpose of social activism and conducted research on comparative religious rhetoric in relation to femininity and national identity. His doctoral dissertation was entitled *The Perception and Utilization of Symbols of American Heritage by the United States Neo-militia Movement and its Critics.* Since 1999, he has taught American and British history courses in the UK in addition to the history of English literature, Greek mythology, and other courses on language-related subjects at the Chih Lee Institute of Science and Technology in Taiwan. Dr. Voulgarakis' current research focus is linguistic human rights as well as immigration policies and trends in Greece. He is a member of the editorial team of the *Asia Journal of Global Studies* (AJGS), the official journal of the Asia Association for Global Studies (AAGS).

Biagio Zammitto has been an attorney at the Brussels Bar for the last five years. He decided to focus his career on human rights issues by dedicating his research to the role of transnational companies in a globalized world and to the international liability of states, both of which were the subjects of a memorandum he wrote at the end of his Master's in Human Rights for Professor Olivier De Schutter, UN Special Rapporteur on the right to food.

1
Introduction

Derrick M. Nault

Globalization as an area of scholarly inquiry has generated a voluminous literature (Berger and Huntington, 2002; Bhagwati, 2007; Held and McGrew, 2007; Scholte, 2005; Steger, 2003). So too has human rights (Davies, 1988; Freeman, 2002; Griffin, 2008; Power and Allison, 2006), a vast field with an even longer history (Hunt, 2007; Ishay, 2004). It comes as somewhat of a surprise, therefore, to discover that relatively few books have explicitly focused on the interrelationship of globalization and human rights.[1]

Perhaps the lack of works on globalization and human rights might be explained by the ubiquitous and often imprecise use of the term "globalization." As might be expected when large numbers of people discuss an issue by employing a word that can mean "anything, everything and nothing" (Munck, 2000, p. 84), not all that has been written on globalization is informative or insightful. In fact, some critics have gone so far as to dismiss debates on globalization as "globaloney" (Veseth, 2006), "global babble" (Abu-Lughod, 1997), and intellectual "folly" (Rosenberg, 2002). But if much theorizing on globalization has been vague or unhelpful, this in itself does not offer sufficient justification for jettisoning the term. Indeed, as Scholte (2005) observes, it could suggest the reverse—that much more work remains to be done in terms of refining concepts and gathering evidence to assess the meaning and implications of globalization (p. xvii).

In spite of its contested nature, globalization remains a useful term for describing a process that commenced around the sixteenth century CE. Since the time of Columbus' first explorations, all the world's major regions have been increasingly drawn into a global system of commercial, cultural, and ecological exchanges that has drastically transformed how human beings live and view the world around them. The Spanish

Conquest, the transportation of slaves from Africa to the Americas, the establishment of British East India Company rule in South Asia, the Partition of Africa by the European powers, and World Wars I and II are but a few examples of the power of globalization to interpenetrate and shape human lifeworlds. In our own time, technological advances in transportation, information technology, and communications mean that an earthquake-related disaster in Haiti can generate sympathy and attract millions of dollars in donations from around the world ("Haiti Donations Exceed $644 Million," 2010), a volcanic eruption in Iceland can cause devastating economic losses for a flower industry in Kenya (Pflantz, 2010), a 47-year-old spinster from Scotland can become a worldwide singing sensation as a result of an online video clip from a British talent show (Parry, 2009), and the leader of a small fundamentalist Islamic group can orchestrate a terrorist plot from a remote region of Afghanistan that kills nearly 3000 persons in the United States and continues to influence the foreign policy of the world's most powerful nation (Wright, 2007).

As the above examples attest, globalization has been taking place for several centuries and continues to have far-reaching implications for human populations worldwide. However, there are still areas of inquiry in the scholarly literature on globalization that remain insufficiently developed. One such gap in the literature concerns human rights. The Universal Declaration of Human Rights (UDHR), proclaimed by the United Nations in 1948, may maintain that "the inherent dignity and...the equal and inalienable rights of all members of the human family is the foundation of freedom, justice and peace in the world" (as cited in Morsink, 2000, p. 313), yet how human rights can be enforced internationally, what human rights-related institutions and policies are appropriate on a global scale, and how human rights are affected by contemporary worldwide economic, political, and cultural exchanges are issues that globalization researchers have barely begun exploring. Indeed, the noted political scientist and human rights expert Jack Donnelly has opined that "a surprisingly small percentage" of works within the "immense" literature on globalization have explicitly focused on the relationship of globalization to human rights (Donnelly, 2007, p. 210). Monshipouri, Englehart, Nathan and Philip, (2003) concur, adding that "The linkage between human rights and globalization is far from obvious and theories that link them are underdeveloped" (p. xxvi).

The purpose of this edited volume is to explore the relevance of globalization for human rights in the developing world, also known as the Global South. The reason for this focus is simply that the dignity, well-being, and freedom of individuals are most at risk in countries that have yet to achieve developed nation status. Unemployment, socioeconomic inequality, inadequate access to healthcare and education, and limited or absent political freedoms pose threats to human rights in both developed and developing nations, but they present particularly grave challenges for peoples in Sub-Saharan Africa, Asia, the Middle East, and Latin America—the world regions that are covered in this book. It is here where populations arguably have the most to lose or gain through globalization. If globalization is managed effectively, it potentially could lift millions out of poverty while granting them greater political freedoms; if, on the other hand, it forms part of a hegemonic project that merely advances Western or other narrow economic and political interests, then vast numbers of the world's citizens stand to see what limited rights they may currently hold eroded yet further. In addition to examining what impact globalization is actually having on human rights in the Global South, what actions should be taken to support and extend rights in the developing world in an era of globalization is also a question that this book seeks to answer.

Defining human rights

Given the theme of this volume, it is appropriate to first define what is meant by human rights. Human rights can be defined in numerous ways, but they are generally thought of as rights that people possess by virtue of being human. Such rights are said to apply to everyone, irrespective of gender, religion, ethnicity, occupation, level of wealth, or national origin. Universal for all times and places, regardless of what governments may do or what laws may be in place, human rights can never be abrogated or taken away. They are essential for and due to everyone if they are to live dignified lives. As defined by Schmitz and Sikkink (2002):

> Human rights are a set of principled ideas about the treatment to which individuals are entitled by virtue of being human. Over time, these ideas have gained widespread acceptance as international norms defining what was necessary for humans to thrive, both in terms of being protected from abuses and provided with the elements to live a life in dignity.... The human right discourse is universal in character and includes claims of equality and non-discrimination. (p. 517)

To further understand what is meant by human rights it is helpful to divide rights into categories. A distinction is often made between two "generations" of human rights—so-called first-generation and second-generation rights. The former refer to political and civil rights. Generally speaking, these rights are meant to protect individuals from state oppression in the form of torture, lack of free speech and political assembly, and arbitrary arrest and detention. First-generation rights derive their name from the fact that they were the first to appear in official documents, the American Declaration of Independence (1776) and French Declaration of the Rights of Man and of the Citizen (1789) being two well-known examples (Wellman, 1999, p. 16). Second-generation rights, as their name implies, are of more recent origin. Inspired by working-class struggles for social justice in industrial Europe in the nineteenth century (Ishay, 2004, pp. 118–172), this generation of rights is economic and social in orientation, emphasizing the right to employment, an adequate standard of living, education, healthcare, and social security.

More recently, a third-generation of rights, linked to independence and post-independence movements in the former "Third World" has been proposed. The aims of these rights are group-oriented and include the right to development, the right to peace, the right to a clean environment, and others. Kabasakal Arat (2006) notes that third-generation rights are often invoked on behalf of people in developing nations who are "struggling against poverty, perpetual warfare, and deteriorating environmental conditions" (p. 39). Karel Vasak, a former chief legal officer with the United Nations Educational, Scientific and Cultural Organization (UNESCO), is credited with initially proposing these rights in the late 1970s. Vasak referred to them as "solidarity rights," emphasizing that they could only be achieved through the combined efforts of individuals, states, groups and organizations in civil society, and the international community (Brems, 2001, p. 482).

Different opinions exist in terms of the validity of these human rights categories as well as the rights themselves. The authors of the UDHR, for example, saw first- and second-generation rights as indivisible (Donnelly, 2003, p. 67). Others maintain that only first-generation rights are acceptable notions as they can be realistically implemented and enforced. Cranston (1973/2002) is of this opinion, arguing that as the first category of rights merely require governments to exercise restraint by not interfering in citizens' lives, they are readily legislated; however, he maintains that "This is no longer the case when we turn to the 'right to work,' the 'right to social security,' and so forth," with such claims especially "vain and idle" for peoples in developing nations (p. 50).

Heinze (1995) observes that if certain reservations have been expressed toward the concept of second-generation rights, the response to third-generation rights has often been one of "outright contempt" (p. 83). An argument often made against the most recent addition to the human rights pantheon is that they represent a possible dilution and devaluation of core rights. To quote Heinze (1995): "[C]ritics fear that if 'everything,' every 'good cause,' becomes elevated to a human right, then human rights lose their distinctiveness among human goods. The more rights there are, the less, it is feared, each right is worth" (p. 83). Other arguments made against third-generation rights are that such rights are not feasible, given the limited resources of the international community, or that advocating them will only lead to disillusionment when such rights go unfulfilled (Wellman, 2002, p. 383).

While scholars will continue to debate how human rights should be defined, the view that certain rights should be supported over others merits a critical response. Indeed, rather than prioritizing or disregarding particular rights, all three generations of rights should be seen as mutually supportive. That these generations of rights are interdependent has been increasingly recognized by UN member states in international agreements. The Vienna Declaration of Human Rights in 1993, for example, states that "all human rights are universal, indivisible and interdependent and interrelated," calling on the international community to "treat human rights globally in a fair and equal manner, on the same footing, and with the same emphasis" (as cited in Donnelly, 2003, p. 188). Critics may be right to point out difficulties in implementing certain generations of rights, but that does not make the aims of such rights any less valid, nor does it make the eventual construction of a workable international legal framework supportive of such rights impossible or something for which we should not strive.

In assessing the validity of particular generations of rights, it is also important to note the power relations behind particular rights emphases. During the Cold War, US reluctance to support economic and social rights while advocating civil and political rights starkly contrasted with Soviet policy, which favored the former over the latter. The support each side gave to particular rights was not based on the inherent value of certain rights over others but rather on ideological and geopolitical considerations (Cumper, 1999, pp. 6–7). In a similar vein, Washington's apparent indifference regarding poor nations' "right to development" does not indicate that such a third-generation right is impractical or undesirable in itself, but rather that conservative forces within the United States fear the creation of a more just and equitable world order in which their interests would not prevail (Felice, 2003, pp. 49–50).

We must not, therefore, accept criticisms of any generation of rights at face value. Rather, the economic and political influences behind such viewpoints should first be assessed, and we should search for ways around obstacles that may impede the realization of all generations of rights. The idea that only certain rights deserve our support, while more desirable than a vision of a world where individuals are accorded no rights, is surely too narrow a focus if we are truly serious about creating a more just, peaceful, and sustainable world.

The origins of human rights

Having defined human rights, we now turn to the question of where human rights come from. On this note, the usual response is that human rights have Western origins. Natural law theories from the seventeenth century, eighteenth-century revolutions in Europe and the American colonies, or the leading role played by the United States and other Western nations in the founding of the United Nations in 1945 are just a few examples from world history that have been cited to support the belief that human rights are a Western innovation. The American human rights theorist Jack Donnelly, one of the most ardent exponents of the Western origins thesis, states: "[T]he Western origins of human rights is a simple historical fact. Human rights initially emerged—were created or 'discovered'—in Europe..." (Donnelly, 1999a, p. 69). Mayer (2002) similarly accepts that "The human rights principles utilized in international law came from the West and are of relatively recent vintage" (p. 120).

While the West has undeniably made vital contributions to the evolution of human rights theory and practice, the notion that it alone "created" or "discovered" human rights and the corresponding principles for international laws is unhelpful and misleading in two respects. First, if human rights are truly universal, it is important to find common ground among cultures and civilizations when determining how rights have evolved over time. Authors who do not accept a shared history of human rights among the world's peoples inadvertently give credence to cultural relativist arguments that contemporary human rights norms represent a Western imposition on non-Western societies. Second, an emphasis on human rights' Western origins obscures how the historical struggles of peoples in the Global South against Western imperialism and colonialism have helped shape present-day human rights discourses and international legal frameworks. In this regard, human rights were not something simply invented in the West and bequeathed to people in the developing world. They were fought for through protest and resistance throughout world history. In other words, the human rights concepts and practices we know today did not germinate in self-contained Western settings from where they flowed outward to the global community.

Ethics and human relations: early contributions

An appropriate starting point for understanding the origins and evolution of human rights is to first look for the earliest expressions of ethics in human relations. Although pre-modern ethics and today's human rights concepts and practices are by no means synonymous, it can nonetheless be argued that human rights in their present form would not exist if pre-modern precursors were not expressed in the form of specific moral codes and even legal frameworks. To argue, therefore, that early affirmations of human dignity bear no relation to human rights as we now know them (Donnelly, 1990b, p. 256) fails to acknowledge their crucial role in the evolution of human rights concepts.

Many world religions in this regard possess ethical features with roots anticipating contemporary human rights discourse by hundreds of years (Traer, 1991). Buddhism, Christianity, and Islam are three prominent examples of religions with non-Western origins that are compatible with human rights. Each of these religions asks adherents to show compassion for fellow human beings, refrain from inflicting harm on others, and perform charitable works. Of course, the language of human rights is not fully developed in early writings associated with these and other world religions, yet they nonetheless contain embryonic features of what we presently understand as human rights.

Buddhism, with origins in India that date back to 500 BCE, is based on five precepts, four of which correlate with human rights. The five precepts are as follows: (1) Do not kill; (2) Do not steal; (3) Do not engage in sexual misconduct; (4) Do not make false speech; and (5) Do not take intoxicants. As argued by Keown (2002), "A direct translation of the first four precepts yields a right to life, a right not to have one's property stolen, a right to fidelity in marriage, and a right not to be lied to" (p. 192). Keown argues further that other rights "such as the rights to liberty and security can either be deduced from or are extant within the general corps of Buddhist teachings," citing the "right not to be held in slavery" as "implicit in the canonical prohibition on trade in living beings" (p. 192). He rightly concludes that human rights were "not 'imported' into Buddhism but were implicitly present" (p. 192).

Given the West's Judeo-Christian heritage, the ethical foundations of Christianity have occasionally been cited as evidence of human rights' early Western origins (D'Souza, 2007, pp. 67–82). Here, a correlation is made with contemporary human rights ideas and biblical scriptures. Among passages from the Bible that are seen as relating to human rights are those that refer to the sanctity and dignity of all human beings, injunctions for the able to help the poor and suffering, and codes forbidding the taking of human life, deception, theft, and other acts that inflict harm on others. Such references can be interpreted to mean that the Christian religion has had a significant impact on the evolution of human rights thought. However, to suggest that Christianity's roots are strictly Western is somewhat misleading as the earliest centers and believers of Christianity were not in fact located in the West but in Palestine, Syria, Iraq, and Africa (Hart, 2009, p. 443). In this sense, Christianity's contribution to human rights, while important, should be seen as part of a global heritage, not something that can be attributed to Western civilization per se.

Turning to Islam, various Islamic scholars have argued that Islam is not only compatible with human rights but that Western contributions to human rights are derived from Islamic traditions. While such claims cannot be proven without doubt (Mayer, 2002, p. 122), passages from the Qur'an do contain directives on justice, the sanctity of life, religious freedom, and tolerance (Ishay, 2004, p. 34). According to Hassan (2005), the Qur'an also "consistently affirms women's equality with men and their fundamental right to actualize the human potential that they share equally with men" (p. 57). Elsewhere, Hassan (1999) interprets passages from the Qur'an as implying a "right to life," "right to respect," "right to justice," "right to freedom," "right to privacy," "right to acquire knowledge," "right to sustenance," and "right to work" (p. 54). Finally, the Qur'an stresses the unity of humankind, describing the world's diverse races and languages as an expression of God's will. No race or culture is viewed as superior to another, with piety seen as more important than one's origins (Kinberg, 2006, pp. 458–459).

In addition to the above precursors to human rights, numerous scholars have suggested that traditional societies, such as those that once existed in Africa, established behavioral norms and legal codes that are relevant for human rights. Claude E. Welch, Jr (1984), for example, argues that long before the advent of Europeans, Africans valued "the right to life, the right to education, the right to freedom of movement, the right to receive justice, the right to work, and the right to participate in the benefits and decision making of the community" (p. 11). Mutua (2002) mentions the Akans of West Africa and the Akamba of East Africa as two traditional societies that had notions of such rights. According to Mutua, "The belief prevailed in both societies that, as an inherently valuable being, the individual was naturally endowed with certain basic rights" (p. 76). Decisions affecting Akan communities were based on deliberations within an elected council followed by discussions with constituents, who could dismiss leaders they felt did not respect their opinions and needs. When an Akamba person appeared in court, he or she did so before a council of elders and a jury. The jurors, who were conversant in Akamba law, did not hand down judgments but advised the defendant as to what arguments they might use to plead their case. After deliberations in this fashion, elders would render a verdict and call for appropriate settlements such as payment in cattle, land, or labor (pp. 76–77).

That pre-modern, non-Western peoples had the capacity for understanding and respecting rights of some kind can further be gathered from accounts of enlightened leaders who based their rule on ideals of peace and tolerance. Among the most remarkable figures in this respect was Ashoka the Great, who ruled over most of India from 304 to 232 BCE. On stone tablets scattered throughout his kingdom, Ashoka promoted wise governance, righteous behavior, and acceptance of all religious faiths. The Mughal Emperor Akbar governed India in a similar spirit in the sixteenth century CE, when he decreed that "No man should be interfered with on account of religion, and anyone is to be allowed to go over to a religion that pleases him" (as cited in Sen, 2005, p. 18). Notably, at the time Akbar was promoting religious pluralism in India, the Inquisitions in Europe—which witnessed the mass persecution, killing, and expulsion of Jews and Muslims—"were in full bloom" (Sen, 2001, p. 139).

To be sure, to suggest that human rights have existed in their present form since time immemorial would be an exaggeration. Indeed, premodern societies—whether Western or non-Western—were more often characterized by their indifference to than support of human rights. Nevertheless it can be argued that the inklings of human rights notions were in evidence in many regions of the non-Western world long before pivotal events such as the European Enlightenment and the American and French Revolutions. Noting these precursors to human rights is important, for it demonstrates the potential of all members of the human family to understand and support human rights, not just those in Western nations. As will be discussed below, recognizing how subjugated peoples struggled against Western domination is also crucial for understanding how the story of human rights is one shared by all of humanity.

Human rights struggles

As the Spanish were the first Europeans to colonize regions of the New World, commencing their rule in what is today the Caribbean and Latin America, it is here where ethical questions concerning the domination of peoples in foreign lands were first raised. The sixteenth-century Dominican priest Bartolomé de Las Casas, moved by the sufferings of indigenous peoples in Hispaniola and Cuba at the hands of Europeans, was among the first critics of Spanish colonial rule, writing scathing commentaries on settlers' barbarities while calling on King Charles V to implement drastic reforms. The New Laws for the Indies that were promulgated by the Crown to curb Indian slavery and abuses under the *encomienda* system were not singlehandedly brought about by Las Casas, yet contemporary historians generally agree that the changes were heavily influenced by his writings and petitions to the Crown (Zamora, 1993, p. 40).

Moreover, as a result of Las Casas' and other priests' criticisms of Spanish rule, Charles V convened a meeting in 1550 at Valladolid for a series of debates between Las Casas and the theologian Juan Ginés de Sepúlveda, which were among the earliest in existence on human rights. Defending the natives against Spanish aggression, Las Casas argued that Indians were rational members of the human family who did not deserve inhumane treatment. Sepúlveda, on the other hand, depicted Native Americans as barbarians, heathens, and inferiors that the Spanish were bound by duty to enslave and forcibly convert to Christianity. While no official decision resulted from the debate, the questions raised by Las Casas nonetheless prompted the Spanish to reflect on issues of social justice in their colonies. Moreover, the human rights tradition in Latin America can be considered as beginning with Las Casas. For his role in the debates and his other activities, he is aptly referred to as the "Father of human rights" (Duffey, 2001, p. 6).

At the time of Las Casas' protests and petitions, capitalism was just beginning to spread from Europe to other regions of the globe. In this regard, the enslaved Indians that the Dominican priest sought to protect were among the front lines of those exploited to meet an escalating demand for luxury goods and raw materials emanating from Western

Europe. By the seventeenth century, however, it would not be Indians but Africans who would provide the greatest source of slave labor to fuel the growth of capitalism. With Europeans in the Americas finding that Africans were resistant to the diseases devastating Indian populations, easier to control than local slaves, and relatively cheap to replace, an industry was spawned whereby European traders increasingly visited points along the West African coast to secure supplies of African slaves for plantations and mines in the Americas. By the time the slave trade was completely abolished in the late nineteenth century, it was estimated that at least 10 million Africans had been taken from their homelands, transported across the Atlantic Ocean, and sold into slavery (Thomas, 1997, p. 861).

Accounts on the end of the slave trade have tended to emphasize the role outsiders or outside forces played in the process. On the one hand, a great debt is said to be owed to the anti-slavery campaigns of European and American abolitionists (Miers, 2003, p. 4). On the other hand, the changing character and needs of global capitalism are stressed, with the argument being that the key reason for the slave trade's demise was that free labor was more cost-efficient than slave labor (Williams, 1944/1994). Less frequently discussed is how slaves and former slaves induced change through public persuasion and resistance, in the process transforming the slave trade into an international human rights issue.

In Great Britain, Olaudah Equiano was the most well-known former slave who used his ability to speak and write in English to convey his abolitionist viewpoints. An Igbo who was captured as a boy in what is today Southern Nigeria and sold into slavery in Barbados, then Virginia, and finally England, Equiano eventually was able to learn how to read and write, and purchased his freedom. In 1789, he wrote *The Interesting Narrative of the Life of Olaudah Equiano, or Gustavus Vassa, the African, Written by Himself*, which discussed his memories of Africa and, important for the abolitionist cause, the horrors of the middle passage and slavery (Equiano, 1789/2003). Equiano was a prominent member of the Sons of Africa, an abolitionist group of African men in England who included Ottobah Cugoano and Ignatius Sancho, two other former slaves who also expressed their anti-slavery viewpoints in books, articles, petitions, and public speeches. Equiano and the group were instrumental in raising awareness of the plight of slaves, working closely with and greatly influencing British abolitionists and anti-slavery associations (Gordon, 2000, p. 58).

In the Caribbean and Americas, resistance to slavery assumed numerous forms.[2] However, runaway communities and their potential to destabilize slave-based economies proved particularly troubling to slave owners. Europeans' greatest fears were realized in Saint Domingue (today Haiti) shortly after the outbreak of the French Revolution in 1789, when the former slave Toussaint L'Ouverture led a series of uprisings aimed at toppling the colonial plantation system. Although L'Ouverture died in a French prison, other leaders continued the anti-slavery struggle, winning Saint Domingue's freedom in 1803. The effects of this victory would reverberate throughout the Caribbean, the Americas, and Africa. Frederick Douglass, the African American abolitionist and former slave, asserted in 1893 that "the freedom that has come to the colored race the world over" was "largely due to the brave stand taken by the black sons of Haiti ninety years ago." Douglass praised the work of American and British abolitionists and slave societies, but nonetheless stressed that "we owe comparably more to Haiti than to them all" (as cited in Davis, 2001, p. 3).[3]

Donnelly (2007) observes that "a dramatic event that crystalizes awareness often is crucial to making a problem an active subject of international concern and action" (p. 4), suggesting that the Holocaust was the "catalyst that made human rights an issue in world politics" (p. 4). While the Holocaust shocked world opinion and resulted in genocide being declared a crime punishable under international law,[4] it was in fact the transatlantic slave trade and its abolition that first galvanized global public opinion and led to significant changes in international relations and human rights. The first notable development occurred in 1807, when Great Britain passed the Act for the Abolition of the Slave Trade. With this Act, the British navy was granted the authority to actively suppress the slave trade by boarding suspect vessels and releasing captives. Britain subsequently signed a series of bilateral treaties that granted signatory nations similar inspection and release rights. International courts were also convened on both sides of the Atlantic to monitor cases involving slave-trading vessels (Fyfe, 1986, pp. 179–180). The Slavery Abolition Act of 1833 dealt yet another blow to the slave trade by abolishing slavery throughout the British Empire. It took some time for these measures to be felt worldwide, but along with slave resistance and public opinion they helped end the slave trade and slavery in French colonies in 1848, in Cuba in 1860, in the southern United States in 1865, and in Brazil in 1888.

While efforts to end the slave trade raised awareness of human rights issues on a global scale, the anti-slavery struggle turned out to be the beginning of a longer battle of oppressed peoples against Western imperialism and colonial rule. Although Latin American nations had achieved their independence from Spain and Portugal by 1824, by the 1880s the Indian subcontinent was firmly under British rule, Africa was on the verge of being partitioned by the European powers, and regions of East Asia had already fallen prey to what was to be the first wave of numerous European expansionist ventures. Examples of human rights abuses linked to Western nations' domination of their formal and informal empires are too numerous to recount here. However, among the most blatant were Great Britain's Opium Wars in China (1839–42, 1856–60), the mutilation and murder of Africans who did not meet rubber quotas in King Leopold's Congo (1885–1908), the genocide perpetrated by Germans against the Herero people in German South West Africa (modern-day Namibia) (1904–7), the British massacre of unarmed Indians at Amritsar in 1919, and institutionalized racial segregation in South Africa.

Rather than representing a humanitarian act on the part of colonial powers, the independence of India in 1947, Ghana in 1957, and numerous African nations in the 1960s was the result of years of protests and resistance on the part of oppressed peoples. In India, the Non-Cooperation Movement of 1919–20 witnessed a concerted assault against the Rowlatt Acts, a body of laws that restricted press freedoms and allowed for the arbitrary arrest of suspected political dissenters. Gandhi's Salt March in 1929, which ended in the arrest of 90,000 Indians as well as their leader, symbolically sought greater economic freedoms for Indians by attempting to break Britain's monopoly on salt. With Great Britain still reluctant to meet Indians' demands for further autonomy and improved human rights, the Quit India Movement, launched in 1942, sought complete independence for India. At this time, Gandhi implored his countrymen to "act as if you are free and are no longer under the heel of this imperialism," stressing that "We shall either free India or die in the attempt; we shall not live to see the perpetuation of our slavery" (as cited in Gandhi, 2008, p. 467).

The struggle for independence in Africa involved similar acts of defiance against colonial authority and assertions of human dignity. As early as 1915 in the midst of World War I, John Chilembwe, a mission-educated African, questioned why Africans should fight and die in a war that was not in their interests, and led an abortive rebellion in Nyasaland in which he sacrificed his life for the cause of African independence (Collins and Burns, 2007, pp. 331–332). In the 1930s, the Nigerian publication *West African Pilot*, inspired by African Americans' civil rights struggles, decried the hypocrisy of colonial rule in Africa.[5] Among the most well-known advocates of African independence was the Ghanaian leader Kwame Nkrumah, who asserted that "We prefer self-government with danger to servitude in tranquility" (as cited in Farlnger, 1991, p. 18). Nkrumah not only played a key role in achieving independence for Ghana in 1957, but he was also instrumental in promoting Pan-Africanism and Third World solidarity through his writings and speeches, and through international diplomacy as independent Ghana's first president (Birmingham, 1998).

Despite the indignities experienced by peoples under colonialism, it was not until the events of World War II that international attention focused on human rights on a scale matching that of the abolitionist era. In August, 1941, American President Franklin D. Roosevelt and British Prime Minister Winston Churchill met aboard a warship off the coast of Newfoundland and issued a joint declaration affirming that they supported "the right of all peoples to choose the form of government under which they will live," the right to "improved living standards, economic advancement, and social security," and the right of the world's peoples to "live out their lives in freedom from want and fear" (as cited in Lauren, 2003, p. 23). Later dubbed "The Atlantic Charter," the document was viewed in many quarters as a tacit promise of independence and recognition of the rights of colonial subjects. When Churchill claimed that such rights were not intended for British colonies, African and South Asian intellectuals, roundly condemning his words as contradictory and hypocritical, pledged to step up their efforts to achieve independence (Vohra, 2000, p. 163).[6]

That World War II was crucial for the emergence of the United Nations, its subsequent focus on human rights, and our contemporary international human rights framework cannot be denied. However, as shown above, it would be wrong to ignore the human rights contributions and struggles of non-Western peoples in earlier eras. It is equally misleading to suggest that the international human rights regime that emerged following World War II was strictly a Western intellectual and legal project.

It bears mentioning, first of all, that World War II was a world war, not one fought strictly in Europe or with European troops. While the war began as a European conflict, battles in the air, on the sea, and on land soon raged across Asia, North Africa, and the Middle East, in addition to various fronts in Europe. By the time of America's entry into the war in late 1941, notes Roberts (1999), "Only a tiny minority of countries were left out of this vast conflict" (p. 425). The global nature of the conflict meant that soldiers were drawn from a wide array of nations. The British deployed some 374,000 African soldiers, who served in places such as Somalia, Ethiopia, Madagascar, and Burma. France similarly shipped 80,000 African soldiers to France to fight Germany (Meredith, 2006, pp. 8–9). Britain's Indian Army, the largest volunteer military force ever assembled in world history, included some 2 million soldiers who fought in East Africa, the Mediterranean, and Burma (Killingray, 1999, p. 10). In the end, the defeat of fascism was not just a victory for Britain, France, and the United States but also for colonial peoples, who through their military contributions and demands for social justice shattered the myth of European racial superiority (Aicardi de Saint-Paul, 1989, pp. 14–15).

The United Nations was officially founded on June 26, 1945, with the explicit purpose of preventing future conflicts such as World Wars I and II. While US President Franklin Roosevelt convened the first meetings that led to the formation of the United Nations,[7] the participation and input of more than the United States and European powers was required if the United Nations was to fulfill its intended purpose. Thus, 53 countries were represented at its inception, including Thailand, India, the Republic of China, the Philippines, Egypt, Ethiopia, Liberia, and 20 Latin American nations. Accounts of the proceedings at this historic event have usually downplayed or overlooked the role such nations played in establishing the United Nations (e.g., Schlesinger, 2004). However, delegations from Asia and Latin America made several notable contributions that deserve mention. For example, Article 55 of the Charter, which states that the United Nations aims to solve "international economic, social, health, and related problems" while promoting "international and educational cooperation," was a Chinese initiative (Glassner, 1998, p. 163). Of even greater significance were key references to human rights in the preamble and a statement mentioning human rights as a purpose of the United Nations that were largely due to the efforts of Latin American representatives (Cleary, 2007, pp. 2–3).

The UN's Universal Declaration of Human Rights, which was adopted and proclaimed on December 10, 1948, represented yet another important milestone for human rights to which nations of the developing world contributed. Prior to the completion of the Declaration, the committee responsible for its drafting solicited opinions of philosophers from all of the world's major intellectual and religious traditions to ensure that the Declaration was based on universal principles. The committee received 70 responses, which including Hindu, Chinese, and Islamic perspectives along with American and European viewpoints, which were incorporated into the final document (Ishay, 2004, pp. 219–220). The final version of the UDHR, containing a preamble and 30 articles that were drafted following extensive cross-cultural discussions, affirmed that "All human beings are born free and equal in dignity and rights," "are endowed with reason and conscience," and "should act towards one another in a spirit of brotherhood." Though not actually a treaty but a non-binding resolution, the Declaration was intended as "a common standard of achievement for all peoples and all nations" (as cited in Morsink, 2000, pp. 330–331).

By the 1960s, the independence of former colonial nations in Africa and Asia opened up the United Nations to additional members from the developing world. In 1966, UN membership rose to 122, with representation from the South now accounting for the majority of member nations. The change in membership had major implications for the guiding principles of the United Nations, with younger nations calling for additions to and strengthening of the UDHR. The end result of lobbying by developing nations were two covenants in 1966, The International Covenant on Economic, Social and Cultural Rights (ICESCR) and The International Covenant on Civil and Political Rights (ICCPR), two multilateral treaties intended to enshrine human rights into international law (Tomuschat, 2003, p. 64). Taken together with the UDHR, the ICESCR and ICCPR comprise the International Bill of Human Rights, which represent the core values of the United Nations, the starting point for additional human rights covenants, and the basis for the world's contemporary human rights regime.[8]

As should now be evident, human rights were not transmitted from Europe to other world regions lacking such traditions or capacities for understanding. Innate in all human beings and hence universal, human rights form part of a shared global heritage that includes contributions from individuals and peoples from around the world throughout human history. The current international human rights framework associated with the United Nations, moreover, is not static in nature but will continue to evolve and be shaped by the entire human community, with peoples in the developing world continuing to play a prominent role in the process.

Globalization and human rights

Defining globalization

As the relationship of globalization to human rights is a central theme in this book, it is now necessary to define what exactly is meant by *globalization*. Much has been written about globalization—so much that it has become somewhat of an empty catchphrase in the hands of many writers and speakers. If it is to be of any help for understanding the contemporary world, however, the term must be defined with clarity and precision.

As the number of available definitions of globalization is staggering, it is possible only to mention a few that have been proposed to date. For Gray (1998), globalization is "the linking together throughout the world by distance abolishing technologies of cultural, political and economic events" (as cited in van Rekom and Go, 2006, p. 80). Robertson (1992) views it as "both the compression of the world and the intensification of consciousness of the world as a whole" (p. 8). Giddens (1990) similarly suggests it represents "the intensification of worldwide social relations which link distant localities in such a way that local happenings are shaped by events occurring many miles away and vice versa" (p. 64).

Stiglitz (2003) offers a more economic definition than these authors, suggesting globalization is

the closer integration of the countries and peoples of the world . . . brought about by the enormous reduction of costs of transportation and communication, and the breaking down of artificial barriers to the flows of goods, services, capital, knowledge, and people across borders. (p. 9)

One of the more all encompassing definitions is provided by Nederveen Pieterse (2004), who sees globalization

as an objective, empirical process of increasing economic and political connectivity, a subjective process unfolding in consciousness as the collective awareness of growing global interconnectedness, and a host of special globalizing projects that seek to shape global conditions. (pp. 16–17)

While definitions of globalization vary in their emphasis, it is possible to discern several dimensions of globalization that the above and other authors have recognized. First, globalization is characterized by increased interconnectivity of nations and peoples. Whereas individuals and communities at the local level in previous eras had little or no contact with the outside world, today few locales remain isolated from the effects of globalizing processes. Transnational linkages in this respect have been fostered over wider areas by new communications technologies and improvements in transportation modes and costs.

Second, the relations among peoples in different parts of the world have become more intensive. This means that the presence of others and associated social forces beyond the locality can be felt more strongly than in previous eras. For example, the Internet offers cost-efficiencies and technological possibilities unavailable in the age of telegraphs or high-cost telephone communications, making communications among world regions more frequent and more extensive than ever before. The Internet also offers multidimensional communicative options in the form of text, images, and sounds that may be seen as an intensification of global communications.

The second dimension is related to a third—that of increased rapidity. Travel, communications, and exchanges of a political, economic, and cultural nature in particular take place today at a speed that is unprecedented in human history. Thus, a letter sent from England to India in the 1830s took 5–8 months to reach its destination (Thompson, 2003, p. 248) while an email over the same distance today can be transmitted in milliseconds. Air travel today also allows one to traverse the distance from London to New York in just over 7 hours, while such a trip by ship in the 1850s took at least 12 days (Agozino, 2000, p. 39). With the speed of global interchanges greater than before, the frequency and intensity of such transnational relations has also been augmented.

The fourth related aspect of globalization concerns global consciousness. As humanity has been drawn closer together by globalization, people throughout the world have a greater awareness of the globe as a whole and humankind's place within it. On this issue, Scholte (2005) observes that "it seems safe to venture that people today are generally more aware than ever before of the planet as a single place and are more inclined to conceive of the earth as humanity's home" (p. 116). He also adds that:

> A hundred years ago global consciousness was generally limited to fleeting perceptions in elite circles. Today, with globes in the classroom, world weather reports in the news, and global products in the cupboard, transworld dimensions of social life are part of everyday awareness for hundreds of millions of persons across the planet. (p. 116)

Related to this consciousness has been a rise in what Scholte terms "transworld solidarities." Global sympathies and assistance have been aroused by disasters such as food crises, natural disasters, and conflicts on a hitherto unknown scale. Bonds of class, gender, religion, and sexual orientation, among others, have also deepened across borders such that

"People living under conditions of globalization have increasingly constructed significant aspects of their identity in supraterrritorial terms" (p. 116).

When we speak of globalization, therefore, we are referring to a complex phenomenon. While it can be helpful at times to select and emphasize one aspect of globalization such as its economic or technological features, it should also be evident that such circumscribed analyses of globalization provide an incomplete picture of what globalization actually encompasses. In this book, therefore, globalization will be defined as a multifaceted process linked to increased transplanetary interconnectivity, intensified global human interactions, and heightened rapidity of exchanges among individuals, communities, and peoples, with economic, political, social, and cultural implications for all of humanity.

The question of whether globalization represents something new or something that has occurred throughout human history has been fiercely debated. It would be incorrect, however, to suggest that globalization is simply a recent development. More realistically, it can be seen as beginning in the sixteenth century, following European explorations and the emergence of global capitalism. From that period to the present, globalization can be divided into various phases. As periodizing globalization is no simple matter and this book focuses on globalization in the contemporary world, this debate will not be discussed here. However, it could be argued that two phases of globalization have been evident since the end of World War II. The first phase, lasting from 1945 to 1989, was the Cold War era and was characterized by US–USSR rivalries and the global competition of communism versus capitalism. The second phase, the present era, commenced in 1989 and witnessed the rise of the United States as the world's sole superpower, the triumph of neoliberal economics, and a communications revolution made possible by Internet-related technologies. Both of these phases are discussed herein, though the latter period of globalization is this volume's main focus.

Significance for human rights

What, then, is the significance of globalization for human rights in the developing world? Before describing the contents of the present volume, it is helpful to tentatively explore this question.

One area of human rights in which globalization has had clear implications is that of civil and political rights. The role international pressure played in the downfall of apartheid in South Africa provides us with an example of how globalization may act in ways conducive to positive political change. The collapse of institutionalized racism and the advent of free elections in 1992 were brought about by black South Africans' protests and resistance, but also through overseas economic sanctions, sports boycotts, and public opinion. The wave of democracy that swept Africa, Asia, and Latin America in the 1990s was likewise encouraged by global human rights campaigns and support from the international media in tandem with local struggles. The pressure on authoritarian states to democratize, applied by international bodies such as the United Nations and European Union, was also relevant (Giddens, 2006, p. 854).

However, the idea that globalization by its very nature promotes political and civil rights cannot be substantiated. The proliferation of totalitarian governments throughout the Global South that preceded the democratic wave of the 1990s, for instance, was not due to an absence of globalization. On the contrary, it was largely the product of Cold War politics. Aiming to counter Soviet and communist influence in the developing world, the United States and other Western governments provided financial, technical, and military backing to a series of client states known for rampant human rights violations. Among the more notorious dictators bolstered by Western aid were Mobutu Sese Seko in Zaire, Augusto Pinochet in Chile, the Shah of Iran, and Ferdinand Marcos in the Philippines. At present, moreover, China represents the world's most populous non-democratic state. Unmoved by international condemnation of the political repression that followed in the wake of pro-democracy protests in 1989, China continues to repress citizens' political and civil rights in the name of economic growth that is made possible largely through exports to a global market.

The impact of globalization on economic and social rights in the developing world is equally difficult to assess. Increased participation in the global economy has enabled former "Asian tigers" such as Taiwan, South Korea, Singapore, and Malaysia to combine high levels of sustained economic growth with significant improvements in access to education, healthcare, and social security. However, the economic "miracles" in these nations were made possible through a denial of political rights that only began to be rectified from the 1990s. Ghai (1999) observes that "much of the postwar period was accompanied by authoritarian governance, and indeed to a considerable extent economic success was offered as the justification for that type of governance" (p. 255). The Asian Financial Crisis of 1997 further revealed the vulnerability of East Asian economies to external shocks and the potential for globalization to undermine earlier economic and social progress. The

World Bank (2000) noted "sharp declines in middle-class standards of living" (p. 47), increases in urban poverty, and declines in real public expenditures on education and health as some of the side effects of the crisis (p. 48).

That the impact of globalization on economic and social rights has been highly uneven can be gauged by comparing the situation of East Asia with that of Sub-Saharan Africa. Whereas the former tiger economies, despite the 1997 Financial Crisis, have been able to achieve developed nation status through globalization, Sub-Saharan Africa has experienced few net benefits from globalization over the past three decades. In fact, Structural adjustment programs (SAPs) in the 1980s and 1990s proved devastating for most of the region. Under SAPs African states were required to reduce or eliminate tariffs, slash public spending, devalue local currencies, and concentrate on debt repayment. The advent of the Washington Consensus in the 1990s led to more of the same policies. The result was not higher levels of human development but greater poverty, increased unemployment, widespread illiteracy, lower life expectancies, and other social ills. The "lost decade" epithet used to describe Africa's worsening poverty in the 1980s implies positive change thereafter, but careful analysis reveals "a continuation, perhaps acceleration, of the same trends" well into the 1990s (White and Killick, 2001, p. 3). Moreover, only very minor reductions in poverty and improvements in access to education and healthcare have been apparent since the 1990s, with the current global economic crisis threatening to undermine gains where they were in evidence (OECD, 2009, pp. 58–66).

As for globalization and third-generation rights, the United Nations has made attempts to support the right to peace, the right to development, and the right to a clean and healthful environment. After the Human Rights Commission (HRCion) supported a series of resolutions on the right to development in the 1970s, the General Assembly proclaimed the Declaration of the Right to Development in 1986. Similarly, a right to peace was first tabled by HRCion in 1976, with the General Assembly adopting the Declaration of the Preparation of Societies for Life in Peace in 1978 and the Declaration on the Right of Peoples to Peace in 1984. The right to a clean and healthful environment was first mentioned in the concluding Declaration of the UN Conference on the Human Environment in 1972 in Stockholm, Sweden. The World Charter for Nature adopted by the General Assembly in 1982 and the Rio Declaration on Environment and Development in 1992 call on states to respect and do more to protect the environment for citizens (Tomuschat, 2003, pp. 48–50).

But while such initiatives are a step in the right direction, third-generation rights have proven difficult to implement in practice. Efforts by the HRCion to clarify the legal connotations of the right to development have yielded few results, with skepticism from Western nations in particular undermining progress (Tomuschat, 2003, p. 49). While the United States in principle accepted the right to development at the Vienna World Conference on Human Rights in 1993, it has generally stonewalled efforts to put this right on the UN agenda since then (Felice, 2003, pp. 49–50). The right to peace, on the other hand, has waned among the international community following the end of the Cold War (Tomuschat, 2003, p. 49). Finally, the right to a clean environment is difficult to enforce when the holders, bearers, and details of such rights have not been adequately identified (Tomuschat, 2003, p. 52).

The preceding analysis suggests that globalization has implications for human rights, but that the impact is not entirely predictable. The idea that globalization is inherently progressive does not appear to be true. Nor could it be argued that it is intrinsically harmful for developing nations. The point of analyzing globalization's impact on human rights, therefore, should be to do so to find better ways to manage globalization. Such is the intention with which this book was written.

Summary of chapters

This volume brings together contributions from 11 authors that aim to advance our knowledge of globalization and human rights in the developing world. The authors share a concern with understanding how globalization and human rights interrelate and how the latter can be promoted, extended, and safeguarded in world regions where they are under severe threat. They present their viewpoints from an array of fields, including political science, economics, sociology, history, and law. The multi- and interdisciplinary perspectives in this book as such are helpful for highlighting the complexity and interrelatedness of globalization and human rights.

Part I examines the relationship between globalization, the state, and human rights. Within the literature on human rights, differences of opinion exist on the place of the state. On one side of the debate are authors who argue that the state can best enable human rights by showing restraint, such as by not impinging on citizens' right to property or their basic political rights. In opposition to this minimalist viewpoint of the state, other writers stress that the state also has certain duties and obligations to its constituents. Here, issues of social justice are factored into the equation and the state is seen as having a role to play in protecting citizens' human rights as well as not infringing on them. If we accept this second school of thought, a question that arises in regard to globalization is to what extent it enables the state to play this assigned role.

The two chapters in this section offer very different assessments of globalization. Browne Onuoha's chapter on human trafficking in Africa acknowledges that trafficking and human rights infractions are linked to globalization. However, he stresses that internal factors in the form of weak and failed states play a primary role in encouraging human trafficking and its associated abuses. Onuoha suggests that without a reform of the state in Africa, human rights violations linked to human trafficking will remain a feature on the African continent into the foreseeable future. Patrick Strefford's contribution on Myanmar raises questions about the efficacy of Western economic sanctions as a tool for promoting democratization and human rights. According to Strefford, such sanctions serve to isolate Myanmar's citizenry from the world at large and deny them the prosperity and political freedom globalization potentially offers. The marginalization of Myanmar's people also allows the military regime to strengthen its grip over civil society and forestall democratic change. While for Onuoha the main issue is to strengthen the state to promote human rights in Africa, for Strefford it is globalization vis-à-vis Western political and economic engagement that can help actualize such rights in Myanmar.

Part II is concerned with enforcement issues, exploring ways to prevent human rights violations by transnational corporations (TNCs). As Brysk (2005) has observed, non-state actors have been increasingly responsible for affronts to human rights worldwide. This means that "private wrongs" require the same scrutiny that has been granted to state-sponsored violations. Examples of non-state actors as human rights violators run the gamut from Nazi doctors subjecting prisoners to medical experiments during the Holocaust to African nuns participating in the Rwandan Genocide. They also include TNCs in Colombia, Nigeria, and Argentina colluding with state authorities to murder human rights activists and labor leaders. And they include TNCs selling unsafe products and services in developing nations (p. 11).

Onyeka Osuji and Biagio Zammitto offer complementary solutions for countering human rights infractions by TNCs. Osuji notes that TNCs, increasingly concerned with the impact of corporate reputation on profit margins, have begun to publish non-financial reports to indicate their compliance with human rights norms. However, as these reports often amount to a form of deceptive advertising, Osuji suggests that they be made mandatory and regulated to ensure TNCs are not impinging on human rights. Zammitto looks at the issue of TNCs from another standpoint—that of the states where TNCs originate and their responsibility to prevent TNC human rights violations committed abroad. Based on an analysis of the International Covenant on Economic, Social and Political Rights and the International Covenant on Civil and Political Rights (both of which came into force in 1976), Zammitto argues that states have an obligation to control their TNCs and their subsidiaries, to adopt measures to prevent human rights abuses, and to provide appropriate redress to victims of TNC activities.

Part III considers how global capital flows influence human rights. According to Collier and Dollar (2002), the period from the early 1980s to early 2000s was characterized by "unprecedented global economic integration" (p. 23). One notable change that accompanied this integration was rising capital flows to developing nations, which increased from US$28 billion in the 1970s to a high of US$306 billion in 1997. Related to this development, the character of capital flows changed as aid flows were halved and private capital flows came to predominate. Within these latter capital flows, foreign direct investment flows increased while bank loans and other private flows decreased following the debt crises of the 1980s (Collier and Dollar, 2002, p. 42). More recently, the World Bank has indicated that about US$450 billion in capital flows went to developing nations in 2009. Upward trends in capital flows have been so pronounced and economic integration has deepened to such an extent that numerous economists have called for "urgent action" to control capital flows in such regions (Adam, 2010).

Individual chapters by Adugna Lemi and Rab Paterson look at what such capital flows mean for human rights in Africa and Latin America respectively. As good governance has been emphasized as necessary for alleviating Africa's political and economic woes, Lemi analyzes how foreign direct investment (FDI) and official development aid (ODA) impact on governance indicators. Assessing quantitative data on Africa for the years 1975–2002, Lemi concludes that ODA had positive and significant effects on governance, whereas FDI had positive effects that were visible one or two years after FDI firms commenced operations in a host country. Whereas Lemi suggests foreign capital flows have encouraged better governance in Africa, Paterson considers the impact of International Monetary Fund (IMF) loans on Latin America to be detrimental to human rights. He therefore views the emergence of Venezuelan President Hugo Chávez's Bank of the South, a financial institution that arose in response to the IMF and disperses low interest loans to Latin

American states, as a welcome alternative lending institution. If it continues to be successful, argues Paterson, the Bank of the South could inspire imitators elsewhere that could greatly diminish the role of the IMF, reduce crushing debt loads in poor nations, and make true development at last possible across the Global South.

Part IV tackles the phenomenon of genocide in relation to globalization. The first use of the term *genocide* can be traced to Raphael Lemkin, a Polish lawyer of Jewish descent, who in 1944 employed it "to denote an old practice in its modern development...made from the ancient Greek word *genos* (race, tribe) and the Latin word *cide* (killing)" (as cited in Charny, 1999, p. 11). Among the first landmarks in the history of the United Nations, the Convention on the Prevention and Punishment of the Crime of Genocide, formulated in response to the Jewish Holocaust, took effect in 1951. It defined genocide as an act "committed with intent to destroy, in whole or in part, a national, ethnical, racial or religious group" through:

(a)   Killing members of the group;
(b)   Causing serious bodily or mental harm to members of the group;
(c)   Deliberately inflicting on the group conditions of life calculated to bring about its possible destruction in whole or in part;
(d)   Imposing measures intent to prevent births within the group;
(e)   Forcibly transferring children of the group. (as cited in Charny, 1999, p. 11)

The two contributions in this chapter examine genocide in two realms—the physical and cultural. Maureen Hiebert's chapter, focusing on the genocides of Cambodia (1975–9) and Rwanda (1994), suggests that globalization and genocide have a long and intertwined history. On the one hand, exclusionary ideas related to race, nation, and class imported from the West as well as access to arms in global markets contributed to the genocides, as did inaction of the international community. On the other hand, owing to advances in communications, the emergence of a global anti-genocide norm, and the creation of an international human rights regime, genocide is now widely vilified as a crime against humanity and the international community is better equipped to combat it. Yet rising global awareness and the present international human rights regime, concludes Hiebert, offer no guarantee a future genocide like ones in Cambodia or Rwanda will not once again occur. Moving to another area of the world, Bei Dawei and Evangelos Voulgarakis discuss the concept of "linguistic genocide" (or "linguicide") to describe government policies aimed at hastening cultural assimilation and language death and whether or not such policies represent actual genocide as defined by the United Nations. They explore the issue, employing what is arguably a paradigmatic transnational example, namely the suppression of the Kurdish languages in contemporary Iraq, Syria, Iran, and Turkey. While noting that Kurds have suffered (and in some cases continue to suffer) systematic human rights abuses in all four countries, Dawei and Voulgarakis take issue with "linguistic genocide" authors for emphasizing the welfare of languages as opposed to the rights of individuals who use them. Also complicating matters for the authors is that notions of one Kurd identity or language obfuscate the great diversity of languages and dialects that in reality exists among Kurds, implicitly raising the paradoxical issue of Kurdish language "purity" and its potential threat to human rights.

Together the following chapters contain important and provocative ideas written by well-informed authors. They provide fascinating insights into the problems and prospects of globalization while suggesting potential remedies to enhance and protect the freedoms and dignity of people in the developing world. While the debate on globalization and human rights does not end with this book, the contributions contained in this volume point the way to further studies on a subject that is of immense importance for the contemporary world and the future global community.

Notes

1. The key works can be counted on one hand and include Alison Brysk (ed.), *Globalization and Human Rights* (Berkeley: University of California Press, 2002), Mahmood Monshipouri, Neil Englehart, Andrew J. Nathan, and Kavita Philip (eds), *Constructing Human Rights in the Age of Globalization* (Armonk, NY and London: M. E. Sharpe, 2003), Jean-Marc Coicaud, Michael W. Doyle, and Anne-Marie Gardner (eds), *The Globalization of Human Rights* (Tokyo: United Nations University Press, 2003), and Matthew J. Gibney (ed.), *Globalizing Rights* (Oxford: Oxford University Press, 2003).
2. Walvin (1992) mentions such forms of resistance as theft, sabotage, lowered productivity, and revolt (pp. 75–87).
3. Davis (2001) agrees with these sentiments, arguing that:

> The Haitian Revolution was indeed a turning point in history. Like the Hiroshima Bomb, its meaning could be rationalized or repressed but never really forgotten, since it demonstrated the possible fate of every slaveholding society in the New World. The Haitian Revolution impinged on one way or another on the entire emancipation debate from the British parliamentary move in 1792 to outlaw the African slave trade to Brazil's final abolition of slavery ninety-six years later. (p. 4)

4. As outlined in the UN Convention on the Prevention and Punishment of the Crime of Genocide, which was adopted in 1948 and ratified in 1951.
5. Viewing World War II as a struggle against fascism and racism, the *West African Pilot* initially supported African participation on the side of the British Empire. However, it spoke out strongly against the restriction of press freedoms in Nigeria during the war, as this went against the principles of freedom for which the war was allegedly being fought (see Ibhawoh, 2007, p. 151).
6. Mahatma Gandhi wrote to Roosevelt to say that the Charter sounded "hollow...so long as India, and for that matter, Africa are exploited by Great Britain and America has the Negro problem in her own home" (as cited in Borgwardt, 2008, pp. 42–43). The *West African Pilot*, similarly, expressed disappointment with the Charter, calling it "The Atlantic Chatter": "A *charter* is a document bestowing certain rights and privileges; *chatter*, on the other hand, means to utter sounds rapidly or to talk idly or carelessly" (as cited in Ibhawoh, 2007, p. 154). The *Daily Service*, another West African newspaper, called Churchill "a bundle of contradiction," explaining that "Imperialism and liberty are by no means coterminous" (as cited in Ibhawoh, 2007, p. 154).
7. Although Roosevelt died before the United Nations was founded, he originally devised the organization's name and convened world leaders of Allied governments to sign the Declaration of the United Nations in 1942. Like the Atlantic Charter, the document included explicit references to human rights and was eventually signed by 46 nations.
8. Jack Donnelly, though usually stressing that human rights are Western in origin (Donnelly, 1999a, p. 69; 1999b, pp. 256–257, 2003, p. 63), appears to contradict this stance when discussing the International Bill of Human Rights. He states that as "newly independent countries had a special interest in human rights" the United Nations "thus began to reemphasize human rights." He adds further that the Covenants that resulted along with the Universal Declaration "represent an authoritative statement of international human rights norms...recognized by the international community as necessary for a life of dignity in the contemporary world" (Donnelly, 2007, pp. 6, 8). In stating the issue as such, Donnelly indicates that our contemporary international human rights regime would not exist in its present form were it not for the contributions of developing nations.

References

Abu-Lughod, J. (1997). Going beyond global babble. In A. D. King (ed.), *Culture, globalization and the world system. Contemporary conditions for the representation of identity* (pp. 131–138). Minneapolis: University of Minnesota Press.

Adam, S. (2010, October 5). "Urgent action" needed to control capital flows, StanChart says. *Bloomberg Businessweek*. Retrieved October 10, 2010, from http://www.businessweek.com/news/2010-04-25/-urgent-action-needed-to-control-capital-flows-stanchart-says.html.

Agozino, B. (2000). *Theoretical and methodological issues in migration research: Interdisciplinary, intergenerational and international perspectives*. London: Ashgate.

Aicardi de Saint-Paul, M. (1989). *Gabon: The development of a nation*. London: Routledge.

Berger, P., and Huntington, S. P. (2002). *Many globalizations: Cultural diversity in the contemporary world.* Oxford: Oxford University Press.

Bhagwati, J. (2007). *In defense of globalization: With a new afterword.* New York: Oxford University Press.

Birmingham, D. (1998). *Kwame Nkrumah: Father of African nationalism* (2nd edn). Athens, OH: Ohio University Press.

Borgwardt, E. (2008). *A New Deal for the world: America's vision for human rights.* Cambridge, MA: Harvard University Press.

Brems, E. (2001). *Human rights: Universality and diversity.* Cambridge, MA and Dordrecht, NL: Kluwer Law International.

Brysk, A. (ed.) (2002). *Globalization and human rights.* Berkeley: University of California Press.

Brysk, A. (2005). *Human rights and private wrongs: Constructing a global civil society.* New York and London: Routledge.

Charny, I. W. (1999). *Encyclopedia of genocide.* Santa Barbara, CA: ABC-CLIO, Inc.

Cleary, E. L. (2007). *Mobilizing for human rights in Latin America.* Bloomfield, CT: Kumarian Press.

Coicaud, J.-M., Doyle, M. W., and Gardner, A.-M. (eds.) (2003). *The globalization of human rights.* Tokyo: United Nations University Press.

Collier, P., and Dollar, D. (2002). *Globalization, growth, and poverty: Building an inclusive world economy.* Washington, DC and New York, NY: The World Bank and Oxford University Press.

Collins, R. O., and Burns, J. M. (2007). *A history of sub-Saharan Africa.* Cambridge: Cambridge University Press.

Cranston, M. W. (1973/2002). Human rights, real and supposed. In C. Wellman (ed.), *Rights and duties* (Vol. 5) (pp. 43–53). New York and London: Routledge.

Cumper, P. (1999). Human rights: History, development and classification. In A. Hegarty and S. Leonard (eds.), *Human rights: An agenda for the 21st century* (pp. 1–9). London: Routledge Cavendish.

Davies, P. (ed.) (1988). *Human rights.* London: Routledge.

Davis, D. B. (2001). The impact of the French and Haitian Revolutions. In D. P. Geggus (ed.), *The Impact of the Haitian Revolution in the Atlantic World* (pp. 3–9). Columbia, SC: University of South Carolina Press.

Donnelly, J. (1999a). Human rights and Asian values: A defense of "Western" universalism. In J. R. Bauer and D. A. Bell (ed.), *The East Asian challenge for human rights* (pp. 60–87). Cambridge: Cambridge University Press.

Donnelly, J. (1999b). Post-Cold War reflections on the study of international human rights. In J. A. Rosenthal (ed.), *Ethics & international affairs: A reader* (pp. 242–270). Washington, DC: Georgetown University Press.

Donnelly, J. (2003). *Universal human rights in theory and practice.* Ithaca, NY: Cornell University Press.

Donnelly, J. (2007). *International human rights* (3rd edn). Boulder: Westview Press.

D'Souza, D. (2007). Created equal: The origin of human dignity. In D. D'Souza, *What's so great about Christianity?* (pp. 67–82). Washington, DC: Regnery Publishing.

Duffey, M. K. (2001). *Sowing justice, reaping peace: Case studies of racial, religious, and ethnic healing around the world.* Lanham, MD: Rowman & Littlefield.

Equiano, O. (1789/2003). *The interesting narrative and other writings* (V. Carretta, ed.). New York and London: Penguin Books.

Faringer, G. L. (1991). *Press freedom in Africa*. New York: Praeger Publishers.

Felice, W. F. (2003). *The Global New Deal: Economic and social human rights in world politics*. Boulder, CO: Rowman & Littlefield.

Fyfe, C. (1986). Freed slave colonies in West Africa. In J. D. Fage, J. E. Flint, and R. A. Oliver (eds.), *The Cambridge history of Africa: From c. 1790 to c. 1870* (pp. 170–199). Cambridge: Cambridge University Press.

Freeman, M. (2002). *Human rights: An interdisciplinary approach*. Cambridge, UK and Malden, MA: Polity Press in association with Blackwell Publishers.

Ghai, Y. (1999). Rights, social justice, and globalization in East Asia. In J. R. Bauer and D. A. Bell (eds.), *The East Asian challenge for human rights* (pp. 241–263). Cambridge, UK: Cambridge University Press.

Gandhi, R. (2008). *Gandhi: The man, his people, and the Empire*. Berkeley and Los Angeles: University of California Press.

Gibney, M. J. (ed.) (2003). *Globalizing rights*. Oxford: Oxford University Press.

Giddens, A. (1990). *The consequences of modernity*. Stanford, CA: Stanford University Press.

Giddens, A. (2006). *Sociology* (5th edn). Cambridge, UK and Malden, MA: Polity Press.

Glassner, M. I. (1998). *The United Nations at work*. Westport, CT and London, UK: Praeger.

Gordon, J. U. (2000). *Black leadership for social change*. Westport, CT: Greenwood Publishing.

Gray, J. (1998). *False dawn; The delusions of global capitalism*. New York: The New Press.

Griffin, J. (2008). *On human rights*. Oxford: Oxford University Press.

Haiti donations exceed $644 million, as of February 3. (3 February 2010). *The Chronicle of Philanthropy*. Retrieved May 14, 2010, from http://philanthropy.com/article/Haiti-Donations-Exceed-644/63887

Hart, J. G. (2009). *Which one is. Book 2: Existenz and transcendental phenomenology*. Berlin: Springer Science & Business Media B. V.

Hassan, R. (1999). Muslim women's empowerment: Challenge of the present, hope of the future. In C. Methuen (ed.), *Time, utopia, eschatology* (pp. 43–64). Leuven, BE: Peeters Publishers.

Hassan, R. (2005). Women's rights in Islam: Normative teachings versus practice. In S. Hunter and H. Malik (eds.), *Islam and human rights: Advancing a US-Muslim dialogue* (pp. 43–66). Washington, DC: Center for Strategic and International Studies.

Heinze, E. (1995). *Sexual orientation: A human right*. Dordrecht, NL; Boston, MA; and London, UK: Martinus Nijhoff Publishers.

Held, D., and McGrew, A. (2007). *Globalization theory: Approaches and controversy*. London: Polity.

Hunt, L. (2007). *Inventing human rights: A history*. New York: W. W. Norton.

Ibhawoh, B. (2007). *Imperialism and human rights: Colonial discourses of rights and liberties in African history*. Albany, NY: State University of New York Press.

Ishay, M. R. (2004). *The history of human rights. From ancient times to the globalization era*. Berkeley and Los Angeles: University of California Press.

Kabasakal Arat, Z. F. (2006). *Human rights worldwide: A reference book*. Santa Barbara, CA: ABC-Clio.

Keown, D. V. (2002). Are there human rights in Buddhism? In L. Gearon (ed.) *Human rights and religion* (pp. 180–197). Eastbourne, UK: Sussex Academic Press.

Killingray, D. (1999). Guardians of empire. In D. Killingray and D. E. Omissi (eds.), *Guardians of empire: The armed forces of the colonial powers, c. 1700–1964* (pp. 1–24). Manchester: Manchester University Press.

Kinberg, L. (2006). Contemporary ethical issues. In A. Rippin (ed.), *The Blackwell companion to the Qur'an* (pp. 450–466). Oxford, UK and Malden, MA: Blackwell Publishing.

Lauren, P. G. (2003). *The evolution of international human rights: Visions seen* (2nd edn). Philadelphia: University of Pennsylvania Press.

Mayer, A. E. (2002). Islam and human rights: Tradition and politics. In L. Gearon (ed.) *Human rights and religion* (pp. 120–140). Eastbourne, UK: Sussex Academic Press.

Meredith, M. (2006). *The fate of Africa: From the hopes of freedom to the heart of despair*. New York: Public Affairs.

Miers, S. (2003). *Slavery in the twentieth century: The evolution of a global pattern*. Walnut Creek, CA: AltiMira Press.

Monshipouri, M., Englehart, N., Nathan, A. J., and Philip, K. (eds.) (2003). *Constructing human rights in the age of globalization*. Armonk, NY and London, UK: M. E. Sharpe.

Morsink, J. (2000). *The universal declaration of human rights: Origins, drafting, and intent*. Philadelphia: University of Pennsylvania Press.

Munck, R. (2000). Labour in the global: Challenges and prospects. In R. Cohen and S. M. Rai (eds.), *Global social movements* (pp. 83–100). London: Athalone Press.

Mutua, M. (2002). *Human rights: A Political and cultural critique*. Philadelphia: University of Pennsylvania Press.

Nederveen Pieterse, J. (2004). *Globalization and culture: Global mélange*. Lanham, MD: Rowman & Littlefield.

Organization for Economic Cooperation and Development (OECD) (2009). *African Economic Outloook 2009: Overview*. Paris: African Development Bank/Development Center of the Organization for Economic Cooperation and Development.

Parry, C. (2009, April 17). Susan Boyle: 47-year-old becomes overnight superstar. *Vancouver Sun*, p. 1.

Pflantz, M. (2010, April 19). How the Iceland volcano ash cloud is crippling Kenya's flower industry. *Christian Science Monitor*. Retrieved May 13, 2010, from http://www.csmonitor.com/World/2010/0419/How-the-Iceland-volcano-ash-could-is-crippling-Kenya-s-flower-industry.

Power, S., and Allison, G. (2006). *Realizing human rights: Moving from inspiration to impact*. New York: St. Martin's Press.

Roberts, J. M. (1999). *The Penguin history of the twentieth century*. London and New York: Penguin Books.

Robertson, R. (1992). *Globalization: Social theory and global culture*. London: Sage.

Rosenberg, J. (2002). *The follies of globalization*. London: Verso.

Schlesinger, S. (2004). *Act of creation: The founding of the United Nations*. Boulder, CO: Westview Press.

Schmitz, H. P., and Sikkink, K. (2002) International human rights. In W. Carlsnaes, T. Risse, and B. A. Simmons (eds.), *Handbook of international relations* (pp. 517–537). London, UK; Thousand Oaks, CA; and New Delhi, India: SAGE Publications.

Scholte, J. A. (2005). *Globalization: A critical introduction*. New York: Palgrave Macmillan.

Sen, A. (2001). *Development as freedom*. Oxford: Oxford University Press.

Sen, A. (2005). *The argumentative Indian: Writings on Indian history, culture and identity*. New York: Picador.

Steger, M. B. (2003). *Globalization: A very short introduction*. New York: Oxford University Press.

Stiglitz, J. (2003). *Globalization and its discontents*. New York: W. W. Norton.

Thomas, H. (1997). *The slave trade: The story of the Atlantic slave trade, 1440–1870*. New York: Simon & Schuster.

Thompson, J. B. (2003). The globalization of communication. In D. Held and A. McGrew (eds.), *The global transformations reader: An introduction to the globalization debate* (pp. 246–259). Cambridge, UK: Polity.

Tomuschat, C. (2003). *Human rights: Between idealism and realism*. Oxford: Oxford University Press.

Traer, R. (1991). *Faith in human rights: Support in religious traditions for a global struggle*. Washington, DC: Georgetown University Press.

Van Rekom, J., and Go, F. (2006). Cultural identities in a globalizing world: Conditions for sustainability of intercultural tourism. In P. M. Burns and M. Novelli (eds.), *Tourism and social identities: Global frameworks and local realities* (pp. 79–90). Oxford: Elsevier.

Veseth, M. (2006). *Globaloney*. Lanham, MD: Rowman & Littlefield.

Vohra, R. (2000). *The making of India: A historical survey*. Armonk, NY: M. E. Sharpe.

Walvin, J. (1992). Resistance. In J. Walvin, *Slaves and slavery: The British colonial experience* (pp. 75–87). Manchester: Manchester University Press.

Welch, C. E. (1984). Human rights as a problem in contemporary Africa. In C. E. Welch, Jr. and R. I. Meltzer (eds.), *Human rights and development in Africa* (pp. 11–31). Albany, NY: State University of New York Press.

Wellman, C. (1999). The proliferation of rights: Moral progress or empty rhetoric? Boulder, CO: Westview Press.

Wellman, C. (2002). The proliferation of rights: Moral progress or empty rhetoric? In L. Gearon (ed.) *Human rights and religion* (pp. 368–389). Eastbourne, UK: Sussex Academic Press.

White, H., and Killick, T. (2001). *African poverty at the millennium: Causes, complexities, and challenges*. Washington, DC: World Bank.

Williams, E. (1944/1994). *Capitalism and slavery*. Chapel Hill, NC: University of North Carolina Press.

World Bank (2000). *Global economic prospects and the developing countries*. Washington, DC: International Bank for Reconstruction/World Bank.

Wright, L. (2007). *The looking tower: Al Queda and the road to 9/11*. New York: Vintage Books.

Zamora, M. (1993). *Reading Columbus*. Berkeley and Los Angeles: University of California Press.

Part I

Globalization, the State, and Human Rights

2
Globalization and the Commercialization of Humanity: The State, Trafficking in Persons, and Human Rights Challenges in Africa

Browne Onuoha

Introduction

This chapter discusses African states' lack of capacity to confront the complex phenomenon of the commercialization of human beings and prevent the human rights violations of their citizens associated with human trafficking. The central argument herein is that the ability of states in Africa to control human trafficking and manage associated human rights violations is a function of the states' total capacity to control crime, maintain peace and security within their borders, and ensure good governance. In this regard, African states are seen as lacking. It is further argued that this lack of capacity is directly related to the character of the state in Africa and that the relationship posited by scholars to exist between globalization and the commercialization of humanity as it affects Africa is of secondary importance. Instead, the primary cause giving rise to migration and trafficking is linked to contradictions internal to Africa, which have followed from over three decades of military dictatorship, civil wars, and cross-border conflicts, expropriation and primitive accumulation of African resources embarked upon by African leaders themselves, and the attendant corruption and poverty that have been unleashed by these contradictions. With the trafficking of Africans occurring in such a context, it is apparent that any resolution to the problem will first need to transform the character of the state in Africa itself.

This chapter is presented in three parts. The first part examines the concept of human trafficking and current explanatory frameworks. The second part reviews the place of African states in relation to human trafficking. Here, the character of the state in Africa is emphasized, as is how it impedes any major attempts to combat trafficking in persons and enforce or protect human rights. The third part, the conclusion, stresses that lack of capacity to tackle trafficking is systemic and relates to the state's inability to prevent its agents from intimidating or oppressing its citizens, to maintain peace and security within national borders, provide social services, address poverty, and provide good governance. Any state that is unable to resolve these domestic shortcomings may not be expected to, or be in the position to, fight and control human trafficking and enforce human rights, particularly given the complex network of organizations involved in trafficking, and the opportunities as well as the challenges created by globalization.

Globalization and trafficking in persons

There is a consensus among scholars that trafficking in persons, or the commercialization of humanity, is a phenomenon tied to the socioeconomic and geopolitical transformations in recent years that have witnessed the increasing interconnectivity and interdependence of global markets, of which Africa is not a full but rather a peripheral participant (Beare, 1999; De Dios, 1999; Kempadoo, 2000; Salt and Stein, 1997; Skrobanek and Sanghera, 1996; William, 1999). Trafficking in human persons has been viewed within the broader framework of a rebalancing of the microeconomic gaps that characterize globalization (Bales and Robbins, 2001). For instance, as it concerns Africa, the uneven distribution of global wealth and the corresponding lack of opportunity accompanied by local unemployment, which have been exacerbated by globalization, create a "push" for poor and unemployed Africans to places where there is demand ("pull") for their labor (Salt and Stein, 1997).

However, globalization has affected Africa in many other ways. Since the 1990s, some forms of international aid, which had been given to African governments during the Cold War era, have dwindled. With such reductions, or in some cases outright withdrawals of assistance, budgetary pressures have aggravated African governments' inability to provide social services and meet other obligations for citizens. This paralysis of African states in turn has provoked further exoduses of African peoples as migrants in search of employment, particularly to the Global North (Anderson and Davidson, 2003). The current global social and economic system as such poses difficult challenges for African nations. Implicitly, the geopolitical and socioeconomic order creates in Africa a gap, which provides avenues for persons, in their search for livelihood and sustenance, to be "exploited" by their fellow human beings. This potential for "exploitation" has manifested itself as trafficking in human persons.

In recent years, human trafficking has been called the "new" or "modern" slave trade and linked to the exploitation of what has been termed "disposable people" (Bales, 1999; Truong, 2006, p. 60). Trafficking is perpetrated under coercion, violence, threats, deceit, and fraud—or all of these together. Scholars concede that finding a common definition of trafficking may be difficult because of the complexities of the activities involved, cultural differences, and the values and perceptions of the different stakeholders, including those of the victims as well as those of the traffickers themselves. But there is broad agreement as to the central features of human trafficking. According to a definition by Wijers and Lap-Chew (1997), human trafficking involves

> all acts...in the recruitment and/or transportation of [persons] within and across national borders for work or service, by means of violence or threat of violence, abuse of authority or dominant position, debt bondage, deception or other forms of coercion. (p. 36)

Also, the United Nations (UN) (2000) has provided what may be referred to as an official definition of trafficking. According to the UN:

> trafficking in persons means the recruitment, transportation, transfer, harboring or receipt of persons by means of threat or use of force or other form of coercion, of abduction, of fraud, of deception, of the abuse of power or of a position of vulnerability or of the giving or receiving of payment or benefit to achieve the consent of a person having control over another person, for the purpose of exploitation. Exploitation shall include, at a minimum, the exploitation of the prostitution of others or other forms of sexual exploitation, forced labor or services, slavery, or practices similar to slavery, servitude or the removal of organs. (p. 2)

As well as defining trafficking, the UN has provided principles and guidelines for countering trafficking, particularly with regard to the enforcement of victims' basic human rights and the punishment of traffickers (UN High Commission, 2002). Its definition, principles, and guidelines have enabled the UN to prepare statements on standard conduct known as "best practices," or behaviors and actions expected of nation-states in carrying out measures designed to eradicate human trafficking and enforce the human rights of victims as well as of persons vulnerable to human trafficking. The United States also funds the preparation of annual reports on governments' observance of best practices (US Trafficking in Persons Report, 2008). The reports categorize countries into three "tiers" (and a fourth one, a Special List) in which each tier outlines the degree of compliance each country has demonstrated in its efforts to combat trafficking.

Tier 1 is comprised of countries whose governments fully comply with the Trafficking Victims Protection Acts (TVPA) minimum standards. Minimum standards require governments to provide assistance to victims, and maintain significant law enforcement actions against trafficking offenders. Tier 2 includes countries whose governments do not fully comply with TVPA minimum standards but are making significant efforts to bring themselves into compliance. In countries on the Tier 2 Watch List, it is apparent that: a) the absolute number of victims of severe forms of trafficking is very significant or is significantly increasing; or b) there is a failure to provide evidence of increasing efforts to combat severe forms of trafficking in persons from the previous year; or c) the determination that a country is making significant efforts to bring itself into compliance with minimum standards is based on explicit commitments by the country to take additional future steps over the following year. Tier 3, on the other hand, represents countries whose governments do not fully comply with the minimum standards and are not making significant efforts to do so. A "Special List" is compiled each year of countries for which adequate information could not be obtained about the human trafficking situation, even when there are reasonable suspicions that trafficking is occurring (US Trafficking in Persons Report, 2008). Below, the performance of African countries in eradicating human trafficking is examined in relation to the UN classification system.

There is a large body of literature on all aspects of trafficking in human persons (Anderson and Davidson, 2003; Beare, 1999; Bertone, 2000; Bruckert and Parent, 2002; De Dios, 1999; Kempadoo, 2000; Salt and Stein, 1997; Williams, 1999). Previous studies have generally discussed what may be considered common elements associated with human trafficking and have not offered a framework for analysis of the phenomenon. The frameworks that do exist as explanatory models are rudimentary in nature. In various cases, attempts have been made to examine diverse elements of human trafficking in the form of descriptions of actual trafficking organizations. Details in such treatments include information on the complex network of the organizations, their activities and general functioning, recruitment, transportation, routes taken or destinations, modalities of activities, the traffickers themselves (especially their criminality, involvement in trafficking, and possible consequences), human rights violations, and the interrelation of migration, smuggling, and trafficking. Other details discussed by scholars cover types of work, such as sexual or domestic labor, supply and demand factors ("push and pull" variables), possible numbers of victims of trafficking to date, the preponderance of women and children as victims, the immense profits made by traffickers, and the contributions of non-governmental organizations (NGOs) to combating trafficking in contrast to the culpable indifference of many governments. Also examined are the wars, corruption, poverty, diseases, and other social problems that, as a cluster, spawn trafficking. Finally, various works discuss the difficulties encountered in and best practices required for combating trafficking in persons (Bales, 1999; Beare, 1999; Bertone, 2000; De Dios, 1999; Salt and Stein, 1997; Shronbanek and Sanghera, 1996; Wijers and Lap-Chew, 1997; Williams, 1999).

According to Bruckert and Parent (2003), most scholars of human trafficking have not situated their analyses within the broader context of globalization and its impact on human populations. However, they identify some researchers, including Bertone (2000), Beare (1999), De Dios (1999), Williams (1999), and Kempadoo (2000), who have offered a more thoroughly developed analytical framework that analyzes the global capitalist production system and such issues as the restructuring and population movements linked to labor competitiveness. Kempadoo (2000) is of the view that global restructuring has weakened the powers of nation-states in favor of transnational organizations and that the new international order has had detrimental consequences for national economies, particularly for those of less developed countries in regions such as Africa. The negative impacts include the displacement of large populations (particularly rural dwellers), job losses, low wages, poverty, and disease, especially HIV/AIDS (Kempadoo, 2000, as cited in Bruckert and Parent, 2003). Kempadoo's arguments, however, fail to consider the devastating effects of structural adjustment policies in Africa in the 1980s. As we shall argue shortly, the weakening of the nations and their loss of capacity to govern was already a reality in the 1980s and was only aggravated by the impact of globalization.

If we add these consequences of globalization to the already existing contradictions of war situations in Africa caused largely by years of military rule, corruption, poverty, and disease, it seems almost inevitable that migration and trafficking have emerged as serious problems for Africa and the global community. While the global concern any time human trafficking is discussed is the link thought to exist between human trafficking and human rights abuses on the one hand and with globalization on the other, under the scenarios discussed above, human rights obligations are not likely to be a preoccupation for most governments in Africa. The problem that the world wants resolved directly relates to the interconnections of globalization, human trafficking, and human rights violations, but it remains unclear as to how African states should effect positive change within a context of circumscribed or declining influence.

The issue of rights violations becomes more critical when it is noted that over 27 million persons are victims of one form of trafficking or another (Bales, 1999). In order to address the rights issues, the UN Protocol to Prevent, Suppress and Punish Trafficking in Persons (2000) (in Article 6 of the Protocol) specifies the rights being violated and/or to be enforced. It stipulates that nation-states protect the privacy of victims by making the legal proceedings of their trial confidential, providing victims with adequate information on relevant court and administrative procedures, and offering victims physical and psychological protection, appropriate housing, medical treatment, education, and counseling. Also, in 2002, Anti-Slavery International prepared a document entitled *Human Trafficking, Human Rights: Redefining Victims' Protection*, which was aimed at strengthening the human rights protection of those vulnerable to trafficking as well as trafficking victims (Pearson, 2002). The United Nations, the International Organization for Migration (IOM), the United Nations Children's Fund (UNICEF), and other related international bodies have all shown interest in the issue of human rights as they relate to human trafficking, especially with regard to women, children, and the poor. Such policy measures make it evident that the organizations and agencies have demonstrated their commitment toward ensuring that trafficking is eliminated. Consequently, the expectation is that these international bodies require nation-states, including those in Africa, to fight trafficking and enforce human rights. But the intention of African states to confront human rights challenges and meet related obligations is suspect. Before demonstrating why this is so, let us first examine current understanding of the issue of human rights.

There is extensive debate over human rights in general and what rights—apart from inalienable rights, which are otherwise known as welfare rights—should be enjoyed (Barrow, 1983; Pettit, 1980; Raphael, 1979; Rawls, 1972; Sen, 2004). African governments are not well disposed toward economic and social rights, or welfare rights that refer to housing, shelter, food, health, and so on. Accordingly, it is difficult to convince African leaders that these are their obligations and they therefore should commit resources to enforce or protect such rights. It is also not significant to them that the inability to provide these rights is linked to "push" factors promoting migration and trafficking. According to Sen (2004), the excuse made for disregarding these rights is that they cannot feasibly be enforced; it is argued that there are no institutions with the capacity to realize such rights and no funds to implement them. However, Sen argues that human rights do not depend on affordability to be rights. Human rights do not require promulgation or legislation. The pursuit of human rights is a "motion towards" an end, which may not be stopped. A human right is an end in itself. Thus, social rights, as with other rights, warrant protection. According to Sen, some of these rights are provided through "imperfect obligation" but obligations nonetheless, which must be implemented or provided for. He goes on to say that human rights, even welfare rights, are reasonable ethical demands that even if not legislated upon could still be realized. Most rights, suggests Sen, came to be enjoyed for the first time through that "imperfect obligation" that arises through public recognition, agitation, and monitoring of violations; they are generated through public acknowledgement, public discussions, appraisal, and advocacy. All these are indicative of obligation, even if "imperfect" (Sen, 2004, pp. 338–342). Quoting Rawls (1972), Sen (2004) therefore notes that rights become rights and are viable because of their link to "public reasoning" and their role in "ethical objectivity" (p. 349). In relation to Africa, it would be correct to infer that if states cannot afford these rights now but there is evidence to show that arrangements or plans are being made through structures and institutions to extend such rights, those actions, or programs will demonstrate a government's readiness or willingness to address or enforce human rights. But in most cases in Africa, there is little evidence to show governments' commitment or willingness to introduce measures to address violations of these rights.

It is doubtful whether such debates can alter or affect African leaders' views of human rights. In relation to this issue, we may ask whether African leaders view their constituents as individuals with the rights of citizens. The question becomes necessary as the way African leaders treat their peoples raises the question as to whether citizenship has been won in Africa at all. African leaders do not manifestly respond to the philosophy or theory of citizenship, and African peoples themselves have not vigorously asserted their citizenship nor seem to have sufficiently fought for it (Dorman, Hammett, and Nugent, 2007; Herbst, 1999, 2000; Seely, 2007). Thus, it appears difficult for both leaders and their peoples to appreciate that there are human rights obligations that leaders need to enforce, and that citizens must demand as their right. These disconnections between leadership and responsibility for providing the rights of citizens partly explain why African leaders cannot see the link between providing for economic, social, or welfare rights, and discouraging migration and fighting human trafficking. We shall later draw cases from prisons in Africa to more incisively argue that African leaders do not appreciate human rights as obligations, and therefore discussing or insisting on such rights makes no fundamental impression on them. Later in the chapter, we discuss how these disconnections are rooted in the nature of the state in Africa and how they result in African political leaders being ill-prepared for the obligations of combating trafficking and enforcing the human rights of their citizens.

The character of the state in Africa

The central argument at the beginning of this chapter was that the character of the state in Africa renders states incapable of either confronting trafficking in persons or protecting the rights of victims and those vulnerable to trafficking. A related argument herein is that in spite of globalization and the predominance of neoliberal thought in recent years, the character of the state in Africa has remained largely the same over the past three decades, irrespective of claims to democratization, and thus an analysis of the state still possesses the rigor and predictive power to enable us understand the contemporary African state's relationship to the phenomenon called modern slavery. Our analysis of the state is drawn largely from prominent debates on the state in the 1970s/1980s but also from more recent discussions (Ake, 1981, 1985, 1994; Deng, 1998; Lumumba-Kasongo, 2002; Ottaway, 1999).

The general consensus on the state in Africa has been that it lacks relative autonomy. It is subordinated and privatized by a coalition of dominant power interests, and has remained as previously studied, whether during the period of indigenization policy of the 1970s and early 1980s, the structural adjustment program of the late 1980s, or the deregulation, liberalization, and privatization programs of globalization of the 1990s (Aina, 1996; Beckman, 1992; Gibbon, Bangura, and Ofstad, 1992; Jinadu, 2000; Nabudere, 2000; Onuoha, 1988; Rugumamu, 1999). The state has been used by ruling coalitions for the expropriation of national wealth, with these coalitions recycling themselves in government over time. During their apogee in the 1970s and 1980s, the coalitions were comprised of political, economic, military, and bureaucratic agents. They employed the instrumentalities of the state most of the time for their own interests, especially to retain and control political power. The security agents were firmly under their domain, and not acting for the interests or in the service of the people. Financial and other resources to be allocated were structured and determined by what constituted political capital for further consolidation of political power (Bayart, 1993).

Africa today has not changed significantly from the past. At present there is still no accountability because governance is based on personal rule or a coalition at best. While the constitutions may be adorned with the principal tenets of constitutionalism, these are ignored at will; the rulers choose which court judgments to obey and which to ignore. The state in Africa, therefore, cannot play its mediatory role among competing groups owing to its subordination to these particular interests. The subordination of the state to coalition interests subverts the rule of law, and makes it difficult, if not impossible, for the state to function, in spite of claims of transition to democracy (Ake, 1994, 1996, 2000).

The subordination of the state is further reflected in the manner in which democratization processes are conducted. For instance, elections are marked by fraud and violence because of the inability of the political class to work out acceptable power-sharing arrangements. As a result of orchestrated crises, those in power remain autocratic using the pretext that they wished to ensure the peace and security of the state. The rigging of elections and all manner of electoral corruption and crime are designed to allow dictators to remain in power, at whatever cost. When political parties in power declare publicly that they will rule their countries for 50 years or longer, such pronouncements destroy trust in government, as they represent a mindset that contradicts the values of democracy. They also alert the opposition to prepare for a power struggle since the incumbent is not ready to relinquish authority whether or not the people vote for him. Thus, agents of the state in Africa are both latently and manifestly reckless in politics because they have the state under their subordination. Except in one or two cases in the recent past—such as Botswana and Ghana (given the latter's successful elections from 1992 to 2008)—a genuine transition to democracy in Africa, which would allow the state to play a mediatory role among competing interests in society, has not occurred. In other words, the majority of states in Sub-Saharan Africa still demonstrate the same characteristics as they did during the preceding three decades (Ake, 1994, 1996, 2000; Ottaway, 1999).

The struggle for change led by opposition forces is ongoing. The existence of the opposition, even if symbolic, is perhaps one of the few differences between now and then, but it has not been significant because the victory of the opposition, wherever it has occurred, has not brought about any significant change. Indeed, African states are not changing, even now. The neoliberal thesis of the state—with debate now shifting to "state-building," in terms of the public and private sectors and civil society, or state–society relations, in other words implying mediation—is not evident in Africa in any significant proportion (Chandler, 2006; Fukuyama, 2004a, 2004b; Hehir and Robinson, 2007).

Indeed, during the democratization process in Africa in the early 1990s, Ake (1994) expressed concern over the amount of stress still placed on politics by African leaders. He also emphasized the unchanging nature of the state in Africa. In Ake's opinion, state power in most parts of Africa is constituted in such a way as to

> render democracy impossible. Therefore, more than determining the controllers of state power competitively, what is needed by way of democratization, is the transformation of the state, for in the absence of such transformation, election can only be a choice between oppressors.... [In Africa] the political class shows no interest, even now, in transforming the autocratic post-colonial state.... The experience of democracy so far shows that even the democratic opposition did not make an issue of the nature of the state, including its highly authoritarian constitutions.... [The African state] is a form of state which cannot bend to the services of democracy. (Ake, 1994, pp. 8–9)

Evidently, post-election crises, the very many cases of electoral tribunals, and the conflicts and brutal struggles to form governments in places such as DR Congo, Nigeria, Ivory Coast, Kenya, and Zimbabwe (countries claiming to have democratized) confirm Ake's doubts. While conducting elections, going to the electoral tribunals or courts, and forming governments may be democratic attributes and so may be considered improvements on the authoritarian regimes of the past, the outcomes of elections have not involved any significant differences in the style of leadership and governance or in the lives of the people. Thus, in Africa, nearly 15 years after the assessment of Ake (1994), the nature of the state has not significantly changed, regardless of the claims of transition to democracy. The forms may have changed, such as the introduction of multiparty politics, but the fundamentals remain much the same. In some cases (e.g. Nigeria), the same group that ran the nation aground under military dictatorship controls the so-called democratic movement in their country. Hence, both the state and democracy in Africa are not yet serving the interests of the people. Positive indices of democratic governance claimed in countries like Ghana and Botswana may not be sufficient to change the interpretation of state and politics in the region.

Indeed, an equally critical feature of the state in Africa identified almost immediately after Ake's writing was the high rate of "failures" of African states (Herbst, 1996/1997; Zartman, 1995). According to the "failed state" thesis, some African states at one time or another after political independence became very weak could not command effective central authority, and collapsed for a significant period. Many of them had personal rulers; private armies were organized, national treasuries were plundered, and primitive accumulation occurred where factions had acquired more wealth than their countries. Somalia, DR Congo, Sudan, Liberia, Sierra Leone, Ivory Coast, Ethiopia/Eritrea, Chad, Uganda, Zimbabwe, Burundi, Rwanda, and even Algeria and Nigeria were at one time or the other perceived as "failed states" (Bates, 2001; Chomsky, 2007; Ghani and Lockhart, 2008; Herbst, 1996/1997; Lyons and Samatar, 2003; Rotberg, 2000; Zartman, 1995). Failed states are characterized by civil war, absence of law and order, cross-border conflict, decayed infrastructure, and paralysis of government. In many cases where failed states exist there is a total loss of the capacity to govern. Moreover, even when peace is apparent in such states, wars, crises, and conflicts can erupt as a result of minimal provocation.

In the *2008 Report of Failed States*, African states represented 12 out of the 35 most critical state failures worldwide. In 2005, 2006, and 2007, out of the 20 most critical failures for each year, Africa comprised 11 in both 2005 and 2006 and 12 in 2007. There are serious contestations about the objectivity of the indices used in reaching the perception and classification of state failure, presently compiled and produced by The Fund for Peace (2008). It is even suggested that the entire thesis and the reports produced have become more political- than research-based ventures (Bates, 2001; Chomsky, 2007; Ghani and Lockhart, 2008; Lyon and Samatar, 2003). But irrespective of the debates, biases, and other possible inadequacies of the reports, the evidence of political crises, instability, hunger, diseases, and endless wars in Africa reveal nothing significantly different from the classifications of The Fund for Peace and earlier scholarly works based on the state failure thesis, which identified African nations as among the foremost cases of state failure (Herbst, 1996/97; Zartman, 1995).

Manifestations of state failure in Africa should not come as a surprise. Between the period of political independence in the 1960s and the early 1990s, most states in Africa were under military rule, embroiled in or on the verge of civil and other wars. Others were under one-party rule, civilian dictatorships, or political strongmen. Thus, the character of the state in Africa is not unconnected with about three decades of one-party dictatorship in many countries of Africa, an era of military occupation of most parts of Africa, and a long period akin to a war situation. It was a period when primitive accumulation, corruption, and lack of accountability were norms in government throughout most of Africa, as we observed above. Indeed, virtually all African countries were immersed in war situations or adversely affected by social upheavals of some variety (Ake, 1978; Zartman, 1995).

The socioeconomic and political consequences of such states in Africa and the social disorder confronting them were inevitable as well as debilitating, involving wide and unprecedented population movements and displacements, poverty, hunger, disease, fear, insecurity, disregard for human life, refugees, child soldiers and street children, and, above all, the perpetration of some of the worst cases of human rights abuses known in the world (Flint and De Waal, 2008; Mamdani, 2002; Prunier, 2005; Turner, 2008). These manifestations of socioeconomic crisis were sharpened by the structural adjustment programs of the 1980s—in particular by the heavy debt burden found in every African country—yet such problems were evident before globalization, even if not at the same levels of intensity (Gibbon, Bangura, and Ofstad, 1992; Olukoshi, 1991).

However, the critical implications for the present discussion are that, under the above social circumstances, most governments lost the capacity to govern and to meet obligations regarding the protection of human rights. The capacity of government in this instance refers to the ability a government has, through its powers and functions, to defend its sovereignty through the legitimate use of physical force to ensure law and order and deter external aggression; the same authority and abilities must be in place to formulate and implement policies, especially welfare policies, build and strengthen governmental institutions, and be able to extract and develop a nation's physical, natural, social, cultural and human-resource endowments (Jinadu, n.d.). According to Jinadu (n.d.), the capacity of government

> is also a function of the complementary, indeed reinforcing and con-solidating role of subsidiary associations and groups in mediating the relationship between the state and its institutions on the one hand, and the civil society on the other hand, and in conferring legitimacy on the state.... Capacity, therefore, is a function of the strength or deficit of these attributes, and of the extent to which a political culture of public spiritedness prevails within both the political lead-ership, and citizenry generally.... Capacity depends on the extent to which citizens take their civic responsibility seriously and will defend their own sovereign rights; believe they own the state and belong to it; and have confidence in its ability, through legal and political processes, to manage or contain conflict impartially. (p. 3)

The argument of this chapter is that the absence of these attributes of state capacity has led to an upsurge of uncontrolled migration, human trafficking, and human rights abuses. As will be discussed below, because of the ineffectiveness of states, governments have been unable to formulate and enact meaningful policies to combat human rights infractions.

The state in Africa, human trafficking, and human rights

The character of the state in Africa, as outlined thus far, makes both the fight against trafficking in persons and the defense of human rights in Africa illusory and unachievable. Governments have long been incapac-itated by a high prevalence of wars and crises as well as by mounting debt burdens. They have also been overwhelmed by extreme poverty, disease, and large-scale population movements. Situations such as these have made smuggling and human trafficking inescapable. Characteris-tically, African political leaders interpret most social issues concerning their societies in a political way, particularly with regard to how such issues may or may not advance the course of access, control, and man-agement of political power, or advance their struggle for power (Ake, 1981, 2000). Accordingly, in their calculations, human trafficking is one of those issues that may not constitute a threat to their quest for or aim to retain power. Therefore, very low priority is given to the fight against trafficking in persons. To African leaders, human trafficking is not a political concern; it has no political costs associated with it, as no matter how examined, it will not add to or subtract from elites' political capital or political currency (Fatton, 1992). Fighting human trafficking will not procure leaders any advantage in their struggle for power, including winning or losing elections. Thus, in Sub-Saharan Africa, no government assigns official responsibility for combating trafficking in persons to any officer above the rank of a director. In most cases, trafficking is handled under the category of illegal entry/illegal aliens under the jurisdiction of the Immigration Department. Also, African governments take little interest in the activities of NGOs combating trafficking in persons, enforcing human rights, and preventing the human rights abuses of persons vulnerable to trafficking (Truong, 2006).

If only to extend the discussion a little further, the issue may be raised as to how many legislative houses in Sub-Saharan Africa have meaningfully discussed or debated human trafficking beyond the mere ratifications of laws or international conventions on human trafficking (Pearson, 2002). Such serious debate would demonstrate genuine concern and commitment toward the eradication of trade in human persons.

Additionally, trafficking in human persons is clandestine and has other features that are difficult and expensive to effectively regulate or monitor, even for the best of governments. Though part of a network, trafficking operates in small and mobile cells that are often camouflaged in such a way as to appear to be legitimate business activities. With such apparent complexity, how many African states have the budget, manpower, commitment, and political will to direct attention to trafficking, or identify and apprehend members of such a network of clandestine organizations? Certainly, this is not a simple task for the weak and unstable governments that are found across Africa.

Also, because trafficking is secretive, law enforcement agents must receive special training in order to combat it. Government agents, in turn, need to acquire expertise, and marry this with patience and dedication, in order to be able to identify and apprehend traffickers. In this respect, African governments lack the organization and sophistication required to contain the network of organizations that characterize the clandestine world of traffickers. Even if such sophisticated training and agents were available, government officials could be compromised in their duties through the tempting bribes traffickers are known to offer (Salt and Stein, 1997). Also related to corruption issues—and perhaps more fundamental—is the fact that most African governments are unable to prevent their law enforcement agents from taking bribes. A government that is unable to prevent its law enforcement agents from taking bribes is not likely to have the power to combat trafficking in persons. Accordingly, governments with high degrees of corruption will not be able to resolve the contradictions in their societies in such a way as to protect citizens' rights.

Incidentally, African governments have been under the spotlight of Transparency International since its inception in 1993, with reports from the organization indicating that the level of corruption associated with African governments and their leaders is so high that fighting human trafficking under the circumstances may be very difficult, if not impossible. According to the 2008 Transparency International Corruption Perceptions Index (CPI), there are 18 African countries in the list of the 50 most corrupt nations. Since the production of the CPI began in the 1990s, Africa has occupied the topmost positions every year. While the CPI are only "perceptions," the experiences and evidence in the individual countries in Africa in particular confirm more than question the CPI's substance, as may be demonstrated by the massive accumulation of the wealth of the people by their leaders. In any case, that the governments in Africa are corrupt is no longer an issue; the point is how to arrest the devastating effects decades of corruption have had for society, including the opportunities the situation creates for criminals trafficking in human persons. Put differently, corruption represents one of the major factors encouraging migration and human trafficking. It could be argued that corruption is largely responsible for mass poverty, diseases, and ignorance in Africa, and leads the vulnerable to accept being trafficked. On the other hand, it is the same poverty, disease, and ignorance created by governments' corruption that governments, in turn, are expected to address in order to mitigate the "push" factors that cause the vulnerable to be trafficked. In other words, if poverty and ignorance are some of the major causes of trafficking, or are inextricably related to trafficking, it may mean that trafficking may not end or be reduced soon as most African states do not have the capacity to address the poverty and ignorance that they helped create, in large part through their corrupt practices.

Indeed, when one examines the literature on human trafficking in Sub-Saharan Africa, one observes that what scholars are calling on African governments to do in order to combat trafficking are the things the governments in that region have not been able to achieve in nearly 50 years of political independence—the eradication of poverty and ignorance as well as the provision of social services in the form of education and healthcare. The implication is that trafficking in persons will persist because most of these governments do not have the capacity to provide the services needed to make its demise possible. In fact, many governments face worse situations now than a decade ago in terms of their socioeconomic and political indices of development (World Bank, 2008–9). However, it may need to be emphasized that the lack of capacity is to a large extent self-inflicted, resulting from the yearly pillage of the resources of these countries by their leaders.

As for reducing the high levels of poverty that contribute to human trafficking, micro-credit schemes have been suggested as a partial solution (Schubert and Slater, 2006). In this regard, a 2002 report by UNICEF indicates that only Cameroon and Togo had micro-credit financial assistance schemes in place at that time to reduce poverty (UNICEF Report, 2002, pp. 23–24). A more recent study conducted in 2008 shows that 11 more countries have introduced micro-credit facilities. But for most of the 13, problems such as corruption, disease (HIV/AIDS), and political meddling are defeating the entire purpose of the poverty-alleviation facilities (Wali, 2009). Thus, instead of micro-credit schemes, it is NGOs in Africa that are meaningfully involved in the fight to reduce poverty and disease, with the aim of stemming the conditions leading to human trafficking (Truong, 2006). The same lack of commitment to best practices by African states is reflected in the US *Trafficking in Persons Report* of 2008 on combating trafficking, which was mentioned earlier. Most African countries were either Tier 2 or on the Tier 2 Watch List, both of which indicate a lack of adequate commitment toward eradicating trafficking. No African country featured among the Tier 1 nations, who are totally committed to eradicating trafficking.

A few other related issues can be raised to add to the suggestion that governments in Africa are unable to seriously fight human trafficking and so offer no solution to related crimes. Apart from failing to deal with the rights of victims of trafficking and the vulnerable, African states are generally known to rank very low on scales measuring respect for human rights. Though some human rights issues find space in their constitutions, African states have not regarded human rights as a necessary official obligation. Governments have ruled with impunity and have no respect for the rule of law that is designed to sustain human rights in every society. African governments can, at will, impose a state of emergency on their peoples, carry out detentions without trial, incarcerate citizens, and abuse and violate the rights of prisoners (Dissel, 2001; Kampala Declaration, 1996; UN Economic Council, 1997/36).

An examination of prisons in Africa and the conditions under which prisoners are held reinforces the argument that African governments have no respect for human rights, and therefore are not in a position to enforce or protect such rights anywhere, or confront and stop groups or individuals such as human traffickers who abuse human rights. Reports on prison conditions in Africa are chilling and question whether any government that treats its prisoners like animals will have regard for victims of human trafficking or those vulnerable to trafficking. Unfortunately, the signing of protocols on human rights by African countries, as well as the fact that a number of African countries have been categorized as Tier 2 and not Tier 3, is not matched by the human rights situations in these countries. The signatures placed on the protocols are worth less than the paper on which they are written. This reflects a similar lack of values attached to constitutions in Africa, and in regard to the rule of law or the practice of democracy on the continent. The rules are one thing, but the practice and patterns of behavior to correspond with the demands of the rules are another. Moreover, with globalization, there is a rush, particularly on the part of developing countries in Africa, to append signatures to high-profile documents in order to secure favorable human rights ratings among the international community, and thus qualify for forms of economic assistance.

According to reports, prison conditions in Africa are the worst in the entire world (Kampala Declaration, 1996). In 1996, Penal Reform International organized a seminar in Kampala, Uganda, where dignitaries signed the Kampala Declaration on Prison Conditions in Africa. The seminar was the first in Africa to address the alarming inhuman conditions in African prisons. A year later, the United Nations Economic and Social Council published a report entitled *The International Cooperation for the Improvement of Prison Conditions*, which had Africa as its main subject. These efforts were aimed at improving the conditions under which prison inmates were kept. The conditions are so bad that African governments may be accused of involvement in inhumanity against their citizens. Citizens are kept for long years in prison custody without trial. Prison yards are dilapidated, and prison cells are overcrowded. Prisons built between 50 and 100 years ago to house 100 inmates now house over 3000 inmates. Hunger, disease, and torture at the hands of prison officials are a common feature of the prisons (BBC News, 2004; Dissel, 2001; IRIN Africa/West Africa, 2009; Penal Reform International, 1996; UN Economic and Social Council, 1997/36; *People's Daily*, 2006; VOA, 2008). The issue of the inhuman treatment meted out to prisoners in Africa has been raised in this chapter to exhaustively argue that governments who allow such treatment of their citizens do not value humanity generally and will not be able to understand why they have an obligation to protect the human rights of their citizens everywhere, including those of the downtrodden and those already victims of human trafficking.

As another way of measuring the understanding, seriousness, and commitment of African governments toward reducing migration and trafficking, it is worth noting that in all of Africa the University of Witwatersrand in South Africa is the only institution known to offer a degree program in migration studies. The University of Ghana in Legon has a Centre of Migration Studies and Research, which coordinates activities and research on migration, but does not offer a degree in migration. This lack of interest or foresight or both among governments in Africa has limited the number of studies on migration and trafficking coming from Africa and hence impeded the acquisition of knowledge concerning the subject matter in Africa. This is in spite of the fact that Africa is home to the most impoverished victims of trafficking. Consequently, very few, if any, of the most authoritative works on migration and trafficking emanate from Africa. While degrees and research on migration may not be sufficient in themselves to solve the ills associated with human trafficking, they demonstrate the seriousness of governments in terms of developing research findings and knowledge that could assist in providing solutions to the problem of human trafficking.

Finally, the impact of structural adjustment programs in the 1980s and neoliberal globalization since the 1990s also needs to be addressed if a solution is to be found to trafficking in persons. A globally concerted effort needs to be made to resolve the subsequent wide gap that has emerged between the Euro-American currencies and those of most African states. The payoff that is expected to accrue to a victim of trafficking out of the few dollars or euros he or she hopes to receive serves as an encouragement to risk being trafficked. Some victims sell their scant belongings back home in addition to borrowing funds to pay to be trafficked. All the risks are taken because the victims believe that the foreign currency they make will pay back their entire debt in a short while. Of course, no thought of failure is admitted. Also, traffickers are encouraged to continue in their crimes because they are aware that with even limited earnings in Europe or America victims should usually be able to pay back the investments made in them (Nnoli, 2006).

Since no one factor is absolutely responsible for trafficking in persons, it is not misleading to suggest that all issues, those remotely and those proximately related to trafficking, need to be re-examined and addressed in order to confront trafficking and prevent corresponding human rights abuses among Africans. But the key factor is the nature of the state in Africa. If the world is serious about combating the new slave trade as it concerns Africa, no other measure can substitute for the reform of African states. A meaningful reform of the state in Africa would ensure a constitutional provision that would insist on the decentralization and devolution of power, whereby political power is not concentrated in one man, the president, or a group of representatives. Such a reform would strengthen the character of the state as an arbiter or an umpire among the interest groups in society, and would also make it both unattractive and unworkable for individuals to dominate the state, state power, or state instruments and agents. The constitution and rule of law as such would be supreme, with the people serving as the base of power. An independent judiciary and a free press would also act as vital elements of the state. The state would not be monopolized by individuals or groups for their own private interests, and thus the state would become a more impartial arbiter in resolving conflicting interests in society. Civil society would reproduce itself as a virile social entity, understanding that it is the ultimate sovereign and is entitled to defend the relative autonomy of the state.

Conclusion

While globalization has debilitated many African economies and created conditions that have facilitated trafficking in persons, the primary factor that has exacerbated human trafficking is the character of the state in Africa, with a related factor being the leadership reproduced by the state. The state across Africa has been ill-prepared and ill-equipped because it has lacked the capacity to effectively enforce and protect the human rights of actual and potential trafficking victims. Therefore, any meaningful solution to trafficking in persons and preventing violations of human rights has to address the character of the state in Africa and the type of political leadership common in the region. If positive changes are to be effected, years of authoritarian politics cannot be ignored; owing to over 30 years of military dictatorship and a period of war—during which militaries fought against their own peoples and pillaged their own nations' wealth—no efforts made so far by democratic governments have been able to redress the devastation, in spite of high expectations among the global community concerning the control of human trafficking.

African leaders have not demonstrated any manifest spirit of nationalism, any sense of mission, and any political will to bring Africa into the twenty-first century; they have not endeavored to cultivate appropriate social values and forms of development. As history has amply demonstrated, no devastation suffered by any society, such as that suffered in Africa from the 1960s to the 1990s, may be overcome in less than half a century.

It is doubtful whether the present leadership in Africa is seriously embarking on remedying the years of dictatorship, war, corruption, and the poverty left in their wake. The social experiences of war to which Africa was subjected have destroyed the values of society that are necessary to sustain development. Until remedies are put in place so that the character of the state is transformed in such a way that it is not subsumed under a particular dominant interest, human trafficking and associated human rights violations will remain a feature of African societies. Only if the state is reformed will the rule of law be possible and all rights respected, including the rights of victims of human trafficking and those vulnerable to trafficking. It should further be stressed that the responsibility for the reconstitution of power associated with the state's reform lies with Africans themselves, who must act as the primary movers of change before any expected global intervention.

References

Aina, T. (1996). Globalization and social policy in Africa. *Council for the Development of Social Science Research in Africa (CODESRIA) Working Paper, 6*. Dakar: CODESRIA.

Ake, C. (1978). *Revolutionary pressures in Africa*. London: Zed Books.

Ake, C. (1981). *Political economy of Africa*. London: Longman.

Ake, C. (1985). *Political economy of Nigeria*. London: Longman.

Ake, C. (1994). Democratization of disempowerment in Africa. *CASS Occasional Monograph, 1*. Suffolk, UK: Malthouse Press.

Ake, C. (1996). *Democracy and development in Africa*. Washington, DC: Brookings Institute.

Ake, C. (2000). *The feasibility of democracy in Africa*. Dakar: CODESRIA.

Anderson, B., and Davidson, J. O. (2003). Is trafficking in human beings demand driven? A multi-country pilot study. *International Organization for Migration (IOM) Migration Research Series, 15*.

Bales, K. (1999). *Disposable people: New slavery in the global economy*. Berkeley: University of California Press.

Bales, K., and Robbins, P. T. (2001). "No one shall be held in slavery or servitude": A critical analysis of international slavery agreements and concepts of slavery. *Human Rights Review, 2*(2), 18–45.

Barrow, R. (1983). *Injustice, inequality and ethics: A philosophical introduction to moral problems*. Brighton: Wheatsheaf Books.

Bates, R. H. (2001). *When things fell apart: State failure in late-century Africa.* Cambridge: Cambridge University Press.

Bayart, J. (1993). *The state in Africa: The politics of the belly.* London: Longman.

BBC News (Online) (29 September 2004). *Kenya prison conditions slammed.* Retrieved 18 February 2009, from http://www.bbc.co.uk/worldservice/africa/.

Beare, M. E. (1999). Illegal immigration: Personal tragedies, social problems and national security threats. In P. Williams (ed.), *Illegal immigration and commercial sex: The new slave trade* (pp. 11–41). London: Frank Cass.

Beckman, B. (1992). Empowerment or repression? The World Bank and the politics of Adjustment. In P. Gibbon, Y. Bangura, and A. Ofstad (eds.), *Authoritarianism, democracy and adjustment: The politics of economic reform in Africa* (pp. 83–105). Uppsala, Sweden: Nordic Africa Institute.

Bertone, A. M. (2000). Sexual trafficking in women: International political economy and the politics of sex. *Gender Issue, 18*(1), 4–22.

Bruckert, C. and Parent, C. (2002). *Trafficking in human beings and organized crime: A literature review.* Paper presented before the Department of Criminology, University of Ottawa, for the Royal Canadian Mounted Police. Retrieved 10 February 2009, from http://www.rcmp-grc.gc.ca/pubs/ccaps-spcca/traffick-eng.htm.

Chandler, D. (2006). *Empire in denial: The politics of state-building.* London: Pluto Press.

Chomsky, N. (2007). *Failed states: The abuse of power and the assault on democracy.* New York: Holt Paperbacks.

De Dios, A. J. (1999). *Macro-economic policies and their impact on sexual exploitation and trafficking of women and girls: Issues, responses and challenges.* Retrieved 10 February 2009, from http://www.catw.-ap.org/Macro.htm.

Deng, L. A. (1998). *Rethinking African development: Towards a framework for social integration and ecological harmony.* Trenton, NJ: Africa World Press.

Dissel, A. (2001). *Prison Conditions in Africa.* Johannesburg: Center for the Study of Violence and Reconciliation. Retrieved 12 February 2009, from http://www.csvr.org.za/docs/correctional/prisonconditions.pdf.

Dorman, S., Hammett, D., and Nugent, P. (eds.) (2007). *Making nations, creating strangers: States and citizenship in Africa.* Boston: Brill.

Fatton, R. (1992). *Predatory rule: State and civil society in Africa.* Boulder: Lynne Rienner.

Flint, J., and De Waal, A. (2008). *Darfur: A new history of a long war.* London and New York: Zed Books.

Fukuyama, F. (2004a). *State-building, governance and world order in the twenty-first century.* Ithaca, NY: Cornell University Press.

Fukuyama, F. (2004b). The imperative of state-building. *Journal of Democracy, 15*(2), 17–31.

Ghani, A., and Lockhart, C. (2008). *Fixing failed states: A framework for re-building a fractured world.* Oxford University Press.

Gibbon, P., Bangura, Y., and Ofstad, A. (eds.) (1992). *Authoritarianism, democracy and adjustment: The politics of economic reform in Africa.* Uppsala, Sweden: Nordic Africa Institute.

Hehir, A., and Robinson, N. (eds.) (2007). *State-building: Theory and practice.* London: Routledge.

Herbst, J. (1996–1997/Winter). Responding to state failure in Africa. *International security, 21*(3), 120–144.

Herbst, J. (1999). The role of citizenship laws in multiethnic societies: Evidence from Africa. In Joseph, R. (ed.), *State, conflict and democracy in Africa* (pp. 267–284). Boulder: Lynne Rienner.

Herbst, J. (2000). *State and power in Africa: Comparative lessons in authority and control.* Princeton: Princeton University Press.

Integrated Regional Information Networks (IRIN). (1 March 2009). *Benin: Prison conditions.* Retrieved 9 February 2009, from http://www.irinnews.org/Report. aspx?Reportld=79523.

Jinadu, A. (2000). Globalization and the new partnership: An African perspective. In G. Lachapelle and J. Trent (eds.), *Globalization, governance and identity: The emergence of new Partnerships* (pp. 67–82). Montreal: Les Presses de l'Université de Montréal.

Jinadu, A. (n.d.). *Globalization and State Capacity in Africa.* Paper presented at the 7th African Leadership Forum. Retrieved 28 February 2009, from http://www.undp.org/africa/agf/documents/en/background_info/papers/ Paper4-GlobalizationandStateCapacityinAfrica.pdf.

Kampala declaration on prison conditions in Africa. (1996). Retrieved 14 February 2009, from http://www.penalreform.org/kampala-declaration-on-prison-conditions-in-africa.html.

Kempadoo, K. (ed.) (2000). *Global sex workers: Rights, resistances and redefinition.* New York: Routledge.

Lumumba-Kasongo, T. (2002). Re-conceptualizing the state as a leading agent of development in the context of globalization in Africa. *African Journal of Political Science, 7*(1), 79–108.

Lyons, T., and Samatar, A. I. (2003). *Somalia: Collapse, multilateral intervention and strategies for political reconstruction.* Washington, DC: Brookings Institute.

Mamdani, M. (2002). *When victims become killers: Colonialism, nativism, and the genocide in Rwanda.* Princeton and Oxford: Princeton University Press.

Nabudere, D. W. (ed.) (2000). *Globalization and the post-colonial African state.* Harare: African Association of Political Science.

Nnoli, O. C. (2006). *The dynamics and contexts of trafficking in persons: A national perspective.* Unpublished master's thesis, University of Lagos, Nigeria.

Olukoshi, A. (ed.) (1991). *Crisis and adjustment in the Nigerian economy.* Lagos: JAD Publishers.

Onuoha, B. (1988). *Indigenization in Nigeria, 1972–1983: Resources and income re-distribution.* Unpublished doctoral dissertation, University of Lagos, Lagos, Nigeria.

Ottaway, M. (1999). *Africa's new leaders: Democracy or state reconstruction?* Washington, DC: Carnegie Endowment for International Peace.

Pearson, E. (2002). *Human trafficking, human rights: Redefining victim protection.* London: Anti-Slavery International.

Penal Reform International. (1996). *The Kampala declaration on prison conditions in Africa.* Retrieved 12 February 2009, from http://www.penalreform.org/ kampala-declaration-on-prison-Conditions-in-Africa.html.

People's Daily (2 September 2006). Ministers agree to improve prison conditions in Africa. Retrieved 10 February 2009, from http://English.peoplesdaily.com. cn/data/Kenya.html.

Pettit, P. (1980). *Judging justice: An introduction to contemporary political philosophy.* London: Routledge and Kegan Paul.

Prunier, G. (2005). *Darfur: The ambiguous genocide.* Ithaca, NY: Cornell University Press.

Raphael, D. D. (1979). *Problem of political philosophy.* London: Macmillan.

Rawls, J. A. (1972). *Theory of justice.* London: Oxford University Press.

Rotberg, R. I. (ed.) (2000). *When states fail: Causes and consequences.* Princeton: Princeton University Press.

Rugumamu, S. M. (1999). Globalization, liberalization and Africa's marginalization. *African Association of Political Science (AAPS) Occasional Papers, 3*(1).

Salt, J., and Stein, J. (1997). Migration as a business: The case of trafficking. *International Migration, 35*(4), 467–494.

Schubert, B., and Slater, R. (2006). Social cash transfer in low income African countries: Conditional or unconditional. *Development Policy Review, 24*(5), 571–578.

Seely, J. C. (2007, February). *Limiting access to citizenship in Sub-Saharan Africa.* Paper presented at the 48th Annual Convention of the International Studies Association, Chicago, Illinois.

Sen, A. (2004). Elements of a theory of human rights. *Philosophy and Public Affairs, 32*(4), 315–356.

Skrobanek, S., and Sanghera, J. (1996). Sex trade and globalized trafficking in women. *Atlantis, 21*(1), 95–99.

Truong, T. (2006). *Poverty, gender and human trafficking in Sub-Saharan Africa: Rethinking best practices in migration management.* Paris: UNESCO Project to Fight Human Trafficking in Africa.

Turner, T. (2008). *The Congo wars: Conflict, myth and reality.* London and New York: Zed Books.

UNICEF Report (2002). *Child trafficking in West Africa. Policy responses.* Florence, Italy: UNICEF Innocenti Research Centre.

United Nations (1997). *Economic and Social Council Resolution 1997. International cooperation for the improvement of prison conditions.* Retrieved 18 February 2009, from http://www.un.org/documents/ecosoc/res/1997/eres 1997-36.htm.

United Nations (2000). *Protocol to prevent, suppress, and punish trafficking in persons, especially women and children: Supplementing the United Nations convention against transnational organized crime.* Retrieved 15 February 2009, from http:// www.uncji.org/documents/...2/Convention_%20traff_eng.pdf.

United Nations High Commission (2002). *For human rights principles and guidelines on human rights and trafficking, E/2002/68/Add.1.* Retrieved 12 February 2009, from http://www1.umn.edu/humanrts/.../traffickingGuidelinesHCHR. html.

US Trafficking in Persons Report (4 June 2008). Retrieved 10 February 2009, from http://www.state.gov/g/tip/rls/tiprpt/2008.

Voice of America (VOA) (11 September 2008). *Prison Conditions in Cameroon Fuel Escape Attempts.* Retrieved 18 February 2009, from http://www.voanews.com/ english/.../2008-09-11-voa28.cfm?...09.

Wali, M. (2009). Poverty alleviation and micro-credit in Sub-Saharan Africa. *International Business and Economic Research, 8*(1), 1–9.

Wijers, M., and Lap-Chew, L. (1997). *Trafficking in Women, forced labor and slavery-like practices in marriage, domestic labor and prostitution.* Utrecht, Netherlands: Foundation Against Trafficking.

Williams, P. (ed.) (1999). *Illegal immigration and commercial sex: The new slave trade.* London: Frank Cass.

World Bank (2008–2009). *African Development Indicators.* New York: World Bank.

Zartman, W. I. (ed.) (1995). *The disintegration and restoration of legitimate authority.* Boulder: Lynne Rienner Publishers.

3
Exclusionary Globalization: Sanctions, Military Rule, and Non-Democratization in Myanmar

Patrick Strefford

Introduction

When Cyclone Nargis devastated Myanmar's Irrawaddy Delta in May 2008, the disaster and its aftermath served as a poignant reminder of the deeply entrenched polarization between the military government and the general population that has long characterized Myanmar's internal politics. The response of the international community to the crisis revealed how Myanmar's international relations remained equally troubled. Despite the obvious and overwhelming need for swift and comprehensive humanitarian assistance, politics soon engulfed the aid agenda and the citizens of Myanmar were left on their own to struggle with the disaster.

While there can be no doubt that the government of Myanmar, being the highest authority in the nation, bears ultimate responsibility for the mismanagement of the country, it is equally clear that the international community has also played a significant role in aggravating Myanmar's woes. As will be argued in this chapter, one major way in which Western nations have contributed to the ongoing humanitarian crisis in Myanmar is through international sanctions aimed at toppling the nation's military regime. Rather than heralding political reforms and improved human rights as intended, the sanctions have in fact led to more political tensions, social dislocation, and economic misery for Myanmar's citizens, while making democracy a highly unlikely prospect.

The application of sanctions and the resulting increased international isolation of Myanmar have occurred during an intensive phase of what is commonly termed "globalization." While international barriers to the movement of goods, services, ideas, and labor have been steadily and purposefully reduced worldwide, those same barriers in the case of Myanmar have been maintained and reinforced. Paradoxically, it is the leading proponents of contemporary globalization—Western liberal democracies, the United States in particular—that have concurrently perpetuated the sanctions policies intended to exclude Myanmar from the global community. In this instance, one thread of globalization has entailed Western states striving to promote political change in Myanmar while the people of Myanmar are prevented from engaging in freer economic, political, and cultural exchanges with the outside world. This "exclusionary globalization" associated with sanctions is impeding the inclusive form of globalization—integration into global markets and the international community of nations—Myanmar actually requires to democratize and improve the human rights of its citizens.

Democracy and dictatorship in Myanmar

The primary justification for sanctions has been the government of Myanmar's oppression of its citizens and its prevention of a transition to democracy against popular demands. While the citizens of Myanmar do indeed desire democracy, public protests in Myanmar have been ignited by hardships aggravated by failed economic policies rather than by purely philosophical political ideals. The widespread demonstrations and resulting popular movement for democracy in 1988, which were directly caused by the demonetization of 1987 that saw wealth and life savings vanish (Mya Maung, 1991, p. 224), brought down the Ne Win dictatorship. Likewise, the anti-government demonstrations of 2007 were sparked by the government's decision to remove fuel subsidies. Myanmar citizens thus support democracy as the form of government that can best provide the environment for the economic development that will allow them to improve their lives. That being the case, it seems illogical to focus exclusively on the political aspects of development—as is the case with the reasoning behind sanctions against Myanmar—while ignoring other interconnected economic or social dimensions.

The government of Myanmar today is a military dictatorship under Senior General Than Shwe, dedicated to its own preservation. Further, officers within the *Tatmadaw* (Burmese military) see their institution as the only one able to keep the nation intact. This perception has been instilled in the leadership since independence, reinforced through the early years of failed democracy, and sharpened through its long fight against widespread insurgencies. In the eyes of the *Tatmadaw*, the nation's survival is intrinsically and irrevocably linked to its own. While a democratic transition is obviously a threat to their authoritarian hold on political power, the *Tatmadaw* believe that democracy is a threat to the survival of the union itself, a presumption based on the experience of failed democratic rule during the 1950s. There is no social contract between the citizens and government in Myanmar, and for this reason the legitimacy of the government is widely questioned. There is no rule of law and the *Tatwadaw*'s military government—the State Peace and Development Council (SPDC)—rules by decree. As is commonly known, human rights abuses are widespread. Although many other governments are also rightly criticized for human rights violations, Myanmar's record of state terrorism and human rights abuses is among the worst in the world. In the preamble to Amnesty International's 2008 Annual Report, for example, Myanmar is described as a "human rights flashpoint" demanding "immediate action" (Amnesty International, 2008). Darfur, Zimbabwe, Gaza, and Iraq are also mentioned, as are Pakistan, China, and Saudi Arabia. But none of these countries have sanctions against them, and do in fact receive considerable foreign assistance despite their widely recognized human rights violations. The self-preservation priority of the *Tatmadaw* is vividly shown when considering that the majority (upwards of 40 per cent) of the national budget goes to the 500,000-strong *Tatmadaw* (Thawnghmung, 2003, p. 40). In terms of the rationale behind the actions of the SPDC, Stephen McCarthy, employing Aristotelian thought to explain "tyranny in Burma," argues that it is necessary for such rulers to eliminate "high thoughts and trust" within their society (McCarthy, 2006). In this way, the *Tatmadaw* have stifled the growth of civil society and limited access to education, both of which are crucial for democratic transition.

Globalization and democracy

There are numerous definitions of globalization, but in its most basic sense it means the transformation of local, regional, or national conditions into ones that are global. However, this does not really help us understand the mechanics or impact of globalization. Broadly speaking, globalization is a process with political, economic, technological, and social components. It is the "growing interpenetration of states, markets, communication, and ideas across borders" (Brysk, 2002, p. 1), while also encompassing the "breaking down of barriers to the flow of goods, services, [and] capital" (Stiglitz, 2002, p. 18). Globalization implies integration, and especially economic integration. Giddens (1990) suggests that globalization is the "intensification of worldwide social relations," (p. 64) and this includes the growing magnitude of transnational relationships. This intensification is, of course, connected to the accelerated pace of global interactions that has resulted from technological advances in travel, communications, and financial transactions.

What impact globalization has for the developing world is a topic of intense debate. While some critics argue that globalization has meant nothing but unmitigated disaster for the Global South (e.g. Chossudovsky, 2003; Petras and Veltmeyer, 2001), once-common ideas such as retreating from the global economy to promote development are no longer viewed as viable. As Stallings (1995) puts it, delinking as a strategy "will not be the basis for growth but of increasing poverty" (p. 388). More realistically, the issue is more one of managing globalization in such a way that more sustained economic development can take place and benefit the greatest number of people as possible in impoverished world regions (Sen, 2002). Moreover, while economic development is not impossible without globalization, the evidence suggests it is far less likely to occur in places with little or no contact with the outside world (Dollar and Kraay, 2002; Sen, 2002). It is also evident that higher levels of economic development and improved communications linked to globalization are more likely to give rise to greater political freedoms in otherwise isolated and economically backward states (Lopez-Cordova and Meissner, 2008).

The notion that economic development leads to democratization is not new; it dates back to the 1950s. At this time, the American political scientist Seymour Martin Lipset was among the first theorists to make the connection, arguing that "the more well-to-do a nation, the greater the chances that it will sustain democracy" (Lipset, 1959, p. 105). More recent research has supported Lipset's proposition (Barro, 1999; Diamond, 1992; Huntington, 1991). While such findings do not mean that countries at lower levels of economic development cannot be democratic, it does mean that democratic forms of government are underpinned by the economic, political, and social capacities that increase with economic development within state and civil society. Also promoting democracy, an expanded middle class emerges in tandem with economic development to demand political rights commensurate with its elevated economic power (Lin and Nugent, 1995).

Regarding the linkages between globalization, economic development, and democratization, numerous works have noted a positive correlation. A study by Lopez-Cordova and Meissner (2008), for example, suggests that "open countries have been more strongly democratic over the long run" and that a "move from autarky to the average level of openness could eventually raise a country's democracy measure from three to five points over the long run" (p. 553). Lin and Nugent (1995) similarly argue that "both a financially independent middle class and the integration of the domestic economy with the world economy are at the same time both necessary conditions for and natural effects of economic success in the modern world" (p. 2336). A relatively open economy (a major attribute of contemporary globalization), in this view, is a precondition of economic development. An open economy can also be seen as a component of successful democratic transition and consolidation, while a closed economy under an authoritarian regime is likely to reduce the possibility of democratic transition.

In 1991, Samuel P. Huntington outlined what he termed a "third wave of democratization," which began in the mid-1970s and continues to this day. In Asia such democratic transitions took place in South Korea, Taiwan, and the Philippines. According to Huntington, there are five causative factors that account for democratic transition, one of which follows Lipset's theory stipulating that economic modernization and development provide the social forces and capacity to push for democratic transition (Huntington, 1991).

Egalitarian societies are also more likely to be democratic (Acemoglu and Robinson, 2000, p. 1194). This means that where the distribution of income and assets is unequal, the holders of power will try to prevent the adoption of more redistributive policies that undermine their monopolistic position. As will be shown later, the *Tatmadaw* in Myanmar are in such a position. Acemoglu and Robinson (2000) further argue that policies resulting in a more equal society, such as access to education for the poor, will support efforts to democratize (p. 1129). It seems plausible to assume, therefore, that official development aid (ODA) specifically targeting education and health could be justified not only on short-term humanitarian grounds, but also on the grounds of supporting a medium- to long-term democratic transition and consolidation. Huntington (1991, p. 69) has also argued that improved education (a necessary component of economic modernization) can promote democratization as well.

Polarization: exclusionary sanctions versus constructive engagement

After the popular democracy movement was violently crushed by the military in 1988, the United States, Japan, and the European Union imposed sanctions on what was then called Burma. These sanctions began with a freeze on economic aid. In response to the military's refusal to honor the results of the 1990 elections, the European Union and the United States introduced an arms embargo in the early 1990s. At the same time, Western states began to block loans and grants to the region from international financial institutions such as the World Bank, the IMF, and the Asian Development Bank. The United States prohibited visas for senior members of the Burmese military and their families in 1996, and banned any new investments in Burma the following year.

The Burma Freedom and Democracy Act (BFDA) became US law in 2003, and has since been renewed annually. It includes a ban on all imports from Myanmar, a ban on the export of financial services to the nation, a freeze on the assets of certain financial institutions, and the extension of previous visa restrictions. In addition to this, President George W. Bush issued a number of executive orders economically targeting senior Myanmar government officials and companies (such as the Union of Myanmar Economic Holdings Ltd and the Myanmar Economic Corporation) that are owned or controlled by the military government. US sanctions against Myanmar have been accompanied by often highly emotive criticism of the Myanmar government. For example, Adam Szubin, director of the Treasury Department's Office of Foreign Assets Control, said in 2008, "The regime's refusal to protect and allow relief to reach the Burmese people as Cyclone Nargis devastated their country is but another example of the regime's heartless neglect of its people" (US Department of the Treasury, 29 July 2008, HP-1105). First Lady Laura Bush gave a rare speech conference just two days after Cyclone Nargis hit Myanmar offering a scathing criticism of that country's poor human rights record, lack of progress on democratization, and failure to allow humanitarian aid to reach disaster victims. Yet the First Lady's condemnations proved counterproductive in that they alienated Myanmar government officials—the only ones positioned to allow the realization of such goals. Indeed, it has been argued that the First Lady's comments severely hindered the swift and comprehensive disbursal of humanitarian aid (Cho, 2008). Yet regardless of such high-profile rhetoric, much criticism from within the United States of official US relations with Myanmar has been directed at the sanctions policy. For example, a report compiled for the Council for Foreign Relations (2003) recommended that "in view of Burma's massive public health crisis, the United States should increase humanitarian assistance to Burma" (p. 2).

In 1996 the European Union adopted its Common Position on Burma/Myanmar, which was renewed annually until 2004, when it was expanded. The Common Position includes a ban on arms sales, a ban on technical or financial assistance "related to military activities," a visa ban and assets freeze on a total of 430 persons connected to the military government in Myanmar, and a ban on any new investment in Myanmar. In 2007, the new Common Position included a ban on imports from Myanmar's logging and mining sectors. While the European Union has expanded sanctions against Myanmar, there seems to also be a growing recognition that the humanitarian situation in Myanmar warrants some type of engagement with the military. For example, a 2005 independent report for the European Commission has admitted that, regarding development in Myanmar, "external sanctions and the insufficient international assistance have worsened the situation" (Supporting Burma/Myanmar's Reconciliation Process, 2005, p. 1). The Australian government has initiated what it terms "the strongest financial measures available under existing Australian legislation against countries or individuals that are not subject to UN Security Council sanctions" (Smith MP, Ministerial Statement: Burma, 2008). The Australian financial sanctions specifically target 418 individuals, including members of Myanmar's State Peace and Development Council, cabinet ministers, and senior military figures.

Canada, for its part, has initiated far broader sanctions similar in scope to those of the United States, resulting in the implementation of the Special Economic Measures (Burma) Regulations in December of 2007. The measures include a ban on all exports to Myanmar (excluding humanitarian goods), a ban on all goods imported from Burma, a freeze on the assets of specified Myanmar leaders, a ban on new investments, a prohibition on financial services to and from Myanmar, and a prohibition on the export of any technical data to Burma. The sanctions even go so far as to include a prohibition on Canadian-registered ships or aircraft from docking or landing in Myanmar, and a prohibition on Myanmar-registered ships or aircraft from docking or landing in Canada, or even passing through Canada (*Canada Gazette*, 26 December 2007).

Importantly, of course, there are no United Nations Security Council sanctions against Myanmar. This is the case because China has always vetoed efforts to implement such sanctions. Premised largely on its desire to counter this Chinese influence, Japan has attempted to tread a fine line between the hard-line sanctions of the West and the constructive engagement policy of the Association of Southeast Asian Nations (ASEAN). Takeda has termed this Japan's "sunshine policy" toward the Myanmar government (Takeda, 2001). This has entailed using ODA both as a conduit for diplomacy and as a "carrot and stick" to encourage positive developments in Myanmar; according to the Japanese Ministry of Foreign Affairs (MOFA), this means "working patiently and persistently for improvements through ongoing dialogue with the present regime" (MOFA, 1997). Importantly, these improvements are specifically mentioned to be "national reconciliation," "democratization," and "human rights" (MOFA, 1997). In 2002, adopting the principle that economic reform can lead to political reform, the Japanese government also tried to support economic reform in Myanmar with projects such as the Myanmar-Japan Cooperation Program for Structural Adjustment of the Myanmar Economy. This project was "expected to encourage economic reform and induce an environment conducive to democratization" (MOFA, 2001). Support for ASEAN is also a key factor underlying the Japanese approach.

ASEAN has, also under the imperative of countering Chinese influence, engaged with the Myanmar government. The admission of Myanmar into ASEAN in 1997 completed the first step of Southeast Asian integration, and is the most tangible example of the engagement policy at work. ASEAN has traditionally followed a policy of non-interference in the domestic politics of its member states, and this has allowed ASEAN to remain mute regarding any negative internal developments in Myanmar. However, the deadlock in Myanmar has provided the biggest challenge yet to such a policy, and ASEAN has broken with its principle of domestic non-interference on a number of occasions. In the 2007 Joint Communiqué of the 40th ASEAN Ministerial Meeting in Manila, the foreign ministers "expressed concern on the pace of the national reconciliation process and urged Myanmar to show tangible progress that would lead to a peaceful transition to democracy in the near future" (ASEAN, 2007). In line with ASEAN's constructive engagement policy, ASEAN investment in Myanmar between 1995 and 2005 amounted to US$1.05 billion, and accounted for about one-quarter of total foreign direct investment (US$3.97 billion). Japanese FDI in Myanmar amounted to US$119 million, and Chinese FDI equaled US$156 million. Even though most Western governments actively discourage FDI in Myanmar, US FDI during the same period was US$406 million. Investment from the EU-15 stood at a staggering US$1.85 billion and was therefore more than the combined FDI from ASEAN, China, the United States, and Japan (ASEAN, 2004). Such levels of FDI from those very same states that enforce sanctions raises serious questions about the sanctions policies, and has led to a number of civil society boycotts and divestment campaigns. The Burma Campaign UK, for example, publishes a "dirty list" of companies that have invested in Myanmar. According to Burma Campaign UK (2007), "since we launched this campaign in 2002 over 100 companies have withdrawn from the country."

Interestingly, such campaigns are often compared to those civil society campaigns against apartheid-era South Africa in the 1970s and 1980s. While there can be little doubt that Aung San Suu Kyi commands a moral authority on par with Nelson Mandela, there are a number of very important differences between the situation in South Africa under apartheid and the situation in Myanmar at present. Even though Myanmar's government is responsible for heinous and considerable human rights violations, it is specious to compare the military regime to that of South Africa's apartheid era. As apartheid was widely considered a racist crime against humanity, South Africa was at that time surrounded by states that were outwardly hostile or, at the very least, deeply suspicious; this stands in stark contrast to Myanmar's neighbors, who *all* favor engagement. In the case of apartheid South Africa, external support came from Western governments—the United Kingdom and the United States in particular. This support was offered to South Africa despite widespread human rights violations, a lack of progress toward genuine democracy, the South African development of nuclear weapons, and considerable worldwide protests, demonstrations, and boycotts against apartheid. Even in the mid-1980s, both President Reagan and Prime Minister Thatcher followed constructive engagement policies, vetoing attempts to impose UN economic sanctions. It was not until the late-1980s that both governments began to apply pressure on the South African government to end apartheid. The situation in Myanmar is different enough that the assumption that the success of sanctions and civil society action against the apartheid regime in South Africa justifies similar actions against Myanmar today can be questioned.

Policy failure and exclusion

The stated purpose of the sanctions against Myanmar's government has been to encourage democratic transition and improve the human rights situation for the general populace. Initiated nearly 20 years ago, the sanctions have been steadily expanded. However, there is no evidence that the Myanmar government has succumbed to this policy. The size of the *Tatmadaw* actually increased continually through the 1990s and now stands at around 500,000 persons, and the military has suppressed a number of public demonstrations since 1988. The SPDC has not recognized the results of the 1990 elections, which saw the opposition National League for Democracy (NLD) win a landslide victory. The writing of a new constitution, a prerequisite for any type of democratic transition according to the SPDC, is firmly under the control of the military in the National Convention. The National Convention met sporadically throughout the 1990s and early twenty-first century, but did finally produce a draft constitution that was put to a referendum in 2008 (directly after Cyclone Nargis). The constitution guarantees the *Tatmadaw* a central role in Myanmar politics and government. It seems that the military government is stronger than ever, and for this very reason it must be concluded that sanctions against Myanmar have failed.

Importantly, the sanctions policy of Western states has been completely undermined by states within the region. Under the prerogative of countering Chinese influence in Myanmar, *all* neighbors of Myanmar now follow some type of engagement policy. Indeed, India, Malaysia, and Russia, as well as ASEAN, are all trying to "woo" the military dictatorship of Myanmar away from its "strong relationship" with China (Clark, 2003, p. 130). As the West attempted to force the Myanmar government into submission by removing access to financial resources, China stepped in offering arms, technology, and investment. Cross-border trade has enabled development in the inland Yunnan Province, which is hugely beneficial considering that Chinese economic development is overwhelmingly concentrated in the southern and eastern coastal regions. Cross-border trade and Chinese economic penetration of upper Myanmar is so intense that it is often said that there is a "Chinese colonization" of the border region stretching down to Mandalay (Bert, 2004, p. 226). Inevitably, such support from China has necessitated concessions from Myanmar, and in this regard China has been one of the main beneficiaries of the sanctions.

In this way, Myanmar has become increasingly dependent on China, and this provides the Chinese government with political and economic leverage. The Chinese have supported infrastructural development projects in Myanmar that analysts say will assist in facilitating Chinese economic and military access to the Indian Ocean. Chinese–Myanmar military cooperation is extensive; China has provided the *Tatmadaw* with jet fighters, tanks, and other military hardware. Not only does this undermine Western sanctions, but also shows the ability of the Myanmar military to defy them. Importantly, this dependence on China is completely contrary to the traditional military perspective of domestic control over land and resources (which has its roots in colonial history and was later manifested as Ne Win's Burmese Way to Socialism). The sanctions left the military with few options but to grant such concessions to their Chinese backers.

Both China and then-Burma were labeled as "pariah states" back in the late-1980s—especially following Beijing's violent responses to Tiananmen Square and the short-lived Summer of Democracy—but subsequent sanctions against China were soon dropped. While this reflects the immense international importance of the Chinese economy, and even though most who champion human rights and democratic development in Myanmar are far more restrained when it comes to those very same issues in China, it seems illogical to pursue a sanctions policy that directly benefits a country guilty of the very same violations used to justify the sanctions. Furthermore, as previously mentioned, it is increased Chinese influence in Myanmar that has provided the imperative for other regional neighbors and global powers to also engage with the government in Yangon.

It is evident that sanctions have failed to force the government of Myanmar to recognize the results of the 1990 election and hand over power to the NLD; indeed, the regime remains more deeply entrenched than ever, supported by its powerful Chinese ally. Foreign policy and diplomacy, like most government policy, is largely premised on the principle of cause and effect. That is, policies are usually initiated with stated goals and desired outcomes. If a policy does not result in the stated goal, then the policy is faulty and must be changed to one that—based on an analysis of the factors causing failure—is more likely to succeed. In the case of Myanmar, Western sanctions are not leading to the intended results, and are hence faulty. More importantly, the sanctions have actually brought about exactly the opposite reaction to that originally intended. Finally, the significance of this failure is further compounded by what the United Nations Children's Fund terms the "silent emergency" that is currently unfolding in Myanmar (UNICEF, 2009).

The humanitarian and public health crisis

In 2005, Myanmar ranked 129th in the Human Development Index (HDI). The nation's infant mortality rate per 1000 live births was 76 in 2003, and the under-five mortality rate was 107 per 1000 live births. For both of these interconnected indicators, Myanmar's performance was worse than one would expect from its overall HDI. In other words, when compared to other developing countries, even those that have a significantly lower overall HDI, Myanmar performed poorly. Importantly, these statistics are evidence that public health in Myanmar is an issue of serious concern. HIV/AIDS is also an issue; a report published in 2003 characterized Myanmar as having a generalized epidemic of HIV in reproductive-age adults (Beyrer et al., 2003). The report concluded that "HIV prevention and care programs are urgently needed in Burma" (p. 317). The Joint United Nations Program on HIV/AIDS (UNAIDS) has also stated that Myanmar has a generalized HIV/AIDS epidemic. Another crisis is endemic malaria, the most important public health problem in Myanmar (WHO, 2007). Malaria is the number one cause of death in Myanmar, accounting for over 10 per cent of deaths in 2003. Myanmar has the region's highest number of deaths from malaria, accounting for 53 per cent of total deaths there (WHO, 2005). That there are more deaths in Myanmar than in India and Indonesia combined (two of the world's most populous countries) is a vivid indication of the seriousness of malaria in Myanmar.

Many within the international community argue that Myanmar's relatively poor performance in public health is a reflection of ineffective and inappropriate government policies overall. In support of such a perspective, government expenditure on health has remained at a very low level despite the fact that total government health spending increased from 18,891 million kyats in 1990 to 89,778 million kyats in 2000 (ADB, 2006). Total public expenditure on health as a percentage of Myanmar's GDP was 0.4 per cent in 2002, which was lower than regional neighbors with similar levels of socioeconomic development; similarly, per capita health expenditure was also relatively low. While government expenditure has increased significantly, and while it would not be illogical to assume that this is simply a reflection of GDP growth, it seems plausible to assume that such statistics are a broad reflection of government prioritization. If so, this would provide support for the argument put forward by the donor community that the health crisis in Myanmar is the result of failed government policies. However, while it is no doubt true that the government does not prioritize the health of its citizens, as would be expected of a military dictatorship that prioritizes self-preservation, if the West is to maintain the moral high ground underpinning the principles behind sanctions, then it is necessary that it provides real and concrete assistance to alleviate the humanitarian crisis. Despite this imperative, because of the sanctions, official development aid (ODA) to Myanmar is extremely low. According to the *2005 Human Development Report*, Myanmar received US$2.6 per capita in ODA; this means that Myanmar receives less, sometimes far less, per capita than its neighbors.

While the *Tatmadaw* are able to protect themselves against this humanitarian crisis (and do in fact benefit from it), it is illogical to think that such conditions are providing the building blocks for a transition to democracy. The idea that an ongoing humanitarian crisis will eventually lead to the SPDC's implosion seems fatuous after 20 years of failed sanctions. Why is it necessary to continue sanctions indefinitely until this unlikely implosion occurs?

Importantly, of course, the question of whether the West (especially the United States) is willing to carry the sanctions policy to its logical conclusion is largely irrelevant. Assuming that the SPDC collapsed, and even if the United States in particular has the will and the means to rebuild Myanmar in its own image, it is highly unlikely that China would allow that to happen. Equally important, Myanmar's other regional neighbors will never allow the country to collapse into a failed state; preventing such an outcome is one rationale for their engagement policies. With such a counterbalance as this, the sanctions against Myanmar can never succeed. While Myanmar's neighbors are each assisting the SPDC in different ways, the sanctions themselves are actually helping the *Tatmadaw* to maintain totalitarian rule.

Paradox: assisting the military to exclude citizens

The purpose of sanctions is to build walls and prevent the movement of specified goods, services, people, or wealth across a border. In this way, sanctions enforce a closed economy and society, which ultimately serves to limit the population of the sanctioned country from possible interactions with the outside world. While many of the previously outlined sanctions are termed "targeted," meaning that the sanctions are specifically aimed at certain leaders, the bans on trade, FDI, and development assistance inevitably impact the population at large. The 2003 Burma Freedom and Democracy Act, for example, banned all imports from Myanmar, and this meant the closure of textile factories exporting to the US market. Seekins (2005), among others, has argued that "sanctions disproportionately impact the people of Burma, not its military" (p. 444). It can be further argued that sanctions not only hurt those it wishes to assist, but are also assisting those it wishes to hurt.

Sanctions actually support the regime by limiting the people of Myanmar from political, economic, and social contact with the outside world, which is of course exactly what the SPDC desires. Myanmar's government is a military dictatorship—an authoritarian regime. Such governments must, by necessity, control society with a strong hand, constraining all individual freedoms. This preoccupation with security extends to limiting contact between the populace and the outside world, and any regime such as that ruling Myanmar will instinctively attempt to isolate its population. Given Myanmar's colonial heritage and its Cold War policy of non-alignment and isolation, this tendency to favor a closed society is rendered even stronger.

Even though there seems to have been some level of economic growth in Myanmar during the 1990s (during 1990–9, GDP growth averaged 6 per cent) and early twenty-first century (during 2000–6, GDP growth averaged over 12 per cent) (ADB, 2008), and even assuming that such figures are true, *all* the benefits of such growth have accrued only to the *Tatmadaw* or those with connections to the *Tatmadaw*. The *Tatmadaw* themselves have gained from economic exchanges with China and other neighbors, but trade, aid, and investment sanctions restrict economic activities that are not connected to the military, and have therefore reinforced the military's monopolistic control over the economy. Sanctions have countered the lowering of barriers that is supposed to be a characteristic of globalization. Not only are the sanctions hindering the overall development of Myanmar, but they are also specifically hindering the development of its independent business organizations.

While it is necessary for the SPDC to limit cross-border interactions, it is also necessary for it to prevent the development of any institutions, groups, or individual citizens that could challenge its monopoly on power. This means that the SPDC, being an authoritarian regime with limited legitimacy, will pursue policies that enhance its own power, while destroying the power of its competitors. In this way, an authoritarian regime will attempt to repress large sectors of society (McCarthy, 2006, p. 126). This repression will obviously include limiting individual political freedoms, but may also encompass restricting access to health, education, and development opportunities. The sanctions assist the *Tatmadaw* in its efforts to keep the population more manageable by further attacking civil society from all sides; lack of broad economic development, restricted access to health and education, and hampered information flows that result in part from sanctions have all impeded the development of civil society organizations and institutions, and discouraged the advancement of social capital. Such social capital stemming from a pluralistic growth in civil society organizations and non-state institutions could, as asserted by Putnam (2000, p. 288), foster civic engagement which, in the case of Myanmar, could provide a counterbalance over time to the SPDC's monopoly on power. Needless to say, the *Tatmadaw* would do all within its power to prevent the development of social capital, but the question remains as to why the international community is also hindering its development. Even when not involved in political issues, civil society organizations enable collective action that can provide services and foster trust among citizens.

Because of the military's deeply ingrained perspective that it is the only institution capable of preserving the integrity of the nation, maintaining power is more important to it than an increase in economic benefits for society. It is obvious that the *Tatmadaw* in Myanmar have managed to maintain control over the organs of the state despite sanctions. In fact, sanctions have reinforced *Tatmadaw* control by impeding the development of non-military institutions. The sanctions have reinforced the infrastructural power deficit within the state that the military has encouraged in order to perpetuate its power. Sanctions have supported the process of weakening non-military state functions to the point whereby services are not delivered to Myanmar's citizens (Englehart, 2005, p. 623), and the previously outlined poor state of the public health service is a prime example of this. Any services that do exist must be provided through the army in a patron–client mechanism that increases dependence on the military. This means that the only way for citizens to gain access to health or education is through some connection with the military. Corruption is so rampant that the civil service in Myanmar is rife with officials who personally collect fees for services. In this way, considering the considerable growth in the size of the military during the 1990s, it seems that most families, especially in lowland Myanmar, can benefit from having a member in the armed forces (Callahan, 2000, p. 31).

The military has its roots in the fight for the nation's independence, and in the early years of nation-building. As the independence struggle involved battles against multiple insurgent groups, the armed forces' perspective of being the defender of the nation came to be dominated by a preoccupation with internal threats to the nation. The Three Main National Causes ("Non-disintegration of the Union," "Non-disintegration of National Sovereignty," and "Consolidation of National Sovereignty") are reflective of the military mindset. It is natural for states that are relatively new and still in the process of nation-building to regard non-state actors such as civil society organizations with suspicion, if not outright hostility. If state capacity was limited to the point whereby it could not provide services to citizens, and hence civil society organizations rationally attempted to provide such services, this would be an especially delicate issue because state legitimacy depends on the provision of services. The process of building citizen loyalty to the state depends on the state's ability to provide services to its citizens, and if foreign donors exclusively target non-state, civil society organizations as recipients of aid, it is inevitable that the state would regard such actions as threatening. Such trepidation has moved the SPDC to severely restrict any international aid efforts in Myanmar.

Sanctions restrict the possibility of developing any non-military economic entities that may eventually provide a counterbalance to military power. Democracies are, by their very nature, open societies, but the sanctions against Myanmar support the perpetuation of a closed society. A constriction of economic development, the intended outcome of sanctions, has led to a related constriction of social development. This means that civil society and non-military institutions cannot develop and improve their capacity, something that is essential for democracy to grow and flourish in Myanmar.

Exclusionary globalization

The number and influence of civil society organizations advocating for democracy and human rights in Myanmar has increased dramatically in the West since the early 1990s. This has come about largely as a result of global networking and an intensification of worldwide social relations. As an example of this trend, the home page of Burma Campaign UK has links to the websites of 27 related organizations in Europe alone. These organizations are not general human rights or democracy advocacy NGOs, but are purely concerned with democracy and human rights in Myanmar. Such organizations, without exception, support the NLD and other opposition groups, and they are able to utilize networks that stretch around the globe to promote their cause. For instance, during the 2007 protests in Myanmar, the Burma Campaign UK and the Burma Global Action Network used Facebook to designate 6 October 2007 a "Global Day of Action for Burma." Over 200 protests were subsequently held in 30 countries, including a London rally of 10,000 people led by Buddhist monks (Burma Campaign UK, 2007).

While such global social movements and their information networks reveal a positive aspect of globalization in terms of citizens in the West and elsewhere being simultaneously aware of injustices and promoting human rights abroad, the sanctions these movements usually support ironically prevent the people of Myanmar from experiencing greater political freedoms. Civil society organizations in liberal democracies are underpinned by high levels of social capital, as well as by a secure state that is not threatened by political actors who may question or challenge its authority. However, a state that is stable and tolerates freedom among citizens does not emerge in an impoverished context overnight but over time and in tandem with sustained economic development. In the case of Myanmar, such development is highly unlikely without increased aid and investment from wealthy Western nations, something sanctions are designed to prevent.

As the sanctions policy is premised on the narrow principle of achieving an immediate transition to democracy, the military regime feels threatened and reacts by curtailing political freedoms, regardless of the economic implications for the general population. Although based on accurate assessments of human rights infractions in Myanmar, the perpetual demonization of the military government by Western leaders and activists also makes persuading SPDC leaders to adopt democracy an unlikely prospect. With sanctions limiting their interactions with the international community, the citizens of Myanmar will continue to be excluded from any positive impacts of globalization. Yet it is interactions with the outside world that can serve to promote a democratic transition within nations governed by totalitarian governments (Huntington, 1991, p. 86).

Conclusion

In conclusion, not only have the sanctions against Myanmar failed to overturn the military regime, they have also caused considerable hardship to the citizens of Myanmar; paradoxically, they have actually supported the *Tatmadaw* by reinforcing a closed society. This closed society is a necessary precondition in the preservation of tyrannical rule, and in Myanmar this has been accompanied by government assaults on political freedom and the lack of state provision of healthcare and education for Myanmar's citizens. The sanctions have fostered a political environment that is so polarized that even relief for humanitarian disasters often becomes embroiled in recriminations.

The sanctions stem from an exclusionary type of globalization that focuses on the political aspects of development in Myanmar without considering interrelated economic and social factors that would assist in fostering a transition to democracy. The highly politicized issues of democracy and human rights in Myanmar are known in the West to such an extent that groups within Western countries overwhelmingly demand immediate democratic transition in Myanmar. However, they show little regard for the reactions of the current military regime and little awareness of the challenges of democratic transition.

It may indeed be necessary for Western governments to voice displeasure with Myanmar's government when negative developments such as those contrary to international law occur in Myanmar. However, it is equally necessary to provide humanitarian assistance where needed. If democratization and improved human rights are its goals, the international community must shift its emphasis from the short-term effort to undermine the military dictatorship and promote an immediate democratic transition with national elections, to a more realistic effort to alleviate the humanitarian crisis and provide the building blocks for a democratic transition in the medium-term.

In the short-term at least, the international community should provide humanitarian assistance to the peoples of Myanmar, regardless of any political developments. This aid should include support for health and education programs. Such programs will help to alleviate hardship, but will also assist in promoting economic development and democratization. While care must be taken to ensure that the *Tatmadaw* cannot use such funds for its own ends, every effort must be made to improve the quality of life for Myanmar's citizens. If the donor community is serious about alleviating the humanitarian crisis in Myanmar, it will be necessary to improve the capacity of state institutions, and this means aid and particularly technical assistance to organs of state that are responsible for health and education. Strengthening non-military institutions in Myanmar will not only assist in the disbursal of aid, but will also—in the medium-term—provide for the development of non-military state institutions, which will support a transition toward democracy. As part of this process, it may even be necessary to provide certain guarantees to the *Tatmadaw* to ensure its cooperation. Such guarantees will obviously appear distasteful to many within the international community, but the process of assisting in the humanitarian crisis would be greatly enhanced with the cooperation of Myanmar's military government.

The international community must engage the Myanmar government. This does not mean that issues of democracy and human rights should be ignored as they often are when Western states deal with, for example, China and Saudi Arabia. Rather, a holistic approach to development and democratization must accept the reality that the *Tatmadaw* will remain in power despite sanctions, and that dialogue is the only way forward. The fact that the Myanmar government has negotiated settlements with insurgent enemies in the past is a clear indication that it is not adverse to negotiation and dialogue. Furthermore, there is evidence that the *Tatmadaw* can cooperate with the international community. As an example, the Joint Program and Fund for HIV/AIDS, established in 2003, aims to "represent the successful commitment of a variety of partners—international development agencies, the Government of Myanmar, national and international non-governmental organizations, and the United Nations family to find effective ways of helping the people of Myanmar fight AIDS" (UNAIDS, 2005, p. 6). In response to the deadlock that blocked humanitarian assistance to the victims of Cyclone Nargis, Louis Michel, European Commissioner for Development and Humanitarian Aid, visited Myanmar in May, 2008. He reported that "despite the inevitable frustrations, I always believed that an open dialogue offered the best chance of gaining access for the international humanitarian community. I'm delighted that our efforts and especially the efforts of United Nations Secretary General Ban Ki-moon have finally paid off" (Europa Press Release, 2008). Needless to say, dialogue and negotiations with the military in Myanmar will be long and arduous. To help better facilitate engagement, it will be necessary to tone down criticisms of the Myanmar government, and this will be a particular challenge considering the current level of polarization in the international community.

References

Acemoglu, D., and Robinson, J. A. (2000). Why did the West extend the franchise? Growth, inequality and democracy in historical perspective. *Quarterly Journal of Economics*, *115*(4), 1167–1199.

Amnesty Calls Burma 'Human Rights Flashpoint' (28 March 2008). *The Irrawaddy*. Retrieved 4 March 2011, from http://www.irrawaddy.org/cartoon.php?art_id=12338.

ASEAN (2004). *Statistical yearbook 2006*. Retrieved 21 January 2009, from http://www.aseansec.org/13100.htm.

ASEAN (2007). Joint Communique of the 40th ASEAN Ministerial Meeting (AMM) "One caring and sharing community," Manila, 29–30 July 2007. Retrieved 16 January 2009, from http://www.aseansec.org/20764.htm.

Asian Development Bank (2006). *Key indicators 2006: Measuring policy effectiveness in health and education*. Retrieved 12 January 2009, from http://www.adb.org/documents/books/key_indicators/2006/default.asp.

Asian Development Bank (2008). *Key indicators for Asia and the Pacific 2008*. Retrieved 2 February 2009, from http://www.adb.org/Documents/Books/Key_Indicators/2008/default.asp.

Barrow, R. (1999). Determinants of democracy. *Journal of Political Economy*, *107*(6), Part 2 (December 1999), S158–S183.

Bert, W. (2004). Burma, China and the USA. *Pacific Affairs*, *77*(2), 263–282.

Beyrer, C., Razak, M. H., Labrique, A., and Brookmeyer, R. (2003). Assessing the magnitude of the HIV/AIDS epidemic in Burma. [Abstract] *Journal of Acquired Immune Deficiency Syndrome*, *1*(32), 311–317.

Brysk, A. (ed.) (2002). *Globalization and human rights*. Berkeley: University of California Press.

Burma Campaign UK (2007). *Last month in Burma*. Retrieved 1 March 2009, from http://www.burmacampaign.org.uk/index.php/burma/campaigns/crackdown.

Callahan, M. (2000). Cracks in the edifice? Changes in military-societal relations in Burma since 1988. In M. B. Pederson, E. Rudland, and R. J. May (eds.), *Burma/Myanmar: Strong regime, weak state?* (pp. 22–51). Adelaide: Crawford House Publishing.

Canada Gazette (26 December 2007). SPECIAL ECONOMIC MEASURES ACT, Special Economic Measures (Burma) Regulations, *141*(26), Retrieved 1 March 2009, from, http://canadagazette.gc.ca/archives/p2/2007/2007-12-26/html/sor-dors285-eng.html.

Cho, V. (6 May 2008). Laura Bush Comments "Inappropriate" says analyst. *The Irrawaddy*. Retrieved 2 March 2009, from http://www.irrawaddy.org/article.php?art_id=11794.

Chossudovsky, M. (2003). *The globalization of poverty and the New World Order*, 2nd edn. Pincourt, Canada: Global Research.

Clark, A. L. (2003). Burma in 2002: A year of transition. *Asian Survey*, *43*(1), 127–134.

Diamond, L. (1992). Economic development and democracy reconsidered. *American Behavioral Scientist*, *35*(4/5), 450–499.

Dollar, D., and Kraay, A. (January/February 2002). Spreading the wealth. *Foreign Affairs*, *81*(1), 120.

Englehart, N. A. (2005). Is regime change enough for Burma? The problem of state capacity. *Asian Survey*, *45*(4), 622–644.

Europa Press Release (2008). Louis Michel welcomes agreement on humanitarian aid worker access to Myanmar. Retrieved 8 February 2009, from http://europa.eu/rapid/pressReleasesAction.do?reference=IP/08/797&format=HTML&aged=0&language=EN&guiLanguage=en.

Falco, M. (2003). *Burma: Time for change. Report for an Independent Task Force*. Geneva: Council of Foreign Relations Press.

Giddens, A. (1990). *The Consequences of modernity*. Stanford: Stanford University Press.

Huntington, S. P. (1991). *The Third Wave: Democratization in the late twentieth century*. Norma: University of Oklahoma Press.

Lin, J. Y., and Nugent, J. B. (1995). Institutions and economic development. In J. Behrman and T. N. Srinivasan (eds.), *Handbook of development economics* (pp. 2302–2363). Amsterdam: Elsevier Science B. V.

Lipset, S. M. (1959). Some social requisites of democracy: Economic development and legitimacy. *The American Political Science Review*, *53*(1), 69–105.

Lopez-Cordova, E., and Meissner, C. M. (2008). The impact of international trade on democracy. *World Politics*, *60*, 539–575.

Maung, M. (1991). *The Burma road to poverty*. New York: Praeger.

McCarthy, S. (2006). *The political theory of tyranny in Singapore and Burma: Aristotle and the rhetoric of benevolent despotism*. New York: Routledge.

Ministry of Foreign Affairs Press Release (MOFA) (1997). Japan's position regarding the Situation in Myanmar. Retrieved 12 November 2009, from http://www.mofa.go.jp/region/asia-paci/myanmar/myanmar.html.

Ministry of Foreign Affairs Press Release (MOFA) (2001). Yangon workshop on Japan-Myanmar cooperation for structural adjustment of the Myanmar economy. Retrieved September 2009, from http://www.mofa.go.jp/announce/event/2001/11/1121.html.

Petras, J., and Veltmeyer, H. (2001). *Globalization unmasked: Imperialism in the 21st century*. London: Zed Books.

Putnam, R. (2000). *Bowling alone: The collapse and revival of American community*. New York: Simon and Schuster.

Seekins, D. M. (2005). Burma and US Sanctions: Punishing an authoritarian regime. *Asian Survey, 45*(3), 437–452.

Sen, A. (2002). How to judge globalism. *American Prospect, 13*(1), A2, 5.

Smith, S. (2008). Ministerial statement: Burma, 22, Retrieved 21 December 2009, from, http://www.foreignminister.gov.au/speeches/2008/081022_burma.html.

Stallings, B. (1995). The new international context of development. In B. Stallings (ed.), *Global change, regional response* (pp. 349–388). Cambridge: Cambridge University Press.

Stiglitz, J. (2002). *Globalization and its discontents*. New York: W. W. Norton & Co.

Supporting Burma/Myanmar's reconciliation process: Challenges and opportunities. An independent report for the European Commission (2005). Retrieved 2 March 2009, from http://www.burmalibrary.org/docs3/Independant_Report-Burma_Day.htm.

Takeda, I. (2001). Japan's Myanmar policy: Four principles. *Gaiko Forum* (Summer), 53–59.

Thawnghmung, A. M. (2003). Burma: A gentler authoritarianism? *Foreign Policy, 139* (November–December), 39–40.

UNAIDS (2005). Joint Programme for HIV/AIDS in Myanmar and the Fund for HIV/AIDS in Myanmar. Annual progress report. Retrieved September 2009, from http://data.unaids.org/pub/Report/2005/Myanmar_progress_report_03_04_en.pdf.

UNICEF (2009). UNICEF humanitarian action report 2009, mid-year review. Retrieved 2 January 2009, from http://www.unicef.org/har09/files/HAR_Mid-Year_Review_2009.pdf.

US State Department (29 July 2008). Bush signs law to extend sanctions against Burmese leadership. Retrieved 3 November 2009, from http://www.america.gov/st/peacesec-english/2008/July/20080729144559dmslahrellek0.9923365.html.

World Health Organization (WHO) (2005). *Health in Myanmar*. Retrieved 22 February 2009, from http://www.whomyanmar.org/LinkFiles/Health_Information_7HS.pdf.

World Health Organization (WHO) (2007). *Malaria situation in SEAR countries: Myanmar*. Retrieved 1 March 2009, from http://www.searo.who.int/EN/Section10/Section21/Section340_4024.htm.

Part II

Transnational Corporations and Human Rights

4
Transnational Corporations and the Protection of Human Rights: Non-Financial Reporting as an Option

Onyeka Osuji

Introduction

Commentaries on such issues as abuse of corporate power (Clinard, 1990, chap. 1), environmental impact and abuse (Clinard, 1990, pp. 44–47), harmful health and safety practices (Clinard, 1990, p. 915), weak regulations (Monks and Minow, 1991), criminal conduct (Gabrosky and Sutton, 1989), performance of "quasi-governmental" roles (Litvin, 2003, p. 269), performance of "quasi-state" roles (Hertz, 2001, p. 186), and human rights and other abuses (Hartmann, 2002) show that corporate power may be exercised positively or negatively. Awareness of inter-dependence among peoples and nations, a heightened level of social consciousness, and shared values and expectations compel the global community to require of its members a greater degree of conformity and compliance with minimum standards of behavior. As members of the global community and subjects of international law with rights and obligations (Bassiouni, 1980, p. 1), business enterprises, including transnational corporations (TNCs), ought to respect globally shared values and expectations. This is evident from Article 2(2) of the United Nations General Assembly Declaration on the Right to Development (1986), which "imposes" responsibility on all, including states and corporations. However, it appears that, as yet, consequences for TNCs for violating international standards of conduct are few or even non-existent (Kamminga and Zia-Zarifi, 2000, p. 1; Vagts, 1970, p. 739).

As a consequence of the growing recognition of the corporation's role in society, the critical reputation of corporations now extends to social values and expectations. This is the background to the emergence and increasing importance of non-financial reporting for TNCs. As a result, non-financial reporting is now "fashionable and strongly encouraged" by TNCs (Kamminga and Zia-Ziarifi, 2000, p. 9). Such reporting accepts wider corporate responsibility. Compared to financial reporting, corporate non-financial reporting has a short history. This is evident from the historical account by Gray, Owen, and Adams (1996, p. 91). One of the earliest works on corporate social reporting by Dierkes and Bauer was only published in 1973. The subjects, audience, and contents of, and motivation for corporate social reporting, are potentially wide (Gray, Owen, and Adams, 1996, p. 83, Figure 4.1), with the broad area of human rights a major component of non-financial reporting. This area also includes labor standards, non-discrimination issues, and environmental matters. The quantity of environmental reporting rose in the 1990s, while reporting on community, ethical, and employee issues appears to have declined (Miles, Hammond, and Friedman, 2002, p. 139). At present, environmental reporting is apparently the most common corporate non-financial form of reporting (Miles, Hammond, and Friedman, 2002, p. 124).

With an abundance of non-financial reports emanating from TNCs and an increasing tendency for interest groups such as consumers and investors to rely on such reports, concerns with credibility, transparency, legitimacy, public interest and regulatory strategy, and false, deceptive, or misleading non-financial reporting have emerged. This chapter examines these issues in the context of using non-financial reporting as a mechanism for protecting human rights in developing countries. The chapter recommends an approach that acknowledges the dichotomy that exists between reporting and performance and counters the ineffectiveness of codes and other non-binding measures. Such an approach recognizes the regulatory role of disclosure and the role of non-financial reporting as corporate advertising. The quality and credibility of non-financial reports, it is suggested, are assured or improved where disclosure and the advertising roles of non-financial reporting are recognized.

Corporations, reputation, and non-financial reporting

As different historical accounts indicate (e.g. Allen, 2001, p. 18; Bowman, 1996, p. 35; Chandler Jr, 1990; Dunlavy, 2004, p. 66; Lamoreaux, 2004, p. 29; Rapakko, 1997, p. 124; Smith and Walter, 2006, pp. 49–73; Wallis, Sylla, and Legler, 1994, p. 121), the use and legal recognition of the corporate form have been an evolving process. Historically speaking, corporations served as a medium for private ordering and enforcement; legislative intervention was a subsequent development (Whincop, 2001, p. 108). In England, for example, a royal charter was once required to establish a corporation. The royal charter did not affect the private status of the corporation, which essentially used the resources of the members in pursuit of their private interests (Smith and Walter, 2006, p. 49). In fact, prior to 1900, corporations were conceived purely as a means to earn profits (Smith and Walter, 2006, p. 59).

However, non-financial matters are now of increasing importance to modern corporations as profit is no longer an exclusive priority. For example, Friedman (1970) insisted four decades ago that corporate management's "direct responsibility" was profit generation, but also stressed corporations' recognition of "the basic rules of the society, both those embodied in law and those embodied in ethical custom" (p. 32). As Clarke (2004) shows, the shift from sole shareholder concern to the inclusion of other interests assumes that "social capital [involves] an evaluation of a deeper and more complex set of social relationships of the corporation" (p. 23). For some observers (Barry, 1991), the expectation is that "business itself is a moral enterprise" (p. 88).

The result is that a link now exists between "practical social values" and "public expectations" regarding business conduct, a perception that may be expressed in the media, or by special interest and pressure groups (Smith and Walter, 2006, p. 234). Media attention on non-financial matters and the increasing connection between corporate reputation and share prices have made non-financial reputation a board-level issue (Miles, Hammond, and Friedman, 2002, p. 11). "Real" consequences await corporations (Schwartz and Gibb, 1999, pp. xiii, 9) and individual officers in cases of negative press or other reports. Adverse consequences may result where corporations are "blindsided by issues that violated the trust of large segments of the public" (Schwartz and Gibb, 1999, p. xiv). Publications such as the magazine *Multinational Monitor* and others (Mokhiber and Weissman, 1999, pp. 83, 116–118) are dedicated to identifying the perceived worst culprits of corporate abuses on such matters as interference in the political process and infractions against human rights, labor standards, and the environment. Modern corporations are challenged "to find means of enduring value creation without social or environmental harm" (Clarke, 2004, p. 23).

As a consequence, "publicity is a potent weapon" for corporations (Robertson and Nicol, 2002, p. 641). In this regard, modern public relations practice has moved from a traditional marketing process to identification and satisfaction of the needs and interests of customers and other stakeholders (Cingula, 2006, pp. 88–89). Consequently, modern public relations and the concept of corporate governance share the same concerns, in particular, social responsibility issues (Cingula, 2006, pp. 89–90). It is for this reason that corporate social responsibility (CSR) is now regarded as a corporate governance issue (Mitchell, 2007, p. 279).

This is the background within which the concept and practice of CSR have come to flourish. Historical accounts of CSR in the US and the UK indicate as much (Campbell and Vick, 2007, pp. 241–266). CSR emphasizes the social responsibility of enterprises and consists of relevant corporate activity and reporting. Although there exist different concepts of CSR (Abreu and David, 2004, pp. 110–114), CSR undoubtedly has internal and external components. The internal components concern internal participants such as managers, shareholders, and employees only. External components of CSR affect the community and the environment, for example. Thus, Gray, Owen, and Adams (1996) have defined corporate social and environmental reporting (CSER) as "the process of communicating the social and environmental effects of organizations' economic actions to particular interest groups within the society at large" (p. 3). CSER is usually a formal account by the organization, mainly for its internal use although in some cases external disclosure may be required (Gray, Owen, and Adams, 1996, p. 11). As Gray, Owen, and Adams (1996) have identified, a conventional CSER, in essence, is "a formal report, prepared and communicated by an 'organization' about social and environmental aspects of the organization's activities, communicated to the internal and external 'participants' of the organization" (p. 12, Figure 1.3). CSER differs from financial accounting in terms of content, media, purposes, and target recipients (Gray, Owen, and Adams, 1996, p. 3). It assumes a "stakeholder" view of reporting to such recipients as employees, trade unions, and the local community (Gray, Owen, and Adams, 1996, pp. 11–12). CSER usually concerns corporate activities affecting the natural environment, employees, consumers, and the local community, and such social issues as race and gender (Gray, Owen, and Adams, 1996, p. 11).

TNCs, reputation, and non-financial reporting

TNCs now constitute the "dominant form" of business organization (Vernon, 1992, pp. 18, 36) and the trend favors an increasing importance of TNCs internationally. With relative ease, TNCs can pool together, distribute, or exploit production methods, processes, costs, resources, research, management and technical knowledge, and funding across different jurisdictions. In this regard, an apt definition of globalization may be the "accelerating interdependence" of states with TNCs as the "primary agent" (Ostry, 1992, pp. 317–318). The critical observation is that TNCs and not governments in most cases provide "the direct source" of decisions on people's lives (Anderson, 2006, p. 28). As a consequence, Stopford (1994) observes that the actions and behaviors of TNCs that used to be dismissed as "a footnote... are now appearing in the main text" (p. 267).

Globalization and the relevance of non-financial issues to modern corporations, and TNCs in particular, are linked. The key to this relationship is the role of globalization in the generation and spread of ideas. Globalization has been described as "the transnational extension and habituation of local ideas and practices" (Anderson, 2006, p. 19). This may justify the assertion that "transnational influences can and do condition relations of power, conventions, and shared cultural constructions in the domestic sphere" (McNichol, 2006, p. 370). TNCs' role in non-financial issues is an example.

The relative size of TNCs is another critical factor. It appears that a connection exists between company size and level of embrace of CSR (Barnard, Deakin, and Hobbs, 2004, pp. 33–34). In practice, size apparently matters in non-financial reporting. For instance, profit-making for small companies may be different from that for large companies, which may put more emphasis on long-term planning and position (Berle, 1965, p. 29). Such approaches may determine corporate responses to non-financial issues. The larger the size of corporations, the more likely "[s]ize extends business decisions from the purely economic into fields of social movement" (Berle, 1965, p. 30). Large companies and consumer goods companies are more likely to be affected by public interest in non-financial issues than small companies or producers of unbranded goods (Parkinson, 2006, p. 9). Large companies also tend to adopt codes of labor standards since they are more sensitive to criticisms of questionable practices (Servais, 2005, p. 94, para. 199). Evidence suggests that small companies are less conscious of corporate image or positive reputation (Barnard, Deakin, and Hobbs, 2004, pp. 33–35; McLeay, 2006, pp. 236–237).

The realization has encouraged international activity on non-financial issues. For example, as the account by Voiculescu (2007, p. 365) shows, CSR has emerged as an issue on the European agenda. The European Commission (2001) has issued a "Green Paper" on, and with a view to the promotion of, CSR. The European Parliament (1999) has also recommended the adoption of a model code on human rights, environmental protection, and labor standards for European enterprises operating in developing countries. However, these international efforts have not always been successful. Within the World Trade Organization (WTO), developing countries oppose discussions on labor standards (Singh and Zammitt, 2003, p. 1). Commentators such as Singh and Zammitt (2003) argue against compulsory enforcement of labor standards in developing countries. The draft UN Code of Conduct for Transnational Corporations was also aborted as a consequence of disagreements on the content, nature, and legal form of the code (Jägers, 2002, pp. 119–122).

Human rights and corporations

Human rights are a "broad area of concern and ... potential subject matter" (Brownlie, 2003, p. 529). There are four classes of international human rights conventions. Constituting the first class are the "comprehensive" conventions (Brownlie, 2003, p. 529) such as the International Covenant on Economic, Social and Cultural Rights (ICESCR) (1966) and International Covenant on Civil and Political Rights (ICCPR) (1966). In the second category are the "comprehensive regional conventions" (Brownlie, 2003, p. 529) such as the European Convention on Human Rights (1950), the American Convention on Human Rights (1969), and the African Charter on Human and Peoples' Rights (1981). In the third and fourth categories are conventions on specific wrongs such as torture or genocide, and for protecting categories of people such as women or children.

As the International Court of Justice acknowledged in the Barcelona Traction case (1970), it is now beyond doubt that international law recognizes "principles and rules concerning the basic rights of the human person" (p. 32). Human rights obligations are positive or negative, and may relate to conduct or results (Jägers, 2002, p. 75). Classical international human rights law is directed toward states, likely due to the apparent recognition of states as the sole subjects of international law in the early stages of international law formulation. For example, Oppenheim (1905) submitted that international law was meant for regulating states, which were seen as constituting the exclusive subjects of international law (p. 341).

However, international law has progressed beyond this state-only focus and now appears to recognize non-state entities as subjects (MacLeod, 2008). For instance, the United Nations General Assembly (1999) has declared that "all members of the international community shall fulfill, jointly and separately, their solemn obligation to promote and encourage respect for human rights and fundamental freedoms." Articles 16 and 18 of the declaration specifically identify the obligations of non-state entities such as individuals, groups, institutions, and non-governmental organizations. The two articles recognize the responsibility of non-state entities in promoting and safeguarding human rights, fundamental freedoms, and democracy through activities such as education, training, and research. As Weissbrodt and Kruger (2003) indicate, international instruments, such as UN declarations and International Labour Organization (ILO) conventions, exist that specifically identify human rights norms applicable to TNCs.

Business enterprises, including TNCs (Clapham, 2000, p. 190; Kaufman, 2007, pp. 155–241; MacLeod, 2008, pp. 65–76), are subject to observance of a range of human rights norms. Some scholars (e.g. Deva, 2003; Jägers, 2002, pp. 51–73; Joseph, 2000; Muchlinski, 2007a, pp. 518–524, 2007b, pp. 440–447; Ramasastry, 2002, p. 1081; Stephens, 2000; Tófalo, 2006) have identified a tentative list of human rights norms applicable to corporations. Although there are some suggestions apparently to the contrary (e.g. Clapham, 2006, chap. 6; Clapham and Jebri, 2001, p. 339; Muchlinski, 2001, pp. 35–44; Muchlinski, 2007a, pp. 514–518; Ratner, 2001, p. 443), corporate obligations are summarized as obligations to respect, protect, and fulfill human rights (Jägers, 2002, p. 78). The obligation to protect extends to acts of business partners who are noted as "major sources" of human rights violations in many countries (Jägers, 2002, p. 83). The pressure is more on large corporations to fulfill human rights since the obligation to fulfill depends on size and resources (Jägers, 2002, p. 83). Corporations are also obliged "not to cooperate" or be complicit in human rights violations instigated by state agencies or business partners (Jägers, 2002, pp. 78, 92–93). The decision of a US court in *The Presbyterian Church of Sudan* v. *Talisman Energy and the Republic of Sudan* (2005) supports this principle, although *In re South African Apartheid Litigation* (2004) from another US court appears to suggest a contrary position.

In the language of Article 3 of the United Nations Sub-Commission on the Promotion and Protection of Human Rights code (2002), TNCs and other enterprises "shall not engage in nor benefit" from human rights violations. TNCs' violations of human rights standards may be direct or indirect. For instance, support for repressive regimes may amount to indirect violation, while TNCs by act or omission, or through agents such as private security forces, may directly engage in human rights abuses (Human Rights Watch, 1999; Jägers, 2002, p. 53; Leader, 2006,

p. 657). Consequently, Judge Paez held that corporations may be in breach of human rights where they are a "willful participant in joint action with the [s]tate or its agents" (Jagers, 2002, p. 232; *National Coalition Government of the Union of Burma* v. *Unocal, Inc.*, 1997, p. 349). For example, *Doe* v. *Unocal Corp.* (1997) held that corporations that accepted forced labor from state agencies might be held to violate human rights (p. 892). In *Bowoto* v. *Chevron*, it was claimed that a multinational enterprise (TNC) assisted the security services of a repressive Nigerian regime. *Wiwa* v. *Shell* (2000) concerned Shell's alleged complicity in the execution of Nigerian human and environmental rights activists by a Nigerian military regime. The background to *Wiwa* v. *Shell* is discussed by Chandler (1998, p. 72). Clearly, human rights are now a reputational issue for corporations (Williams, 1999, p. 63). As a result, Campbell (2007) has proposed that human rights be a core issue of CSR (p. 529).

Labor standards as human rights

TNCs' role in the promotion of labor standards—that is, the treatment of workers and the physical and social conditions of the workplace—is now recognized. Muchlinski (2007b), for example, provides an overview of TNCs and labor standards (pp. 473–506). Labor standards are of more concern in developing countries (Servais, 2005, p. 311, para. 1061) as appropriate laws on labor standards are either non-existent or weak in such regions and, when laws exist, public and individual enforcement of rules are absent or ineffective. Relevant labor issues to interest groups include those of core labor standards and also those concerning wages, general conditions of work, social security, social policy, industrial relations, and employment and treatment of women, older workers, migrant workers, and indigenous peoples (Servais, 2005, p. 107; Swepston, 2004, pp. 149–155). As is evident from the activities of the ILO and the interest groups, child labor and forced labor attract particularly significant attention (Swepston, 2004, p. 152). The harsh realities of child labor and forced labor may be the reason. For instance, a US court considered forced labor as serious as slave trading (*Doe* v. *Unocal Corp*, 1997, p. 891).

Previous research (Servais, 2005, pp. 21–33) and the founding principles of international labor law indicate that international labor law has a long history. However, the recent special role of TNCs in shaping labor standards is evident in the United Nations Global Compacts with TNCs and the ILO's Tripartite Declaration of Principles Concerning TNCs and Social Policy (1977) (ILO Tripartite Declaration) addressed to TNCs, in cases where labor standards figure prominently.

Judicial and other opinions suggest that some labor rights are regarded as human rights issues. The reasoning is that labor standards of the ILO actually give "practical expression to a number of very important human rights" (Brownlie, 2003, p. 530). A US court in *Doe* v. *Unocal Corp* (1997) recognized the classification of labor rights as human rights. The court found that forced labor and slave trading are analogous and held that international law recognizes the responsibility of the individual human actor in both cases. From Article 10(3) of the ICESCR, it appears that international human rights law recognizes that children and young people should be protected from "economic exploitation [and] employment in work harmful to their morals or health or dangerous to life or likely to hamper their normal development." The nexus between labor rights and human rights is also apparent from Article 8 of the ICCPR and Article 4 of the Universal Declaration of Human Rights (1948). Incidentally, Article 55 of the United Nations Charter (1945) recognizes the need for the promotion of "higher standards of living, full employment, and conditions of economic and social progress and development... [as well as] universal respect for, and observance of human rights and fundamental freedoms for all."

Non-discrimination as human rights

International instruments recognize the principle of non-discrimination on grounds such as race, religion, gender, language, color, nationality, social class, and so on. This principle can be found in Article 2(1) of the ICCPR, the International Convention on the Elimination of All Forms of Racial Discrimination (ICERD) (1966), the Convention on the Elimination of All Forms of Discrimination against Women (1979) (ICEDAW), and the Declaration on the Elimination of All Forms of Intolerance and Discrimination Based on Religion or Belief (DEAFIDBRB) (1982). The Copenhagen Declaration on Social Development and Program of Action (1995) appealed to public and private sectors "to ensure gender equality, equal opportunity and non-discrimination on the basis of race, ethnic group, religion, age, health and disability, and with full respect for applicable international instruments." The principle of non-discrimination clearly applies to TNC operations. As a result, Article 22 of the ILO Tripartite Declaration (1977) expects TNCs to exhibit non-discrimination in their operations.

The recognition of the principle of non-discrimination as an aspect of human rights can be traced to the United Nations Charter (1945). Article 2 of the Charter acknowledges international cooperation "in promoting and encouraging respect for human rights and for fundamental freedoms for all without distinction as to race, sex, language, or religion." The preamble to the Charter also affirms "faith in fundamental human rights, [and] in the equal treatment of men and women." The principle of non-discrimination is also evident in Articles 2(1), 3, 4(1), 20(2), 24(1), and 26 of the ICCPR, Articles 3 and 7 of the ICESCR, Articles 1 and 2 of the Universal Declaration on Human Rights (1948), and Article 2(e) of ICEDAW. These international instruments are clearly human rights instruments that are relevant to TNCs.

Environmental protection as human rights

TNCs have become a focal point for environmental concerns and policies (Muchlinski, 2007b, pp. 539–574; OECD, 2000, chap. 11, para. 5; Sands, 2003). As a consequence, sustainability is a core principle of the International Chamber of Commerce's Business Charter for Sustainable Development (1991). Evidence suggests that businesses in environment-sensitive sectors have three concerns: sustainability, human rights, and local community interests (Gao, 1998, pp. 49–51). For example, human rights organizations have indicted some TNCs for complicity in the present conflict in the Democratic Republic of Congo as a consequence of their involvement in the exploitation of the country's natural resources (Leader, 2008). Such organizations have had recourse to the Organization for Economic Co-operation and Development (OECD) Guidelines to support their position (Leader, 2008).

International environmental law has a relatively short history (Gao, 1998, p. 9), but recognition of collective and individual rights to a healthy environment and participation in environmental decisions are emerging as part of an international legal framework (Francioni, 1991, p. 293). Rights to health, such as those described in the Universal Declaration of Human Rights (1948) and Article 16 of the African Charter on Human and Peoples' Rights (1981), and participation in environmental decisions, as indicated by Principle 23 of the World Charter for Nature (1982), are recognized in legal instruments. Thus, rights to health and participation in environmental decisions are now linked to a safe environment (Francioni, 1991, p. 293).

Considerations of human rights have had a significant influence on the formulation of international environmental law (Gao, 1998, pp. 50–51). Scholars acknowledge that some environmental protection issues are human rights issues (Sinden, 2007, p. 501), and current human rights jurisprudence appears to account for environmental matters (e.g. Schall, 2008, p. 419). The concept of environmental justice links environmental protection and human rights. Environmental justice is "equitable utilization of resources, procedural fairness and a safe and healthy environment" and these components are increasingly regarded as human rights-based (Shelton, 1999, p. 26). As Brownlie (2003) has pointed out, environmental protection issues "do not concern the 'environment' in isolation, but relate to human and social priorities, systems of loss distribution, and the right to development" (p. 273).

Rights to life, health, association, expression, personal liberty, equality, legal redress, information, and participation in public decision-making and governance are regarded as broadly relevant for environmental protection and environmental justice (Shelton, 1999, p. 26). Thus, Shell's alleged complicity in human rights abuses in Nigeria included damage to the environment of the oil-producing areas (Lambooy and Rancourt, 2008). The Charter on Industrial Hazards and Human Rights (1996) drafted by a group of non-governmental organizations also links protection from industrial hazards and pollution to human rights. In European law, the right to a safe environment is increasingly recognized as a fundamental right (Sanchez Galera, 2008). For example, the European Court for Human Rights, in *Hatton* v. *United Kingdom* (2003) and *Giacomelli* v. *Italy* (2007), accepted that an environmental matter can, in principle, justify a claim for breach of rights in respect to private and family life. However, environmental matters are recognized as a distinct class of issues. Although environmental protection and human rights are connected, environmental rights are not a precise category of human rights (Birnie and Boyle, 2002, p. 253).

Human rights, non-financial reporting, and reality of performance

The broad area of human rights including labor standards, non-discrimination issues, and environmental matters occupies a major part of non-financial reporting. Some commentators (Parkinson, 2003, p. 8) and the UK Cabinet Office (2000) have found that certain non-financial issues sufficiently attract attention from campaigners to trigger pressure on enterprises while other issues receive less attention. Child labor and the environment currently attract the most attention (Parkinson, 2003, p. 9). However, this does not mean that other issues are not of public concern.

Economists debate the economic benefits of labor issues such as minimum wage (Card and Krueger, 1994, p. 772, 2000, p. 1397; Neumark and Wascher, 2000, p. 1362), employee training (Acemoglu and Pischke, 1999, p. F112; Becker, 1964), collectivization (Dau-Schmidt, 1992, p. 419; Posner, 1984, p. 988), and even prescriptive rules (Botero, Djankov, La Porta, Lopez-de-Silanes and Schleifer 2004, p. 1339). Regarding these issues, the reality is that threat of adverse publicity can engender corporate action toward addressing health and safety concerns (Clinard, 1990, p. 143).

However, the general view appears to be that the "tale of corporate misconduct conflicts with the glowing image that advertising and other media portray of the corporations" (Clinard, 1990, p. ix). Voluntary codes on corporate conduct and integrity have been described as "empty rhetoric" (Mendes and Mehmet, 2003, p. 132) and "window-dressing ... [with] no evidence that [corporate] behavior has improved or is likely to improve" (Parkinson, 2006, p. 20). Implementation of such codes has been labeled "disappointing" (Mendes and Mehmet, p. 132). Thus, a review of corporate codes undertaken by Paul and Garred (2000) criticizes the ineffectiveness of such codes.

It has been observed that TNCs are often involved in major industrial accidents and cases of inflicting environmental damage, particularly in developing nations (Francioni, 1991, p. 275). One reason for such incidents is the lack of adequate information provided by TNCs (Francioni, 1991, p. 275). In some quarters, it is thought that TNCs' "crimes against health and safety are frightening, shocking and disturbing" (Clinard, 1990, pp. 91–92; Frank, 1985, p. 84; Mills, 1987; Mokhiber, 1988). The abuses that triggered the founding of ILO still exist in various forms (Servais, 2005, pp. 31–32), mainly because corporations appear to prefer host countries with "little regard for worker safety" (Clinard, 1990, p. 141). The Bhopal gas disaster, for example, was a clear-cut case of a TNC attempting to avoid liability for recklessness even where it held prior knowledge of the danger of its operations (Clinard, 1990, pp. 37–159).

Whereas TNCs were once relatively immune to human rights criticisms, these days it is not uncommon that "[a] close inspection of major corporations ... turns up dirty linen that contradicts their claims of integrity" (Clinard, 1990, p. 15). Governmental and non-governmental bodies for examining corporate claims have emerged from the belief that "corporate advertising either misleads or deceives" (Clinard, 1990, p. 11), and TNCs are thought to be unwilling to voluntarily apply or implement international standards of conduct (Rieth, 2004, p. 181), especially in respect to their operations in less developed countries

(Brühl and Rittberger, 2001, p. 22; Kaul, Grunberg, and Stern, 1999, p. xxvi). Such criticisms are apparent during anti-globalization protests, which "illustrate a growing public demand for greater transparency, representation and regulation under the conditions of globalization" (Lipschutz, 1999, p. 259; Lipschutz and Fogel, 2002, p. 115).

Proliferation and ineffectiveness of codes and guidelines

As an index of corporate governance codes by the European Corporate Governance Institute (2009) indicates, such codes have proliferated. Several codes are the product of bilateral agreements, while individual corporate codes number in the thousands (Kline, 1993, pp. 313–314). A corporate code is "the written document by which a company pledges to follow a certain policy and certain principles" (Fasterling, 2006, p. 98). According to Fasterling (2006) such codes attempt, without legal backing, to provide "a systematic array of prospective norms concerning the institutional structure of a company's direction, control, and risk management" (p. 468). Codes are issued by individual corporations alone or in conjunction with other corporations, or by NGOs or even by government agencies (Jägers, 2002, p. 132). Codes have referential (point of reference as recognized by the European Commission's *Fourth Company Law Directive*, 2004), metrical (standards for measurement), and communicational (forum for exchange of ideas) roles (Fasterling, 2006, p. 468).

A significant number of codes directly concern TNCs (Sauvant and Aranda, 1994, pp. 86–87). As Kline (1993) has illustrated, in some cases a TNC may concurrently be affected by several codes from different countries (p. 312, Figure 12.3). However, the problem is that "gaps and overlaps" do occur with the result that consistency and coherence are lacking (Kline, 1993, p. 312). Surveys have revealed "minimal" connection between codes and prevention or elimination of corporate abuses, while such codes "are not real evidence of self-regulation or of [CSR]" (Clinard, 1990, p. 163).

The reason might be that such codes generally function as mere codes of honor. Most, if not all, codes lack enforcement provisions (Hong, 2000; ILO, 1998; Voiculescu, 2006, p. 254). Even where mandatory legal disclosure in accordance with a code is required, lack of verification mechanisms weakens a code's referential function and general effectiveness (Fasterling, 2006, pp. 476, 483–484). Some commentators have rightly argued that codes lacking adequate enforcement provisions are not a "silver bullet solution" (McLeay, 2006, p. 240) but rather "meaningless public-relations gimmicks" (Clinard, 1990, p. 162). Fasterling

(2006) therefore adds that corporations recognize the need for accuracy "solely if it is in their interest" (p. 472).

The United Nations Global Compact is an example of the ineffectiveness of corporate codes in the promotion and enforcement of human rights. As its history shows (Jägers, 2002, pp. 128–130), the Compact was initiated by a United Nations secretary-general as a cooperative venture between the United Nations and some large corporations for the promotion of ten principles in corporate operations. Under the Compact, corporations voluntarily agree to adhere to principles related to human rights, labor standards, environmental protection, and anti-corruption. However, critics argue that enterprises that subscribe to the Global Compact usually act contrary to the principles (Jägers, 2002, pp. 129–130). It has also been noted that corporations apparently complying with these codes of conduct are more often than not the subjects of US regulatory actions for earlier abuses (Clinard, 1990, p. 163).

Guidelines have also emerged as a "regulatory" mechanism for nonfinancial issues relating to TNCs. For example, the European Parliament Resolution on Standards for European Enterprises Operating in Developing Countries came into existence in 1999. Another illustration is the United Nations Norms on the Responsibility of Transnational Corporations and Other Business Enterprises with Regard to Human Rights (2003), of which transnational corporations are a concern (para. 20). Inspired by the prevalence of codes (Commentaries to the OECD Guidelines, 2000, para. 15), OECD Guidelines ("Disclosure" OECD Guidelines, 2000) expressly encourage TNCs to include "value statements of business conduct intended for public disclosure including information on the social, ethical and environmental policies of the enterprises and other codes of conduct to which the company subscribes" (para. 5). TNCs are also encouraged "to apply high quality standards for disclosure of non-financial information including environmental and social reporting where they exist" ("Disclosure" OECD Guidelines, para. 5).

Guidelines are meant to be non-binding, non-mandatory, and non-enforceable from a legal standpoint. The history as well as the negotiation of the OECD Guidelines (2000) clearly confirms this position (Vogelaar, 1980, p. 135). As Servais (2005) has pointed out, statements of policy or principles may be important in some respects, but they are similar to "expressing a political message [with] no legal value" (p. 318, para. 1078). Incidentally, OECD Guidelines are said to be "morally binding" (Blanpain, 2004, p. 210) rather than legal obligations of TNCs.

The Guidelines are said to "lead a 'silent, if not languishing, existence' [with] little attention from the parties concerned" (Jägers, 2002, p. 108). Another set of guidelines, the ILO Tripartite Declaration (1977), is also said to be of "limited" practical effect (Jägers, 2002, p. 110).

Regulatory gap

National company law usually imposes demanding financial disclosure requirements. In most cases, disclosure requirements may "exceed the requirements governing the financial actions themselves" (Gray, Owen, and Adams, 1996, p. 65). In contrast, a "gap" (Gray, Owen, and Adams, 1996) usually exists in non-financial disclosure (pp. 64–65). Despite evidence suggesting increasing corporate engagement in social reporting, the situation is apparently one of partial regulation of CSER with variation from jurisdiction to jurisdiction. The result is that CSER has been labeled a virtually limitless "area of potential activity" (Gray, Owen, and Adams, 1996, p. 82). Elements of social reporting are usually found in annual reports. However, with no attempt to quantify performance or reporting, annual reports usually focus on the "creation of images" of active corporate involvement in relevant activities, for example environmental protection (Crowther, 2004, p. 158). In this regard, a study of the top 100 Australian companies by Bubna-Litic (2008) found that environmental reporting is ineffective without guidance and enforcement by a regulator of some kind.

Information, disclosure, transparency, and accountability

A different approach may recognize the role of effective and transparent information and disclosure as a regulatory and accountability tool. Some scholars, for example Hess (2008), rightly regard disclosure as part of a tripod, including also dialogue and development, which constitutes the pillars of CSR as a governance regulatory tool. Comparative information advantage or disadvantage among market participants often induces regulatory intervention in some areas (Cheffins, 1997, p. 9). Legal intervention in information and disclosure requirements has advantages. It simultaneously addresses information imbalance while permitting market participants to make decisions on choice or quality. For example, a properly informed consumer is not only protected, but is also able to participate fairly and effectively in the market (Howells and Weatherill, 2005, p. 63; Weatherill, 1994). This regulatory technique is also cheaper to enforce (Weatherill, 1994, p. 63).

Availability of information is one of the elements of a perfect market (Ramsay, 2003). Major reasons for external intervention in markets include fairness, competition, and access to and cost of information (Grundmann, Kerber, and Weatherill, 2001; Howells, Janssen, and Schulze, 2005; Smith and Walter, 2006, p. 228; Trebilcock, 2003, p. 68). In financial reporting, for instance, Section 432(2)(d) of the UK Companies Act 1985 recognized regulators' power to appoint inspectors for investigating members' lack of information on company affairs. Apparent information asymmetry between corporations and customers has promoted the concept of "enterprise liability" in American law where strict liability appears to be in disuse (Priest, 1985; Sicilia, 2004, p. 210). As the cases of *Henningsen* v. *Bloomfield Motors, Inc* (1960) and *Greenman* v. *Yuba Power Products, Inc* (1963) show, enterprise liability is based on the notion of corporations' position of advantage in regard to product information.

Although it is generally accepted that a perfect market exists only in theory, the expectation is that legal policy should ideally favor conditions necessary for positive movement toward a perfect market (Cartwright, 1999, p. 8). Since free market economic systems rely heavily on transparency, inaccurate information may distort the market (Smith and Walter, 2006, p. 159). In such a distorted market, market discipline to compel adjustment by underperformers is absent (Smith and Walter, 2006, p. 159). Apart from the terms of the relationship between parties, there is also the need for transparency. The aim is the promotion of fairness. Transparency recognizes the need for "not being positively misled" (Willett, 2007b, p. 75). Incidentally, "[i]n regulatory politics, the party with information is the party with power [since] [a]symmetric information implies asymmetric power" (McLean, 2004, p. 64). This view has received the support of a UK public institution (Department of Trade and Industry, 2004, pp. 22–26) and is included in Article 7 of the European Unfair Commercial Practices Directive (2005).

An effective consumer protection regime maintains measures to ensure that information is sufficiently "accurate, comprehensive and comprehensible" for consumers to make informed choices (Howells and Weatherill, 2005, p. 63). Such a regime ensures, or at least improves, the "estimates of the value" of information (Trebilcock, 2003, p. 73). Where sufficiently relevant information on products or services is available to consumers, incentive may be provided to producers to improve the quality of products or services (Cartwright, 1999, p. 11). An adequately informed consumer is a protected consumer and effective market participant. This notion is now recognized, at least in the European Union, as critical to good consumer protection policy (Howells and Weatherill, 2005, pp. 63–64; Weatherill, 1994). The European Court of Justice in *GB-INNO* v. *CCL* (1990) considered it a principal requirement for an effective consumer protection policy. Deutch (1994) goes as far as to suggest that consumer protection should be linked to human rights as a form of human dignity protection.

Consequently, the existence and enforcement of disclosure obligations are important. It is conceded that laws may not be able to stop or prevent irrational individual decisions. Behavioral economics provides evidence of consumer irrationality (Howells, 2005, pp. 358–362; Offer, 2006, p. 70; Ramsay, 2005, p. 52; Sunstein and Thaler, 2003, p. 1159) and does not discount business awareness and manipulation of such irrationality (Hanson and Kysar, 1999, pp. 1424–1425). Behavioral analysis shows that, in some cases, availability of accurate information may not be sufficient to stop irrationality in individual decision-making. However, at its bare minimum, the law ought to ensure the conditions necessary for effective communication of accurate information (Ramsay, 2003, p. 23). For instance, the European Court of Human Rights has held in *Guerra* v. *Italy* (1998) that human rights rules are now recognized to include positive obligations to maintain conditions for collecting, disseminating, and receiving information on corporate activity. This position of a right may represent a subset of a "general" right to information apparently recognized in *Observer* v. *United Kingdom* (1992) and *Thorgeirson* v. *Iceland* (1992).

Regulation of information and disclosure also promotes shared goals (Ogus, 1994, pp. 15, 19). Regulation of non-financial reporting provides an avenue for enforcing internationally shared values and expectations. Such values include human rights, labor standards, non-discrimination issues, and environmental protection. Mere reporting of these issues ensures awareness of their existence and increases the likelihood of compliance. Avery (2000) observes that bad publicity in regard to any of those values and expectations "can undo hundreds of millions of dollars worth of marketing" (p. 71). Mandatory disclosure achieves policy objectives indirectly by expecting public pressure to lead to desired outcomes. In other words, mandatory disclosure increases "the alignment of company behavior with public pressure" (Parkinson, 2006, p. 18), particularly where adverse consequences may result from disregarding public opinion. For example, obligatory disclosure under the US Toxics Release Inventory resulted in the substantial reduction of emissions from relevant corporations (Fung and O'Rourke, 2000; Parkinson, 2006, p. 18).

Therefore, full disclosure is of "the highest importance" to account-ability and public assurance (*Greenbury Report*, 1995, p. 26, para. 5.2). Accountability is

> the duty to provide an account ... or reckoning of those actions for which one is held responsible [and] involves two responsibilities or duties: the responsibility to undertake certain actions (or forbear from taking actions) and the responsibility to provide an account of those actions. (Gray, Owen, and Adams, 1996, p. 38)

Information is vital to the exercise, for example, of the freedom *from* contract. Freedom *from* contract is "the idea that parties should have freedom to choose *not* to enter into contracts with and, perhaps more aptly, freedom to choose *not* to enter into a contract with any given party" (Willett, 2007a, p. 18). Where consumers or investors, for instance, are properly informed of the human rights performance of a corporation, such persons can decide to do or not to do business with the corporation.

Non-financial reporting as advertising

The suggested approach to non-financial reporting in this chapter rec-ognizes such reporting as corporate advertising. Advertising generally includes "all measures that aim at increasing one's or a third person's sales" (Glinski, 2006, p. 202). The aim of consumer advertising is clearly to attract public attention to particular products or services. However, advertising may not be restricted to products or services. Advertising may also, arguably, attract attention to the reputation of an organiza-tion including the organization's non-financial policies or values. The reason is that "reputational capital" is "a fragile, intangible asset" that "complements—and sometimes surpasses—the material and financial assets" (Fombrun, 1996, pp. 5–6, 10, 32). Reputation is linked with "brand equity" and makes "real" but not always "directly quantifiable" contributions to the value of corporations (Schwartz and Gibb, 1999, p. 10). As a result, "social labeling" may be classified as advertising. Social labeling on products or packaging, or otherwise attached to the producer, indicates "information on the social conditions in which a product was manufactured or a service provided" (Servais, 2005, p. 103, para. 228).

Non-financial reputation is now an important factor considered by consumers and investors, among other interest groups. As a result, reputation management is "essential" to modern corporations (Brammer and Pavelin, 2005, p. 40). As such, modern business organizations are expected to recognize, understand, and express, internally and externally, their distinct identity and brand (Schulz, Hatch, and Larsen, 2000). Here, cause-related marketing is recognized as one variation of reputation management (e.g. Baghi, Rubaltelli, and Tedeschi, 2009). Marketing practitioners acknowledge the importance of CSR in the theory and practice of marketing (Vaaland, Heide, and Gronhaug, 2008). Even within the supply chain, the role of CSR as a marketing tool is increasingly emphasized (Verhees, Kuipers, and Meulenberg, 2008). Public relations practitioners appear to share this view (Demetrious, 2008; Kim and Reber, 2008).

The manner the CSR image is communicated influences consumer behavior (Currás-Pérez, 2008; Marin, Ruiz, and Rubio, 2009), although there may be doubt as to the connection between CSR and consumer trust (Castaldo, Perrini, Migani and Tencati 2009). A manufacturer's reputation evidently influences consumer selection or rejection of products (Cowe and Williams, 2000). The "market" for ethical trading and consumption is also increasing (McBarnet, 2007, pp. 17–19). Consumers engage in "ethical purchase behavior" by selecting "ethical products" and avoiding suppliers on "reputational grounds" or "actively seeking out those with a positive reputation" (Parkinson, 2003, p. 12). Corporations, including TNCs, target the "ethical consumer" and "ethical corporation" market where consumers express "lifestyles and identities" in purchasing decisions (Muchlinski, 2007b, p. 100).

Damage to commercial reputation can have substantial consequences (Ogus, 2006, p. 130; Shapiro, 1982). There is evidence of a growing tendency for people to boycott the products of or speak out against "irresponsible companies" in terms of human rights, environment protection, labor practices, and other areas (Mendes and Mehmet, 2003, p. 231). Attacks on TNCs for perceived abuses and performance in non-financial matters have been well-documented (Klein, 2000; Smith, 1990). Organized consumer boycotts are described as "the most visible and acute form" of consumer response (Parkinson, 2003, p. 12). Results from case studies (Smith, 1990, chap. 8) appear to provide proof for this claim. Research indicates that negative ethical publicity can adversely affect other areas of corporate activity, including earnings and employee morale (Clinard, 1990, p. 178; Fisse and Braithwaite, 1983), and adverse publicity may cause "brand vulnerability" (McBarnet, 2007, p. 16) and even "brand boomerang" (Klein, 2000, p. 345). Evidence for the financial effects of organized consumer boycotts may be limited (Parkinson, 2003, p. 12), but the reactions of targeted businesses indicate substantial and serious consequences (Willets, 1998, p. 216).

As already noted in the preceding section, a legal framework is needed to address unequal bargaining power between consumers and enterprises as a result of consumers' lack of, or difficulty of obtaining, correct information (Oughton and Lowry, 2000, pp. 15, 16, 19; *Report of the Crowther Committee*, 1971; Trebilcock, 1971). The same justifications may apply to "reputational advertising" or advertisement of non-financial reputations since reputation is also a consumer concern. The distinction between product/service and "process information" is difficult to justify since consumers buy "not only products, but also shares of responsibility in the moral and ecological economy that produces them" (Kysar, 2005, p. 641). Incidentally, some policymakers (e.g. Department of Environment, Food and Rural Affairs, 2005, pp. 1–2; Fuchs and Lorek, 2005; Seyfang, 2004) suggest the need for a consumer role in such issues as sustainable development, production, and consumption.

Public interest and credibility

Abuses by large corporations concern a number of interest groups, including consumers and investors (Clinard, 1990, pp. 1, 6, 9). People are particularly worried about the extent and exercise of TNCs' power (Clinard, 1990, pp. 13–14). Public interest generally indicates a combination of public interest in the outcome of proceedings, the claimant's lack of personal (proprietary or pecuniary) interest or at least economically viable interest in the outcome, and the importance of the issues beyond the parties' immediate interests (Schall, 2008, p. 419).

Although doubted by some (e.g. Posner, 1974), public interest protection is one of the usual bases for regulatory intervention (Smith and Walter, 2006, p. 48). As Justice Cory in *R* v. *Wholesale Travel Group* (1991) pointed out, regulatory legislation protects "the public or broad segments of the public [and] involves the shift of emphasis from the protection of individual interests" (p. 219). For example, the "public element" was the trigger factor for the pioneer English corporate criminal statute (Pinto and Evans, 2003, p. 8). Regulatory legislation has further been crucial for protecting vulnerable people from corporate abuses since the Industrial Revolution (*R* v. *Wholesale Travel Group*, 1991, p. 234). Regulatory activity is also influenced by changed opinions or attitudes. For example, Lord Justice Hoffmann observed in *Bishopsgate Investment Management Ltd* v. *Maxwell (No.2)* (1994) that the law evolves "in response to changes in public attitudes to corporate governance" (p. 264).

Recognition of the twin notions of the regulatory role of disclosure and non-financial reporting as advertising would improve or enhance the quality and credibility of such reports. The regulatory aim ought to be the promotion of the credibility of reports and preventing or reducing the abuse of non-financial reporting. It is clear that legal intervention has occurred to promote certain conduct, or to correct abuses (Skeel, Jr, 2006). Credibility of non-financial reports is a legal issue in light of their widespread use, growing importance, and potential for abuse. As noted already, there are surveys that indicate that corporations regularly "lie about any and everything" (Rayman-Bacchus, 2004, p. 28). The aborted *Kasky* v. *Nike* (2002) and the ongoing *Bowoto* v. *Chevron* cases in the US illustrate the legal difficulties concerning non-financial reporting.

Kasky v. *Nike* focused on Nike's response to allegations of operating "sweatshop" factories in South-East Asia. Among other claims made to a number of persons and organizations, Nike suggested that its wages were "on average double the minimum wage" in countries where its factories were located, and its employees were "protected from physical and sexual abuse" (Kazer and Williams, n.d.). Kasky sued Nike, alleging that Nike's claims were false and misleading. The claimant also sought an injunction prohibiting Nike from making false statements and forcing the surrender by Nike of its revenue in California. The California Supreme Court reversed the lower courts' finding of political or non-commercial speech protected under the US Constitution's First Amendment guarantee of free speech and asked the trial court to determine the substantive issue of whether Nike made false and misleading statements. Nike was granted permission to appeal by the US Supreme Court. However, the court later pronounced that its permission was "improvidently granted" on the ground that it was premature for the court to hear a case in which the facts had not been fully developed either in discovery or at trial. The suit was then sent back to the trial court but the parties subsequently settled the case. The main point of the settlement was that Nike agreed to pay US$1.5 million to the Fair Labor Association for workers' programs and independent monitoring of labor practices, particularly in Nike's overseas factories.

In its first non-financial publication after the *Kasky* litigation, Nike documented the conditions of its factories. Its April 2005 report admitted to poor labor standards in a significant number of Nike's factories, especially in Asia (Nike, 2005). Nike's report has been described as an "unusual step" (Baker, 2004, p. 6). Apart from indicating the growing need for "careful" non-financial reports (Joseph, 2004, p. 110), *Kasky* v. *Nike* showed that the credibility of such reports had risen to become a legal issue. This issue of credibility has not been resolved nationally and internationally. However, the increasing reliance on non-financial reports and litigation involving such reports suggest that at some point the law has to address or confront the issue by either recognizing or denying legal liability for such reports.

In *Bowoto* v. *Chevron*, the claimants sued Chevron (now Chevron-Texaco) for human rights abuses and false and misleading information concerning its practices during the period of military rule in Nigeria between 1993 and 1998. In March 2004, the US (federal) District Court, California, rejected Chevron's preliminary objections that Nigeria was the proper forum for trial of the case, the alleged human rights abuses did not violate international law, and Chevron could not be held responsible for the actions of its Nigerian subsidiary. The case is still in the pre-trial stage.

Conclusion

Evidence indicates the growing importance of non-financial issues and reporting nationally and internationally. As a result, in relation to TNCs, the concept of "international corporate social responsibility" is gaining prominence (Muchlinski, 2007b, pp. 101–104). Similarly, the World Bank (Darrow, 2003) and the WTO (Jägers, 2007, p. 177) now often integrate CSR issues (particularly human rights) into discussions and projects. However, a critical issue for ensuring the credibility of non-financial reports has emerged—the impression is that without external pressure, corporations will not be socially responsible and consider the rights of consumers, workers, and the public, or the impact of business operations on the environment (Clinard, 1990, p. 18). Corporate non-financial performance and corporate non-financial reporting do not often coincide, with the result that credibility is an issue. Credibility affects the influence or potential effect of non-financial reporting as a governance tool.

It is generally accepted that "voluntariness is integral to CSR" although that does not necessarily indicate support for deregulation

(Parkinson, 2006, p. 5). The voluntary nature of CSR may not exclude the use of binding legal obligations for its promotion (Parkinson, 2006, p. 6). Similarly, human rights components of non-financial reporting may have legal implications. For example, Jägers (2002) has observed that "[c]orporate human rights obligations are not merely a question of self-imposed obligations emanating from ethical or policy considerations [but] derive from a trend towards a broad and dynamic interpretation of international human rights" law (p. 260). Observing that CSER "is not a precisely definable activity—nor is it likely to become so in the absence of detailed regulation" (Gray, Owen, and Adams, 1996, p. 81), some commentators (e.g. Chandler, 2003; de la Cuesta González and Valor Martinez, 2004; Klein, 2000; Parker, 2007; Shamir, 2004) have called for the regulation of CSR.

This chapter suggests that the key to ensuring the credibility of non-financial reports is the recognition of the regulatory role of effective disclosure in non-financial reporting and the role of non-financial reporting as corporate advertising. Where such reports are credible, the role of non-financial reporting in the promotion and protection of human rights in developing countries is enhanced.

Cases

- Barcelona Traction case (1970) Reports 3
- *Bishopsgate Investment Management Ltd* v. *Maxwell* (No.2) [1994] 1 All ER 261
- *Bowoto* v. *Chevron*, C99-2506 CAL (ND Cal.)
- *Doe* v. *Unocal Corp.*, 963 F.Supp. 880 (C.D. Cal. 1997)
- *GB-INNO* v. *CCL* (Case C-362/88) (1990) ECR I-667
- *Giacomelli* v. *Italy* (2007) 45 EHRR 38
- *Greenman* v. *Yuba Power Products, Inc.* 59 Cal.2d 57, 27 Cal.Rptr. 697, 377 P.2d 897 (Cal. 1963)
- *Guerra* v. *Italy* (1998) 26 EHRR 357
- *Hatton* v. *United Kingdom* (2003) 37 EHRR 28
- *Henningsen* v. *Bloomfield Motors, Inc.* (1960) 32 N.J. 358; 161 A.2d 69
- *In re South African Apartheid Litigation* (2004) 346 F Supp. 2d 538
- *Kasky* v. *Nike* 27 Cal. 4th 939, 946, 45 P.3d 243, 247, 119 Cal. Rptr.2d 296 (Cal. 2002), 123 S. Ct. 2554 (2003)
- *National Coalition Government of the Union of Burma* v. *Unocal, Inc.*, [1997] U.S. Dist. Lexis 2097
- *Observer* v. *United Kingdom* (1992) 14 EHRR 153
- *R* v. *Wholesale Travel Group* (1991) 3 S.L.R. 154 (Canada)

- *The Presbyterian Church of Sudan* v. *Talisman Energy and the Republic of Sudan* (2005) 374 F Supp. 2d 331
- *Thorgeirson* v. *Iceland*, also known as *Thorgeir* v. *Iceland* (1992) 14 EHRR 843
- *Wiwa* v. *Royal Dutch Petroleum Company and Shell Transport and Trading Company*, 226 F 3d 88 (2nd Cir. 2000); No. 96 Civ. 8386 (S.D.N.Y 1998)

International instruments

- African Charter on Human and Peoples' Rights (1981)
- American Convention on Human Rights (1969)
- Convention on the Elimination of All Forms of Discrimination against Women (1979)
- Copenhagen Declaration on Social Development and Program of Action, adopted by the 1995 World Summit for Social Development, Copenhagen: UN Doc.A/CONF.166/9 (1995)
- Declaration on the Elimination of All Forms of Intolerance and Discrimination Based on Religion or Belief, UN GA Res.36/55 (1982) 21 ILM 205
- Declaration on the Right and Responsibility of Individuals, Groups and Organs of Society to Promote and Protect Universally Recognised Human Rights and Fundamental Freedoms, 1999, UN Doc. A/Res/53/144
- European Commission, Directorate-General for Employment and Social Affairs, Unit EMPL/D.1, July 2001
- European Commission, Fourth Company Law Directive, COM (2004) 725 of 27 October 2004
- European Convention on Human Rights (1950)
- European Parliament Resolution on Standards for European Enterprises Operating in Developing Countries, 1999 C 104/180
- European Parliament, Resolution on EU Standards for European Enterprises Operating in Developing Countries: Towards a European Code of Conduct, European Parliament Resolution A4-0508/98, 1999 C 104/180
- International Convention on the Elimination of All Forms of Racial Discrimination, 1966 UN Res.34/180, 34 UN GAOR Supp. (No. 46) 193, UN Doc.A/34/46
- International Covenant on Civil and Political Rights (1966)
- International Covenant on Economic, Social and Cultural Rights (1966)

- Unfair Commercial Practices Directive, Directive 2005/29/EC OJ 2005 L149/22
- United Nations Charter (1945)
- United Nations General Assembly Declaration on the Right to Development, 4 December 1986, GA Res.41/128; Annex 41 UN GAOR Supp. (No. 53), UN Doc.A/41/53
- United Nations Norms on the Responsibility of Transnational Corporations and Other Business Enterprises with regard to Human Rights, UN Doc. E/CN.4/Sub.2/2003/12/Rev.2 (2003)
- Universal Declaration on Human Rights 1948, adopted in UN GA Res. 217A, Article 25(1), (1948) UN Doc. A/810
- World Charter for Nature, adopted in GA Res n.37/7 of 28 October 1982

References

Abreu, R., and David, F. (2004). Corporate social responsibility: Exploration inside experience and practice at the European level. In D. Crowther and L. Rayman-Bacchus (eds.), *Perspectives on corporate social responsibility* (pp. 109–139). Aldershot: Ashgate.

Acemoglu, D., and Pischke, J. (1999). Beyond Becker: Training in imperfect labour markets. *Economic Journal, 109*, F112–F142.

Allen, L. (2001). *The global financial system, 1750–2000*. London: Reaktion Books.

Anderson, G. W. (2006). Corporate governance and constitutional law: A legal pluralist perspective. In S. MacLeod (ed.), *Global governance and the quest for justice. Volume II: Corporate governance* (pp. 27–47). Oxford: Hart.

Avery, C. (2000). *Business and human rights in a time of change*. London: Amnesty International UK.

Baghi, I., Rubaltelli, E., and Tedeschi, M. (2009). A strategy to communicate corporate social responsibility: Cause related marketing and its dark side. *Corporate Social Responsibility and Environmental Management, 16*(1), 15–26.

Baker, N. (2004). All done with mirrors? Transparency and business ethics. *International Bar News, 59*(4), 4.

Barnard, C., Deakin, S., and Hobbs, R. (2004). *Reflexive law, corporate social responsibility and the evolution of labour standards: The case of working time*. Cambridge: ESRC Centre for Business Research, University of Cambridge.

Barry, N. (1991). *The morality of business enterprise*. Aberdeen: Aberdeen University Press.

Bassiouni, C. (1980). *International criminal law: A draft international criminal code*. Rijn: Sijthoff and Noordhoof.

Becker, G. (1964). *Human capital*. Chicago: The University of Chicago Press.

Berle, A. A. (1965). The impact of the corporation on classical economic theory. *The Quarterly Journal of Economics, 79*, 25–40.

Birnie, P. W., and Boyle, A. E. (2002). *International law and the environment* (2nd edn). Oxford: Oxford University Press.

Blanpain, R. (2004). Multinational enterprises and code of conduct. The OECD guidelines for multinational enterprises in perspective. In R. Blanpain (ed.), *Comparative labour law and industrial relations in industrialized market economies* (viii & revised edn) (pp. 191–212). The Hague: Kluwer.

Botero, J. C., Djankov, S., La Porta, R., Lopez-de-Silanes, F., and Schleifer, A. (2004). The regulation of labor. *Quarterly Journal of Economics, 119*(4), 1339–1382.

Bowman, S. R. (1996). *The modern corporation and American political thought. Law, power, and ideology*. University Park: The Pennsylvania State University Press.

Brammer, S., and Pavelin, S. (2005). Corporate reputation and an insurance motivation for corporate social investment. *The Journal of Corporate Citizenship, 20*, 39–51.

Brownlie, I. (2003). *Principles of public international law* (6th edn). Oxford: Oxford University Press.

Brühl, T., and Rittberger, V. (2001). From international to global governance: Actors, collective decision-making, and the United Nations in the world of the twenty-first century. In V. Rittberger (ed.), *Global governance and the United Nations system* (pp. 1–47). Tokyo: United Nations University Press.

Bubna-Litic, K. (2008). Environmental reporting as a communications tool: A question of enforcement? *Journal of Environmental Law, 20*(1), 69–85.

Cabinet Office, Performance and Innovation Unit (2000). *Rights of exchange: Social health, environmental and trade objectives on the global stage*. London: Cabinet Office.

Campbell, T. (2007). The normative grounding of corporate social responsibility: A human rights approach. In D. McBarnet, A. Voiculescu, and T. Campbell (eds.), *The new corporate accountability. Corporate social responsibility and the law* (pp. 529–564). Cambridge: Cambridge University Press.

Campbell, K., and Vick, D. (2007). Disclosure law and the market for corporate social responsibility. In D. McBarnet, A. Voiculescu, and T. Campbell (eds.), *The new corporate accountability. Corporate social responsibility and the law* (pp. 241–278). Cambridge: Cambridge University Press.

Card, D., and Krueger, A. B. (1994). Minimum wages and employment: A case study of the fast-food industry in New Jersey and Pennsylvania. *American Economic Review, 84*(4), 772–793.

Card, D., and Krueger, A. B. (2000). Minimum wages and employment: A case study of the fast-food industry in New Jersey and Pennsylvania: A reply. *American Economic Review, 90*(5), 1397–1420.

Cartwright, P. (1999). Consumer protection in financial services: Putting the law in context. In P. Cartwright (ed.), *Consumer protection in financial services* (pp. 1–24). London: Kluwer.

Castaldo, S., Perrini, F., Migani, N., and Tencati, A. (2009). The missing link between corporate social responsibility and consumer trust: The case of fair trade products. *Journal of Business Ethics, 84*(1), 68–84.

Chandler Jr, A. D. (1990). *Scale and scope: The dynamics of industrial capitalism*. Cambridge, MA: Harvard University Press.

Chandler, G. (1998). Oil companies and human rights. *Business Ethics: A European Review, 7*(2), 69–72.

Chandler, G. (2003). The curse of "corporate social responsibility". *New Academy Review, 2*(1), 31–34.

Charter on industrial hazards and human rights (1996). Retrieved 5 February 2009, from http://www.globalpolicy.org/socecon/envronmt/charter.htm.

Cheffins, B. R. (1997). *Company law. Theory, structure and operation.* Oxford: Clarendon.

Cingula, M. (2006). Corporate governance as a process-oriented approach to socially responsible organizations. In P. U. Ali, and G. N. Gregoriou (eds.), *International corporate governance after Sarbanes-Oxley* (pp. 65–94). Hoboken, NJ: John Wiley.

Clapham, A. (2000). The question of jurisdiction under international criminal law over legal persons: Lessons from the Rome Conference on an International Criminal Court. In M. T. Kamminga and S. Zia-Zarifi (eds.), *Liability of multinational enterprises under international law* (pp. 139–195). The Hague: Kluwer.

Clapham, A., and Jebri, S. (2001). Categories of corporate complicity in human rights abuses. *Hastings International and Comparative Law Review, 24,* 339–349.

Clapham, A. (2006). *Human rights obligations of non-state actors.* Oxford: Oxford University Press.

Clarke, T. (2004). Introduction: Theories of governance—Reconceptualizing corporate governance theory after the Enron experience. In T. Clarke (ed.), *Theories of corporate governance. The philosophical foundations of corporate governance* (pp. 13–20). London: Routledge.

Clinard, M. B. (1990). *Corporate corruption. The abuse of power.* New York: Praeger.

Consumer credit: Report of the committee (Crowther Committee) (1971). Cmnd 4596.

Cowe, R., and Williams, S. (2000). *Who are ethical consumers?* Manchester: The Co-operative Bank.

Crowther, D. (2004). Corporate social reporting: genuine action or window dressing. In D. Crowther and L. Rayman-Bacchus (eds.), *Perspectives on corporate social responsibility* (pp. 140–160). Aldershot: Ashgate.

Currás-Pérez, R. (2008). Corporate social responsibility communication: Image and identification with the company as antecedents of consumer behaviour. *International Review of Public and Non-profit Marketing, 5*(2), 193–194.

Darrow, M. (2003). *Between light and shadow: The World Bank, the International Monetary Fund and international human rights Law.* Portland: Hart.

Dau-Schmidt, K. G. (1992). A bargaining analysis of labor law and the search for equity and industrial peace. *Michigan Law Review, 91*(3), 419–514.

de la Cuesta González, M., and Valor Martinez, C. (2004). Fostering corporate social responsibility through public initiative: From EU to the Spanish case. *Journal of Business Ethics, 55,* 273–293.

Demetrious, K. (2008). Corporate social responsibility: New activism and public relations. *Social Responsibility Journal, 4*(1/2), 104–119.

Department of Environment, Food and Rural Affairs (DEFRA) (2005). *Securing the future: Delivering the UK sustainable development strategy.* London: The Stationery Office.

Department of Trade and Industry (2004). Extending competitive markets: Empowered consumers, successful business. Retrieved 5 February 2009, from http://www.berr.gov.uk/files/file23787.pdf.

Deutch, S. (1994). Are consumer rights, human rights? *Osgoode Hall Law Journal, 32*(3), 537–557.

Deva, S. (2003). Human rights violations by multinational corporations and international law: Where from here? *Connecticut Journal of International Law, 19*, 1–57.

Dierkes M., and Bauer, R. A. (eds.) (1973). *Corporate social accounting.* New York: Praeger.

Dunlavy, C. A. (2004). From citizens to plutocrats: Nineteenth century shareholder voting rights and theories of the corporation. In K. Lipartito and D. B. Sicilia (eds.), *Constructing corporate America. History, politics, and culture* (pp. 66–93). Oxford: Oxford University Press.

European Corporate Governance Institute. Retrieved 5 February 2009, from http://www.ecgi.org/codes/all_codes.php.

Fasterling, B. (2006). Prospects and limits of corporate governance codes. In P. U. Ali, and G. N. Gregoriou (eds.), *International corporate governance after Sarbanes-Oxley* (pp. 467–484). Hoboken, NJ: John Wiley.

Fisse, B., and Braithwaite, J. (1983). *The impact of publicity on corporate offenders.* Albany: University of New York.

Fombrun, C. (1996). *Reputation: Realizing value from the corporate image.* Boston: Harvard Business School Press.

Francioni, F. (1991). Exporting environmental hazard through multinational enterprises: Can the state of origin be held responsible? In F. Francioni and T. Scovazzi (eds.), *International responsibility for environmental harm* (pp. 275–298). London: Graham & Trotman.

Frank, N. (1985). *Crimes against health and safety.* New York: Harrow & Heston.

Friedman, M. (13 September 1970). The social responsibility of business is to increase its profits. *New York Times*, p. 6.

Fuchs, D., and Lorek, S. (2005). Sustainable consumption governance: A history of promises and failures. *Journal of Consumer Policy, 28*(3), 2612–2688.

Fung, A., and O' Rourke, D. (2000). Reinventing environmental regulation from the grassroots up: Explaining and expanding the success of the toxics release inventory. *Environmental Management, 25*, 115–127.

Gabrosky, P., and Sutton, A. (eds.) (1989). *Stains on a white collar: Fourteen studies in corporate crimes or corporate harm.* Sydney: Federation Press.

Gao, Z. (1998). Environmental regulation of oil and gas in the twentieth century and beyond: An introduction and overview. In Z. Gao (ed.), *Environmental regulation of oil and gas* (pp. 3–58). London: Kluwer.

Glinski, C. (2006). Self-regulation of transnational corporations: Neither meaning in law nor voluntary. In S. MacLeod (ed.), *Global governance and the quest for justice. Volume II: Corporate governance* (pp. 197–220). Oxford: Hart.

Gray, R., Owen, D., and Adams, C. (1996). *Accountability. Changes and challenges in corporate social and environmental reporting.* Hemel Hempstead: Prentice Hall.

Grundmann, S., Kerber, W., and Weatherill, S. (eds.) (2001). *Party autonomy and the role of information in the internal market.* Berlin: De Gruyter.

Hanson, J., and Kysar, D. (1999). Taking behaviorism seriously: Some evidence of market manipulation. *Harvard Law Review, 112*, 14,201–14, 572.

Hartmann, T. (2002). *Unequal protection. The rise of corporate dominance and the theft of human rights.* US: Rodale Inc.

Hertz, N. (2001). *The silent takeover: Global capitalism and the death of democracy.* London: Heinemann.

Hess, D. (2008). The three pillars of corporate social reporting as new governance regulation: Disclosure, dialogue and development. *Business Ethics Quarterly*, *18*(4), 4474–4482.

Hong, J. (2000). Enforcement of corporate codes of conduct: Finding a private right of action for international laborers against MNCS for labor rights violations. *Wisconsin International Law Journal*, *19*, 41.

Howells, G. (2005). The potential and limits of empowerment by information. *Journal of Law and Society*, *32*(3), 349–370.

Howells, G., and Weatherill, S. (2005). *Consumer protection law* (2nd edn). Aldershot: Ashgate.

Howells, G., Janssen, A., and Schulze, R. (eds.) (2005). *Information rights and obligations: A challenge for party autonomy and transactional fairness*. Aldershot: Ashgate.

Human Rights Watch (1999). *The price of oil, corporate responsibility and human rights violations in Nigeria's oil producing communities*. New York: Human Rights Watch.

International Chamber of Commerce (1991). Business charter for sustainable development. *Environmental Policy and Law*, *21*, 35.

International Labour Organization (1998). Corporate Codes of Conduct. Retrieved 5 February 2009, from http://itcilo.it/english/actrau/telearn/iglobal/ilo/code/main.htm.

International Labour Organization (1977). *Tripartite declaration of principles concerning multinational enterprises and social policy*. Geneva: International Labour Organization.

Jägers, N. (2007). Bringing corporate social responsibility to the World Trade Organization. In D. McBarnet, A. Voiculescu, and T. Campbell (eds.), *The new corporate accountability. Corporate social responsibility and the law* (pp. 177–206). Cambridge: Cambridge University Press.

Jägers, N. M. C. P. (2002). *Corporate human rights obligations: In search of accountability*. Antwerpen: Intersentia.

Joseph, S. (2000). An overview of the human rights accountability of multinational enterprises. In M. T. Kamminga and S. Zia-Zarifi (eds.), *Liability of multinational enterprises under international law* (pp. 75–93). The Hague: Kluwer.

Joseph, S. (2004). *Corporations and transnational human rights litigation*. Oxford: Hart.

Kamminga, M. T., and Zia Ziarifi, S. (2000). Introduction. In M. T. Kamminga and S. Zia-Zarifi (eds.), *Liability of multinational enterprises under international law* (pp. 1–13). The Hague: Kluwer.

Kaufman, C. (2007). *Globalisation and labour rights. The conflict between core labour rights and international economic law*. Oxford: Hart.

Kaul, I., Grunberg, I., and Stern, M. A. (1999). *Global public goods: International cooperation in the 21st century*. New York: Oxford University Press.

Kazer, A. K. and Williams, C. A. (n.d.) The future of social reporting is on the line—Nike v Kasky could undermine the ability to require accurate reporting. Retrieved 5 February 2009, from http://www.business-ethics.com/nikevkasky.htm.

Kim, S. Y., and Reber, B. H. (2008). Public relations' place in corporate social responsibility: Practitioners define their role. *Public Relations Review*, *34*(4), 337–342.

Klein, N. (2000). *No Logo*. London: Flamingo.

Kline, J. M. (1993). International regulation of transnational business, providing the missing leg of global investment standards. *Transnational Corporations*, 2(1), 153–164.

Kysar, D. A. (2005). Preferences for processes: Process/product distinction and the regulation of consumer choice. *Harvard Law Review, 118*, 525–641.

Lambooy, T., and Rancourt, M. E. (2008). Shell in Nigeria: From human rights abuse to corporate social responsibility. *Human Rights and International Legal Discourse, 2*(2), 229–275.

Lamoreaux, N. R. (2004). Partnerships, corporations, and the limits on contractual freedom in U.S. history: An essay in economics, law, and culture. In K. Lipartito and D. B. Sicilia (eds.), *Constructing corporate America. History, politics, and culture* (pp. 29–65). Oxford: Oxford University Press.

Leader, D. (2008). Business and human rights—Time to hold companies to account. *International and Comparative Law Review, 8*(3), 447–462.

Leader, S. (2006). Human rights risks and new strategies for global investment. *Journal of International Economic Law, 9*, 657–705.

Lipschutz, R. D. (1999). From local knowledge and practice to global governance. In M. Hewson and T. J. Sinclair (eds.), *Approaches to global governance theory* (pp. 259–286). Albany, NY: SUNY Press.

Lipschutz, R. D., and Fogel, C. (2002). Regulation for the rest of us? Global civil society and the privatization of transnational regulation. In R. B. Hall and T. J. Biersteker (eds.), *The emergence of private authority in global governance* (pp. 115–140). Cambridge: Cambridge University Press.

Litvin, D. (2003). *Empires of profit: Commerce, conquest and corporate responsibility.* New York: Texere.

MacLeod, S. (2008). The United Nations, human rights and transnational corporations: Challenging the international legal order. In N. Boeger, R. Murray, and C. Villiers (eds.), *Perspectives on corporate social responsibility* (pp. 65–84). Cheltenham: Edward Elgar.

Marin, L., Ruiz, S., and Rubio, A. (2009). The role of identity salience in the effects of corporate social responsibility on consumer behaviour. *Journal of Business Ethics, 84*(1), 65–78.

McBarnet, D. (2007). Corporate social responsibility beyond law, through law, for law: The new corporate accountability. In D. McBarnet, A. Voiculescu, and T. Campbell (eds.), *The new corporate accountability. Corporate social responsibility and the law* (pp. 9–57). Cambridge: Cambridge University Press.

McLean, I. (2004). The history of regulation in the United Kingdom: Three case studies in search of a theory. In J. Jordana and D. Levi-Faur (eds.), *The politics of regulation. Institutions and regulatory reforms for the age of governance* (pp. 45–66). Cheltenham: Edward Elgar.

McLeay, F. (2006). Corporate codes of conduct and the human rights accountability of transnational corporations: A small piece of a larger puzzle. In O. De Schutter (ed.), *Transnational corporations and human rights* (pp. 219–240). Oxford: Hart.

McNichol, J. (2006). Transnational NGO certification programs as new regulatory forms: Lessons from the forestry sector. In M. Djelic and K. Sahlin-Andersson, (eds.), *Transnational governance-Institutional dynamics of regulation* (pp. 349–374). Cambridge: Cambridge University Press.

Mendes, E., and Mehmet, O. (2003). *Global governance, economy and law-waiting for justice.* London: Routledge.

Miles, S., Hammond, K., and Friedman, A. L. (2002). *Social and environmental reporting and ethical investment.* London: The Association of Chartered Certified Accountants.

Mills, S. L. (ed.) (1987). *Corporate violence: Injury and death for profit.* Totowa, NJ: Rowman and Littlefield.

Mitchell, L. E. (2007). The board as a path towards corporate social responsibility. In D. McBarnet, A. Voiculescu, and T. Campbell (eds.), *The new corporate accountability. Corporate social responsibility and the law* (pp. 279–306). Cambridge: Cambridge University Press.

Mokhiber, R., and Weissman, R. (1999). *Corporate predators. The hunt for mega-profits and the attack on democracy.* Monroe, ME: Common Courage Press.

Mokhiber, R. (1988). *Corporate crime and violence: Big business power and the abuse of the public trust.* San Francisco: Sierra Club.

Monks, R. A. G., and Minow, N. (1991). *Power and accountability. Restoring the balance of power between corporations, owners and society.* London: HarperCollins.

Muchlinski, P. T. (2001). Human rights and multinationals—Is there a problem? *International Affairs, 77*(1), 31–48.

Muchlinski, P. T. (2007a). Corporate social responsibility and international law: The case of human rights and multinational enterprises. In D. McBarnet, A. Voiculescu, and T. Campbell (eds.), *The new corporate accountability: Corporate social responsibility and the law* (pp. 431–458). Cambridge: Cambridge University Press.

Muchlinski, P. T. (2007b). *Multinational enterprises and the law* (2nd edn). Oxford: Oxford University Press.

Neumark, D., and Wascher, W. (2000). Minimum wages and employment: A case study of the fast-food industry in New Jersey and Pennsylvania: Comment. *American Economic Review, 90*(5), 1362–1396.

Nike (2005). *2004 corporate social responsibility report.* Retrieved 5 February 2009, from http://www.nikebiz.com/.

OECD (2000). *Guidelines for multinational enterprises.* Paris: OECD.

Offer, A. (2006). *The challenge of affluence: Self-control and well being in the United States and Britain since 1950.* Oxford: Oxford University Press.

Ogus, A. (2006). *Costs and cautionary tales. Economic insights for the law.* Oxford: Hart.

Ogus, A. I. (1994). *Regulation: Legal form and economic theory.* Oxford: Clarendon.

Oppenheim, L. F. (1905). *International law.* London: Longman.

Ostry, S. (1992). The domestic domain. The new international policy arena. *Transnational Corporations, 1*(1), 7–26.

Oughton, D., and Lowry, J. (2000). *Textbook on consumer law* (2nd edn). London: Blackstone Press.

Parker, C. (2007). Meta-regulation: Legal accountability for corporate social responsibility. In D. McBarnet, A. Voiculescu, and T. Campbell (eds.), *The new corporate accountability. Corporate social responsibility and the law* (pp. 207–240). Cambridge: Cambridge University Press.

Parkinson, J. (2003). Disclosure and corporate social and environmental performance: Competitiveness and enterprise in a broader social frame. *Journal of Corporate Law Studies, 3,* 3–39.

Parkinson, J. (2006). Corporate governance and the regulation of business behaviour. In S. MacLeod (ed.), *Global governance and the quest for justice. Volume II: Corporate governance* (pp. 1–26). Oxford: Hart.

Paul, J. A., and Garred, J. (2000). *Making corporations accountable: A background paper for the United Nations financing and development process*. Retrieved 5 February 2009, from http://www.globalpolicy.org/publications/pubsindex. htm#2000.

Pinto, A., and Evans, M. (2003). *Corporate criminal liability*. London: Sweet & Maxwell.

Posner, R. A. (1974). Theories of economic regulation. *Bell Journal of Economics, 5*, 335–358.

Posner, R. A. (1984). Some economics of labor law. *University of Chicago Law Review, 51*(4), 988–1011.

Priest, G. L. (1985). The invention of enterprise liability: A critical history of the intellectual foundations of modern tort law. *Journal of Legal Studies, 14*, 461–527.

Ramasastry, A. (2002). Corporate complicity: From Nuremberg to Rangoon— An examination of forced labor cases and their impact on the liability of multinational corporations. *Berkeley Journal of International Law, 20*, 91–159.

Ramsay, I. (2003). Consumer redress and access to justice. In C. E. F. Rickett and T. G. W. Telfer (eds.), *International perspectives on consumers' access to justice* (pp. 17–45). Cambridge: Cambridge University Press.

Ramsay, I. (2005). From truth in lending to responsible lending. In G. Howells, A. Janssen, and R. Schulze (eds.), *Information rights and obligations: A challenge for party autonomy and transactional fairness* (pp. 47–65). Aldershot: Ashgate.

Rapakko, T. (1997). *Unlimited shareholder liability in multinationals*. The Hague: Kluwer.

Ratner, S. R. (2001). Corporations and human rights: A theory of responsibility. *Yale Law Journal, 111*, 443–545.

Rayman-Bacchus, L. (2004). Assessing trust in, and legitimacy of, the corporate. In D. Crowther and L. Rayman-Bacchus (eds.), *Perspectives on corporate social responsibility* (pp. 21–41). Aldershot: Ashgate.

Rieth, L. (2004). Corporate social responsibility in global economic governance: A comparison of the OECD guidelines and the UN global compact. In S. A. Schirm (ed.), *New rules for global markets—Public and private governance in the world economy* (pp. 177–192). Basingstoke: Palgrave Macmillan.

Robertson, G., and Nicol, A. (2002). *Media law* (4th edn). London: Sweet & Maxwell.

Sanchez Galera, D. M. (2008). Fundamental rights and private law in Europe. A fundamental right to the environment. *European Review of Private Law, 16*(5), 759–778.

Sands, P. (2003). *Principles of international environmental law* (2nd edn). Cambridge: Cambridge University Press.

Sauvant, K. P., and Aranda, V. (1994). The international legal framework for international corporations. In A. A. Fatouros (ed.), *Transnational corporations: The international legal framework* (pp. 83–115). London: Routledge.

Schall, C. (2008). Public interest litigation concerning environmental matters before human rights courts—A promising future concept? *Journal of Environmental Law, 20*(3), 417–453.

Schulz, M., Hatch M. J., and Larsen, M. H. (2000). *The express organization—Linking identity, reputation, and the corporate brand.* Oxford: Oxford University Press.

Schwartz, P., and Gibb, B. (1999). *When good companies do bad things. Responsibility and risk in an age of globalization.* New York: John Wiley.

Servais, J. (2005). *International labour law.* The Hague: Kluwer.

Seyfang, G. (2004). Consuming values and contested cultures: A critical analysis of the UK strategy for sustainable consumption and production. *Review of Social Economy, 62*(3), 323–638.

Shamir, R. (2004). Between self-regulation and the alien tort claims act: On contested concept of corporate social responsibility. *Law and Society Review, 38,* 635–663.

Shapiro, C. (1982). Consumer information, product quality, and seller reputation. *Bell Journal of Economics, 13,* 20–35.

Shelton, D. (1999). Environmental justice in the postmodern world. In K. Bosselman and B. J. Richardson (eds.), *Environmental justice and market mechanisms. Key challenges for environmental law and policy* (pp. 21–29). The Hague: Kluwer.

Sicilia, D. B. (2004). The corporation under siege: Social movements, regulation, public relations, and tort law since the second world war. In K. Lipartito and D. B. Sicilia (eds.), *Constructing corporate America: History, politics, and culture* (pp. 188–222). Oxford: Oxford University Press.

Sinden, A. (2007). Power and responsibility. Why human rights should address corporate environmental wrongs. In D. McBarnet, A. Voiculescu, and T. Campbell (eds.), *The new corporate accountability: Corporate social Responsibility and the law* (pp. 501–528). Cambridge: Cambridge University Press.

Singh, A. and Zammitt, A. (2003). *Globalisation, labour standards and economic development.* Cambridge: ESRC Centre for Business Research, University of Cambridge.

Skeel, Jr, D. A. (2006). Icarus and American corporate regulation. In J. Armour and J. A. McCahery (eds.), *After Enron: Improving corporate law and modernising securities regulation in Europe and the US* (pp. 129–154). Oxford: Hart.

Smith, N. C. (1990). *Morality and the market. Consumer pressure for corporate accountability.* London: Routledge.

Smith, R. C., and Walter, I. (2006). *Governing the modern corporation. Capital markets, corporate control and economic performance.* New York: Oxford University Press.

Stephens, B. (2000). Corporate accountability: International human rights litigation against corporations in US Courts. In M. T. Kamminga and S. Zia-Zarifi (eds.), *Liability of multinational enterprises under international law* (pp. 209–229). The Hague: Kluwer.

Stopford, J. M. (1994). The growing interdependence between national corporations and governments. *Transnational Corporations, 3*(1), 53–76.

Study Group on Directors' Remuneration (1995). *Greenbury report.* London: CBI.

Sunstein, C., and Thaler, R. (2003). Libertarian paternalism is not an oxymoron. *University of Chicago Law Review, 70,* 1159–1202.

Swepston, L. (2004). International labour law. In R. Blanpain (ed.), *Comparative labour law and industrial relations in industrialized market economies* (viii & revised edn) (pp. 141–164). The Hague: Kluwer.

Tófalo, I. (2006). Overt and hidden accomplices: Transnational corporations' range of complicity for human rights violations. In O. De Schutter (ed.), *Transnational corporations and human rights* (pp. 335–358). Oxford: Hart.

Trebilcock, M. (1971). Consumer protection and the affluent society. *McGill Law Journal, 16*, 263–265.

Trebilcock, M. J. (2003). Rethinking consumer protection policy. In C. E. F. Rickett and T. G. W. Telfer (eds.), *International perspectives on consumers' access to justice* (pp. 68–100). Cambridge: Cambridge University Press.

United Nations Sub-Commission on the Promotion and Protection of Human Rights (2002). *Human rights principles and responsibilities for transnational corporations and other business enterprises.* UN Doc.E/CN.4/Sub.2/2002/XX, E/CN.4/Sub.2/WG.2/WP.1.

Vaaland, T. I., Heide, M., and Gronhaug, K. (2008). Corporate social responsibility: Investigating theory and research in the marketing context. *European Journal of Marketing, 42*(9/10), 927–953.

Vagts, D. F. (1970). The multinational enterprise: A new challenge for transnational law. *Harvard Law Review, 83*(4), 739–792.

Verhees, F. J. H. M., Kuipers, A., and Meulenberg, M. T. G. (2008). Marketing potential of corporate social responsibility in supply chains. *Journal on Chain and Network Science, 8*(2), 143–152.

Vernon, R. (1992). Transnational corporations. Where are they coming from, where are they headed? *Transnational Corporations, 1*(2), 7–35.

Vogelaar, T. W. (1980). The OECD guidelines: Their philosophy, history, negotiation, form, legal nature, follow-up procedures and review. In N. Horn (ed.), *Legal problems of codes of conduct for international enterprises* (pp. 127–139). London: Kluwer-Deventer.

Voiculescu, A. (2006). Towards an acquisition of human rights by way of business practices. In S. MacLeod (ed.), *Global governance and the quest for justice. Volume II: Corporate governance* (pp. 239–262). Oxford: Hart.

Voiculescu, A. (2007). The other European framework for corporate social responsibility: From green paper to new uses of human rights instruments. In D. McBarnet, A. Voiculescu, and T. Campbell (eds.), *The new corporate accountability. Corporate social responsibility and the law* (pp. 365–398). Cambridge: Cambridge University Press.

Wallis, J. J., Sylla, R. E., and Legler, J. B. (1994). The interaction of taxation and regulation in nineteenth-century U.S. banking. In C. Goldin and G. D. Libecap (eds.), *The regulated economy: A historical approach to political economy* (pp. 121–144). Chicago: University of Chicago Press.

Weatherill, S. (1994). The role of the informed consumer in European community law and policy. *Consumer Law Journal, 2*, 49–69.

Whincop, M. J. (2001). *An economic and jurisprudential genealogy of corporate law.* Aldershot: Ashgate.

Weissbrodt, D., and Kruger, M. (2003). Norms on the responsibilities of transnational corporations and other business enterprises with regard to human rights. *American Journal of International Law, 97*, 901.

Willetts, P. (1998). Political globalisation and the impact of NGOs upon transnational companies. In J. V. Mitchell (ed.), *Companies in a world of conflict: NGOs, sanctions and corporate responsibility* (pp. 195–226). London: Earthscan.

Willett, C. (2007a). *Fairness in consumer contracts. The case of unfair terms.* Aldershot: Ashgate.

Willett, C. (2007b). General clauses on fairness and the promotion of values important in services of general interest. In C. Twigg-Flesner, D. Parry, G. Howells, and A. Nordhausen (eds.), *The yearbook of consumer law 2008* (pp. 67–106). Aldershot: Ashgate.

Williams, S. (1999). How principles benefit the bottom-line: The experience of the co-operative bank. In M. Addo (ed.), *Human rights standards and the responsibility of transnational corporations* (pp. 63–68). The Hague: Kluwer.

5

The Duty to Protect Against Human Rights Violations Committed Abroad by Transnational Corporations and their Subsidiaries

Biagio Zammitto

Introduction

More and more human rights violations committed by transnational corporations (TNCs) have been reported over the past few years, most of which remain unpunished.[1] To further illustrate the importance of this issue, it is worth noting that a special representative was designated by the secretary-general of the United Nations to advance solutions to TNC human rights abuses.[2]

When a violation of human rights is committed, the governing state of the territory where it occurred is expected to prosecute the author of the violation and allow the victims access to justice. However, victims often remain without remedy in their own country. Many countries have very little means to fight against human rights violations committed by TNCs: some are bound by economic obligations such as bilateral investment treaties, some are themselves instigators or accomplices of the violations, and some simply lack the financial resources to offer a fair trial to the victims or to investigate allegations of wrongdoing.

This chapter aims to explore a specific way to redress these kinds of violations. Close observation shows that most TNCs are based in Western countries that have the structural and financial means to redress any tort. The question then is whether these countries have control over the foreign activities of their TNCs and their subsidiaries abroad and, if so, to what extent. Are states free to regulate the foreign activities of TNCs and their subsidiaries based outside state territory? Does this regulation have limits as it concerns offering a remedy to the victims of violations committed abroad?

There are four classic examples of extraterritorial jurisdiction (De Schutter, 2006, pp. 22–24): (1) the regulation of activities that have a substantial, direct, and foreseeable impact on the territory of a state, (2) the principle of active and passive personality, (3) the threat to fundamental interests of the nation, and (4) the universal jurisdiction for some international crimes such as genocide, war crimes, and crimes against humanity.

The principle of active personality can be applied to national TNCs: states are free to regulate their activities abroad on this basis and to punish them in front of their courts in case of human rights violations. They may, thus, offer an effective remedy to their victims. However, this principle cannot be extended to subsidiaries based abroad. In its famous Barcelona Traction arrest, the International Court of Justice stated that a company should not be confused with its shareholders.[3] In the same way, the personality of the subsidiary must not be confused with the parent (Meeran, 1999, p. 161). It is possible to "lift the veil" in the case of abuse of personality, but this is somehow exceptional (De Schutter, 2006, p. 37; Meeran, 1999, pp. 161–170).

By process of elimination, the only useful principle for legal jurisdiction over TNC subsidiaries would be that of universal jurisdiction, as the other possibilities seem too anecdotal. Universal jurisdiction is generally limited to severe international crimes classified as *jus cogens*. This is not the case with most human rights cases, which are less severe. In the meantime, this strict limitation does not seem to have inescapable grounds in international law. In fact, there does not seem to be any restriction to the prescriptive and adjudicative powers of the state. The International Permanent Court of Justice sustained this point of view in the Lotus case.[4] Additionally, those powers do not hinder the noninterference principle or the sovereignty of other states, as long as the prescriptive or adjudicative state does not claim to impose the legislation or the jurisdictional decision it took on another state without its agreement (executive power) (De Schutter, 2006, pp. 9–10). A state could consequently legislate as widely as it wishes, even in situations outside its territorial borders, and still not find itself in violation of the sovereignty of third states that remain free to recognize (or not) the validity of such legislation on their territories, and to give it some effect. The same reasoning applies to jurisdictional decisions (De Schutter, 2006, p. 28).

It is interesting to note that states already regulate the behavior of their TNCs and subsidiaries abroad in different fields, such as tax law and competition law. Moreover, English courts have asserted that parent companies may be held liable for violations of human rights committed abroad by their foreign subsidiaries as a breach of their due diligence obligations (Kamminga, 2003, p. 18). Another example of extraterritorial regulation can be found in the United States with the Alien Tort Claim Act.[5] This act provides, at least in theory, an effective remedy to human rights violations against any foreigner, even against foreign companies. However, the exception of *forum non conveniens* moderates this principle a great deal (Norberg, 2005, p. 744).

States are therefore free to regulate the foreign activities of their TNCs or their subsidiaries established abroad, but they almost never put this possibility into practice to address human rights violations and their victims, as they delimit their criminal jurisdiction to their own territory, except in occasional unusual cases.

Having established that Western states can indeed control the behavior of their TNCs, the next step is to examine whether or not states have a duty to do so. In other words, do they have a responsibility to protect people against human rights violations committed abroad and, if so, to what extent?

The state's duty to protect and its limits according to the International Covenant on Economic, Social and Cultural Rights

The ICESCR and the duty to protect

Article 2 §1 of the International Covenant on Economic, Social and Cultural Rights (ICESCR) is written as follows:

> Each State Party to the present Covenant undertakes to take steps, individually and through international assistance and co-operation, especially economic and technical, to the maximum of its available resources, with a view to achieving progressively the full realization of the rights recognized in the present Covenant by all appropriate means, including particularly the adoption of legislative measures.

The Committee on Economic, Social and Cultural Rights (CESCR) has deduced from this Article that the states not only have a duty to respect the rights recognized in the Covenant, but also a positive obligation to protect these rights. Therefore, the Committee did not hesitate to affirm in its General Comment No. 12, regarding the right to adequate food, that:

The right to adequate food, like any other human right, imposes three types or levels of obligations on States parties: the obligations to *respect*, to *protect* and to *fulfill*. In turn, the obligation to *fulfill* incorporates both an obligation to *facilitate* and an obligation to *provide*. The obligation to *respect* existing access to adequate food requires States' parties not to take any measures that result in preventing such access. The obligation to *protect* requires measures by the State to ensure that enterprises or individuals do not deprive individuals of their access to adequate food. (CESCR, 20th session, 1999, General Comment 12, The right to adequate food (art. 11), E/C.12/1999/5, §15)

This general obligation has been confirmed in General Comment No. 14, regarding the right to the highest attainable standard of health,[6] General Comment No. 15, regarding the right to water,[7] General Comment No. 18, regarding the right to work,[8] and General Comment No. 19, regarding the right to social security.[9] The dimension of this obligation has been particularly specified in General Comment No. 16, regarding the equal rights of men and women:

19. The obligation to protect requires States parties to take steps aimed directly at the elimination of prejudices, customary and all other practices that perpetuate the notion of inferiority or superiority of either of the sexes, and stereotyped roles for men and women. States parties obligation to protect under article 3 of ICESCR includes, *inter alia*, the respect and adoption of constitutional and legislative provisions on the equal right of men and women to enjoy all human rights and the prohibition of discrimination of any kind; the adoption of legislation to eliminate discrimination and to prevent third parties from interfering directly or indirectly with the enjoyment of this right; the adoption of administrative measures and programmes, as well as the establishment of public institutions, agencies and programmes to protect women against discrimination.

20. States parties have an obligation to monitor and regulate the conduct of non-State actors to ensure that they do not violate the equal right of men and women to enjoy economic, social and cultural rights. This obligation applies, for example, in cases where public services have been partially or fully privatized. (CESCR, 34th session, 2005, General Comment 16, The equal right of men and women to the enjoyment of all economic, social and cultural rights [art. 3 of the International Covenant on Economic, Social and Cultural Rights], E/C.12/2005/4, §19–20)

It is clear from these general comments that the duty of the state goes beyond refraining from violating the rights granted to individuals in the Covenant. It has, in addition, an obligation to prevent third parties from encroaching upon the rights of its members. Third parties as used here include individuals, groups, and also companies, the latter, of course, being of particular concern.

The measures that must be employed by the state in order to fulfill its obligation to protect are all of a legal nature: the state must regulate the behavior of private persons, notably by prohibiting the violation of rights recognized in the Covenant. These measures must be deterrent in nature, which means that in some cases criminal sanctions should be attached to the violation of rights committed by private persons stipulated in the Covenant. These measures would not be effective if they did not provide victims of violations committed by third parties with the right to an effective remedy and access to obtain redress before courts, contingent with any criminal penalties awarded to the guilty party.

Finally, the state has an obligation to check the behavior of non-state actors in order to ensure they do not violate the provisions of the Covenant. This obligation implies a duty to control the behavior of third parties in a proactive way, to be informed, notably through investigations, in order to prevent and, where appropriate, to punish the violations committed by private persons.

The ICESCR and the extent of the duty to protect

Interpretation of the provisions of the Covenant

It is interesting to note as this section begins that the ICESCR contains no provision that defines its territorial scope.[10] On the contrary, the wording of Article 2§1 of the Covenant contains an explicit reference to international assistance and cooperation as a means to ensure the full exercise of the rights guaranteed therein. Like any international agreement, the Covenant is subject to the provisions of the 1969 Vienna Convention on the Law of Treaties (VC), the rules of which are regarded as customary and consequently apply even to the conventions concluded before its enforcement.

Article 29 provides that unless a different intention appears from the treaty or is otherwise established, states parties are bound to their entire territory. The foregone conclusion seems to be that the Covenant is designed to apply only within the territory of each contracting party. Be that as it may, Article 29 VC is interpreted as requiring states parties to an international convention to apply it at least in their territory, but not confining it to that territory. Therefore, this provision does not prevent an extraterritorial application of the Covenant.

Articles 31 and 32 VC supply the rules to follow in order to interpret the provisions of an international convention, notably to determine whether or not it has to be applied outside the territory of the contracting parties. Beyond the common sense of the terms of the treaty, the context, the subject, and the aim must also be taken into account. The preamble of an international convention must also contextually be taken into account in view of its interpretation. In this case, the preamble of the Covenant contains clear references to the universality of human rights, to obligations ensuing from the Charter of The United Nations, and to the Universal Declaration of Human Rights, of which the Covenant is an application. The combination of Articles 55 and 56 of the UN Charter also imposes upon the states a duty to observe "universal respect for, and observance of, human rights and fundamental freedoms for all."

In accordance with the preamble of the Universal Declaration of Human Rights, the states "have pledged themselves to achieve, in cooperation with the United Nations, the promotion of universal respect for and observance of human rights and fundamental freedoms." Therefore, in the context of its material provisions, the Covenant could be interpreted as imposing onto states obligations pertaining to extraterritorial settings, even at a universal level. As a matter of course, states must also respect their other obligations as stipulated by the UN Charter, particularly the obligation to recognize the sovereignty of their peers and the attendant obligation of non-interference. It has been noted that the regulation of TNCs and their subsidiary companies, and the effort to control their activities abroad, is not to be construed as interference in the internal affairs of the states where they perform their activities, nor should this be seen as a violation of the sovereignty of those states. Finally, it can be said that the obligations to respect and protect as advocated by the Covenant also apply to the activities of the transnationals and their subsidiary companies abroad—insofar as the states where they have their registered offices have the means to regulate their behavior—and to punishing them if necessary.

General comments of the Committee

The CESCR has progressively elaborated on its general comments, devoting more and more attention to the international obligations of states. It has subsequently reaffirmed that their duty to protect also applies abroad. In its General Comment No. 8, related to economic sanctions, the Committee has already written that:

> [E]ffective monitoring, which is always required under the terms of the Covenant, should be undertaken throughout the period that sanctions are in force. When an external party takes upon itself even partial responsibility for the situation within a country (whether under Chapter VII of the Charter or otherwise), it also unavoidably assumes a responsibility to do all within its power to protect the economic, social and cultural rights of the affected population. (CESCR, 17th session, General Comment 8, The relationship between economic sanctions and respect for economic, social and cultural rights, E/C.12/1997/8, §13)

Furthermore, the international obligations of individual states regarding the right to food, including the obligation to respect and protect this right abroad, have been defined as follows:

> In the spirit of article 56 of the Charter of the United Nations, the specific provisions contained in articles 11, 2.1, and 23 of the Covenant and the Rome Declaration of the World Food Summit, States parties should recognize the essential role of international cooperation and comply with their commitment to take joint and separate action to achieve the full realization of the right to adequate food. In implementing this commitment, States parties should take steps to respect the enjoyment of the right to food in other countries, to protect that right, to facilitate access to food and to provide the necessary aid when required. (CESCR, General Comment 12, §36)

This extraterritorial obligation to protect was refined in General Comment No. 14, regarding the right to health,[11] General Comment No. 15, regarding the right to water,[12] and General Comment No. 18, regarding the right to work.[13] But it is probably in the recent General Comment No. 19 that the Committee has most explicitly addressed the extraterritorial dimension of the obligation to protect, with marked reference to the TNCs:

> States parties should extraterritorially protect the right to social security by preventing their own citizens and national entities from violating this right in other countries. Where States parties can take steps to influence third parties (non-State actors) within their jurisdiction to respect the right, through legal or political means,

such steps should be taken in accordance with the Charter of the United Nations and applicable international law. (CESCR, General Comment 19, §54)

It is at this juncture that the notion of jurisdiction appears; now it remains to be determined how this notion ought to be interpreted.

Content of the extraterritorial obligations

Careful analysis shows that states parties to the Covenant have an obligation to respect and protect the economic, social, and cultural rights of people living within their territory as well as abroad. It is not enough that they merely abstain from directly violating those rights; in addition they must protect those rights abroad insofar as they can. The obligation to protect is limited only by the duty to respect the sovereignty of third states. Yet regulation and control of transnationals and subsidiary companies active abroad does not have to present itself as a violation of the principle of sovereignty. When states have the ability to impose standards of behavior onto third parties abroad, they are obligated to exercise this ability on pain of violating their obligations with regard to the Covenant; in so doing, they fulfill their international responsibilities.

In very concrete terms, states have a primary obligation to take legislative or statutory measures that establish prohibited behavior in order to prevent violations of the Covenant by TNCs and their subsidiary companies abroad. To make sure this prohibition is effective, states are required to impose sanctions (if necessary, criminal sanctions). However, they are also required to ensure that when violations are observed or reported, the veracity of the violations is investigated and verified, and then steps are taken to apply sanctions. Finally, all victims, without distinction, must be given access to an effective resort against those violations in order to obtain redress.

The duty to protect and its limits according to the International Covenant on Civil and Political Rights

The duty to protect according to the ICCPR

Article 2 of the International Covenant on Civil and Political Rights (ICCPR) is drafted as follows:

1. Each State Party to the present Covenant undertakes to respect and to ensure to all individuals within its territory and subject to its jurisdiction the rights recognized in the present Covenant, without

distinction of any kind, such as race, color, sex, language, religion, political or other opinion, national or social origin, property, birth or other status.

2. Where not already provided for by existing legislative or other measures, each State Party to the present Covenant undertakes to take the necessary steps, in accordance with its constitutional processes and with the provisions of the present Covenant, to adopt such laws or other measures as may be necessary to give effect to the rights recognized in the present Covenant.

3. Each State Party to the present Covenant undertakes:

(a) To ensure that any person whose rights or freedoms as herein recognized are violated shall have an effective remedy, notwithstanding that the violation has been committed by persons acting in an official capacity;

(b) To ensure that any person claiming such a remedy shall have his right thereto determined by competent judicial, administrative or legislative authorities, or by any other competent authority provided for by the legal system of the State, and to develop the possibilities of judicial remedy;

(c) To ensure that the competent authorities shall enforce such remedies when granted.

As a result of these provisions states must *ensure* individuals have the benefit of these rights, in addition to respecting the rights recognized by the Covenant. They must adopt the necessary laws to give effect to these rights and provide an efficient remedy against the violation of these rights.

The ICCPR Human Rights Committee, organ of control of the Covenant, has specified the extent of the obligations provided by Article 2 in General Comment No. 31. After affirming that the obligations resulting from Article 2 do not have any horizontal effect and do not bind the private individuals, the Committee lists the obligations borne by the state:

[T]he positive obligations on States Parties to ensure Covenant rights will only be fully discharged if individuals are protected by the State, not just against violations of Covenant rights by its agents, but also against acts committed by private persons or entities that would impair the enjoyment of Covenant rights in so far as they are amenable to application between private persons or entities. There may be circumstances in which a failure to ensure Covenant rights as required by article 2 would give rise to violations by States Parties of those rights, as a result of States Parties permitting or failing to take appropriate measures or to exercise due diligence to prevent, punish, investigate or redress the harm caused by such acts by private persons or entities. States are reminded of the interrelationship between the positive obligations imposed under article 2 and the need to provide effective remedies in the event of breach under article 2, paragraph 3. (CCPR, 80th session, 2004, General Comment 31, Nature of the general legal obligation on States Parties to the Covenant, CCPR/C/21/Rev.1/Add.13, §8)

These positive obligations are detailed in the following paragraphs:

The Committee attaches importance to States Parties establishing appropriate judicial and administrative mechanisms for addressing claims of rights violations under domestic law.... Administrative mechanisms are particularly required to give effect to the general obligation to investigate allegations of violations promptly, thoroughly and effectively through independent and impartial bodies.... A failure by a State Party to investigate allegations of violations could in and of itself give rise to a separate breach of the Covenant. Cessation of an ongoing violation is an essential element of the right to an effective remedy ... [and] the Covenant generally entails appropriate compensation. The Committee notes that, where appropriate, reparation can involve restitution, rehabilitation and measures of satisfaction, such as public apologies, public memorials, guarantees of non-repetition and changes in relevant laws and practices, as well as bringing to justice the perpetrators of human rights violations.... In general, the purposes of the Covenant would be defeated without an obligation integral to article 2 to take measures to prevent a recurrence of a violation of the Covenant. Accordingly, it has been a frequent practice of the Committee in cases under the Optional Protocol to include in its Views the need for measures, beyond a victim-specific remedy, to be taken to avoid recurrence of the type of violation in question. Such measures may require changes in the State Party's laws or practices.... Where the investigations ... reveal violations of certain Covenant rights, States Parties must ensure that those responsible are brought to justice. As with failure to investigate, failure to penalize perpetrators of such violations could, in and of itself, give rise to a separate breach of the Covenant. (CCPR, General Comment 31, §15–18)

This General Comment confirms the Committee's case law, according to which: "the courts of States parties are under an obligation to protect individuals... whether this occurs within the public sphere or among private parties" (CCPR, *Franz Nahlik* v. *Austria*, Communication No. 608/1995, UN Doc. CCPR/C/57/D/608/1995 (1996), §8.2). The state therefore has an obligation to protect individuals against violations of the Covenant made by third parties, including private companies. This obligation can be broken down into separate obligations that are more specific:

- an obligation to *prevent* the violations, which implies—in addition to implementing laws forbidding behaviors that are contrary to the rights recognized in the Covenant—the duty to examine, on a proactive basis, violations that would be made by private entities;
- an obligation to *investigate*, which may consist of opening a law inquiry, especially when the allegations of violation arise, with a certain degree of plausibility, from the victim itself or in case the public authorities are informed by other means, notably in the framework of their duty to seek information;
- an obligation to *penalize* the violations when they are established, which requires that criminal penalties are provided and actually applied;
- an obligation to *repair* that must grant the individual, through a legal remedy, assurance that an end is put to the violation and that the damage is appropriately compensated.

The extent of the duty to protect according to the ICCPR

As described above, the extraterritorial obligations resulting from the ICESCR are very broad. But is the situation similar as regards political and civil rights?

The obligation to respect: A universal application?

One of the fundamental differences between the two covenants is that the Covenant on Economic, Social and Cultural Rights does not provide for any territorial limit as regards its scope of application, whereas rights alluded to in the Covenant on Civil and Political Rights seem more restricted. Article 2 §1 of this Covenant reads as follows: "Each State Party to the present Covenant undertakes to respect and to ensure to all individuals within its territory and subject to its jurisdiction the rights recognized in the present Covenant."

A hasty understanding of this provision could lead one to believe that the Covenant is meant to apply to the territory of each state party, considered separately. States would therefore have no extraterritorial obligation. As detailed below, such a strict interpretation is not predominant. This provision must be split into two different parts. On the one hand, the state has an obligation to respect the rights recognized in the Covenant; on the other hand, it has to "ensure to all individuals within its territory and subject to its jurisdiction the rights recognized in the ... Covenant." The "territorial" restriction applies only to the obligation to *ensure* these rights and not to the obligation to *respect* them (Künnemann, 2004, p. 228). In order to obtain a different interpretation, the provision should have stipulated, for example, that the states undertake to respect and ensure the rights recognized in the Covenant regarding all the individuals in their territory and under their jurisdiction. However, this is not the case.

Therefore, as regards the obligation to respect, the Covenant does not provide for any territorial limitation. It is then possible to refer, *mutatis mutandis*, to comments relating to the ICESCR and assume that they apply to the obligation to respect provided by the Covenant on Civil and Political Rights. In support of this assertion it should be observed that the context surrounding the two covenants is completely identical. In other words, states must submit to the obligation to refrain from violating, in their territory and in foreign territories, the civil and political rights laid down in the Covenant. It must be noticed, nonetheless, that the Human Rights Committee does not acknowledge this distinction and considers equally the obligations to respect and to ensure provided by Article 2, §1 of the Covenant (General Comment 31, §10). We will see, hereafter, how the Committee has interpreted the word *jurisdiction* in its case law.

The notion of jurisdiction: focus on the Committee's case law

The Human Rights Committee considers equally the obligations to respect and to ensure, considering—at least implicitly—that states have to submit to these two obligations only toward individuals "within their territory" and individuals "subject to their jurisdiction." However, one should not deduce from this that these obligations do not apply outside the territory of the concerned state.

The first point to consider is the fact that the Committee and part of the doctrine[14] interprets these conditions in a disjunctive way. In its General Observation No. 31 (§10), the Committee has asserted that:

States Parties are required by article 2, paragraph 1, to respect and to ensure the Covenant rights to all persons who may be within their territory and to all persons subject to their jurisdiction. This means that a State party must respect and ensure the rights laid down in the Covenant to all individuals within the power or effective control of that State Party, even if the individuals are not situated within the territory of the State Party. As indicated in General Comment no. 15, adopted at the twenty-seventh session (1986), the enjoyment of Covenant rights is not limited to citizens of States Parties but must also be available to all individuals, regardless of nationality or statelessness, such as asylum seekers, refugees, migrant workers and other persons who may find themselves in the territory or subject to the jurisdiction of the State Party. This principle also applies to those within the power or effective control of the forces of a State Party acting outside its territory, regardless of the circumstances in which such power or effective control was obtained, such as forces constituting a national contingent of a State Party assigned to an international peace-keeping or peace-enforcement operation.

The contentious case law of the Committee on Human Rights is, in this respect, edifying. In the cases *Celiberti de Casariego* v. *Uruguay* and *Lopez Burgos* v. *Uruguay*, investigated on the same day, the Committee considered that:

Article 2 (1) of the Covenant places an obligation upon a State party to respect and to ensure rights "to all individuals within its territory and subject to its jurisdiction," but it does not imply that the State party concerned cannot be held accountable for violations of rights under the Covenant that are committed upon the territory of another State by its agent, whether with the acquiescence of the Government of that State or in opposition to it.... [I]t would be unconscionable to interpret the responsibility under article 2 of the Covenant, as permitting a State party to perpetrate violations of the Covenant on the territory of another State, when it would not perpetrate these violations on its own territory. (Committee on Human Rights, *Celiberti de Casariego* v. *Uruguay*, Communication 56/1979 [29 July 1981] §10.3; Committee on Human Rights, *Lopez Burgos* v. *Uruguay*, Communication 52/1979 [29 July 1981] §10.3)

This point of view was sustained by the International Court of Justice when it was moved to express itself on the question in an advisory opinion of 9 July 2004. This opinion related to the legal consequences of the construction of a wall in occupied Palestinian territory.[15] The court ruled in the following terms:

> The Court would observe that, while the jurisdiction of States is primarily territorial, it may sometimes be exercised outside the national territory. Considering the object and purpose of the International Covenant on Civil and Political Rights, it would seem natural that, even when such is the case, States parties to the Covenant should be bound to comply with its provisions....In conclusion, the Court considers that the International Covenant on Civil and Political Rights is applicable in respect of acts done by a State in the exercise of its jurisdiction outside its own territory.

States therefore have obligations with regard to not only individuals who are within their territory but also those who are subject to their jurisdiction. The jurisprudence quoted above supports the idea that this last concept can have extraterritorial implications.

The concept of "jurisdiction" reinterpreted and adapted to the obligation to protect

The criterion retained by the Committee to establish whether an individual falls within the jurisdiction of a state is the level of authority or the effective control exerted by the state on this individual (Lawson, 2004, p. 93). Could this criterion be applied to a victim of TNC activities abroad? Could it be said that this victim is under the authority or the effective control of the state on the territory of which the TNC is based?

The criterion of effective control is not really adapted to the duty to protect. It was indeed developed by the Committee with regard to times when the state violated its obligation to respect and not its duty to protect (although I believe that with attentive reading of Article 2 §1 of the Covenant, the obligation to respect does not depend on the fact that the victim is within the territory, or is subject to the jurisdiction of the state that makes the violation, but is essential in any situation).

What about the concept of authority? It is certain that the state exerts an authority over the TNCs based in its territory even when they act abroad directly or by the means of subsidiary companies. As I have already illustrated, the state has the faculty to regulate the behavior of transnationals and their subsidiary companies, and even offer remedy to their victims abroad when they violate international human rights laws. By this faculty, the state exerts a form of authority on these victims that renders them subject to its jurisdiction.

We are conscious that such an interpretation is particularly extensive and goes beyond what the Committee agreed. It results in the transformation of the faculty of the state into an obligation for the latter; however, this interpretation does not seem deprived of any foundation. First of all, as already pointed out, Article 31 of the Vienna Convention on the right of the treaties forces one to interpret the provisions of the Covenant according to common sense. However, the ordinary interpretation of the word "jurisdiction" is the legally recognized ability of a public authority to take legal decisions under given conditions. That is to say, at the moment when the state has the legally recognized ability to take a legal decision that has an influence on an individual, the latter becomes subject to the jurisdiction of the state, wherever the individual is, and whether the legal decision is taken or not.

In view of this, the context of the International Covenant on Civil and Political Rights is the same as the International Covenant on Economic, Social and Cultural Rights. Its purpose is to translate the principles of the Universal Declaration of the Human Rights into a compulsory instrument for states. Its preamble contains an explicit reference to the Universal Declaration as well as to the obligations rising from the Charter of the United Nations to promote the universal and effective respect of human rights and freedoms. These references to universality call for an extensive interpretation of the field of application of the Covenant.

Does similar conception expose the states to an exorbitant responsibility? Not necessarily. It forces them, on the one hand, to respect the human rights on their territory and abroad, an obligation that is clearly affirmed by the Committee. As the Committee argues, it would be unreasonable that the Covenant could be interpreted as making it possible for states to commit violations abroad that they could not commit in their own territory. It forces them, in addition, to take measures to prevent third parties on whom they exert an influence from committing violations abroad. These obligations do not seem exorbitant.

In conclusion, although the Committee affirmed that the Covenant could extend, in certain circumstances, the obligation to respect, which falls on states beyond their borders, it has not as yet had occasion to come to a conclusion about the specific case of the obligation to protect, leaving the door open to various interpretations. However, when taken in context, the provisions of the Covenant regarding the concept of jurisdiction can be interpreted as imposing upon states the duty to regulate the activities of the TNCs and their subsidiaries abroad by prohibiting them from violating the provisions of the Covenant, and by ensuring that victims—without distinction—have access to effective remedy, which grants them recourse and the ability to obtain adequate redress.

Conclusion

In order to maintain human rights, it is not sufficient to simply require states to refrain from committing human rights violations. They must also take preventative measures to protect individuals upon whose rights TNCs might encroach. This duty to protect has many ramifications.

The states in question must first take preventive measures aimed at preventing human rights violations committed by third parties, in particular by adopting legislative standards that are likely to control their behavior. In order to make these measures effective, the states must match them with sanctions and must guarantee victims an effective remedy against violations. This remedy should itself guarantee cessation of these violations and adequate compensation for damage sustained. At the very least, these sanctions must be of a penal nature when applied to the most serious violations and states should prosecute as soon as the violations are brought to their attention. The states must carry out investigations in order to identify the authors of these violations.

These obligations are not limited to violations committed in the territory of the state. The Committee on Economic, Social and Cultural Rights extended them to the activities of TNCs abroad, without reservation. The states in the territory where TNCs are based must thus take all measures aimed at regulating the behavior of these companies, punishing their abuses, and offering to their victims, whatever their country of origin, an effective remedy against these violations within their legal bodies.

In conjunction with this finding, the ICCPR Human Rights Committee has also recognized that the provisions of the International Covenant on the Civil and Political Rights can have an extraterritorial effect. Although it did not affirm it, the Committee did not abnegate that this extension can also apply to the obligation to protect. Generally speaking, the two international covenants have created for the member states obligations toward any individual likely to fall under their influence—in proportional measure to this influence—wherever this individual is located.

According to this interpretation, the duty to *respect* forces states to abstain from directly committing human rights violations with regard to any individual, without reference to the territory in which these violations are committed. Moreover, the duty to *protect* forces states to take measures with regard to third parties on whom they exert any authority, measures which must be proportional to their level of authority, and must be aimed at preventing these third parties from committing human rights violations.

If it is obvious that as states exert an influence on TNCs that are incorporated on their territory, and thus have the obligation to impose strict standards of control as regards human rights, they can also exert this influence on their subsidiaries. There is nothing to prevent states, for example, from imposing the obligation of due diligence on TNCs, under which they will be obligated, under penalty of engaging their responsibility, to police the behavior of their subsidiary companies as regards human rights abroad. Insofar as they have this faculty, states must exert it under penalty of violating their own international liabilities.

Notes

1. See, among others, De Schutter (2006, pp. 1–39), Kamminga (2003, pp. 9–19), Sornarajah (2001, pp. 491–512).
2. Special representative John Ruggie's report, 7 April 2008 (UN DOC A/HRC/8/5).
3. I. C. J., *Barcelona Traction, Light and Power Co. Case* (*Belgium* v. *Spain*), 5 February 1970. See also De Schutter (2006, p. 31).
4. I. P. C. J., *Lotus Case* (*France* v. *Turkey*), 7 September 1927. The question of the validity of a universal jurisdiction law was addressed to the International Court of Justice in two cases involving, respectively, Belgium and France. In the first case, the Court did not answer this specific question (C. I. J., *Democratic Republic of Congo* v. *Belgium*, 14 February 2002). In the second case, the Court has not answered yet.
5. See, among others, Frydman (2007, pp. 301–321) and Norberg (2005, pp. 739–745).
6. CESCR, 22nd session, 2000, General Comment 14, The right to the highest attainable standard of health (art. 12 of the International Covenant on Economic, Social and Cultural Rights), E/C.12/2000/4, §33: "The right to health, like all human rights, imposes three types or levels of obligations on States parties: the obligations to *respect, protect* and *fulfill*. In turn, the obligation to fulfill contains obligations to facilitate, provide and promote. The obligation to *respect* requires States to refrain from interfering directly or indirectly with the enjoyment of the right to health. The obligation to *protect* requires States to take measures that prevent third parties from interfering with article 12 guarantees."
7. CESCR, 29th session, 2002, General Comment 15, The right to water (arts. 11 and 12 of the International Covenant on Economic, Social and Cultural Rights), E/C.12/2002/11, §23 and 24: "23. The obligation to *protect* requires State parties to prevent third parties from interfering in any way with the enjoyment of the right to water. Third parties include individuals, groups, corporations and other entities as well as agents acting under their

authority. The obligation includes, *inter alia*, adopting the necessary and effective legislative and other measures to restrain, for example, third parties from denying equal access to adequate water; and polluting and inequitably extracting from water resources, including natural sources, wells and other water distribution systems. 24. Where water services (such as piped water networks, water tankers, access to rivers and wells) are operated or controlled by third parties, States parties must prevent them from compromising equal, affordable, and physical access to sufficient, safe and acceptable water. To prevent such abuses an effective regulatory system must be established, in conformity with the Covenant and this General Comment, which includes independent monitoring, genuine public participation and imposition of penalties for non-compliance."

8. CESCR, 34th session, 2005, General Comment 18, The right to work (art. 6 of the International Covenant on Economic, Social and Cultural Rights), E/C.12/GC/18, §25: "Obligations to *protect* the right to work include, *inter alia*, the duties of States parties to adopt legislation or to take other measures ensuring equal access to work and training and to ensure that privatization measures do not undermine workers' rights. Specific measures to increase the flexibility of labour markets must not render work less stable or reduce the social protection of the worker. The obligation to protect the right to work includes the responsibility of States parties to prohibit forced or compulsory labour by non-State actors."

9. CESCR, 39th session, 2008, General Comment 19, The right to social security (art. 9 of the Covenant), E/C.12/GC/18, §45: "The obligation to protect requires that State parties prevent third parties from interfering in any way with the enjoyment of the right to social security. Third parties include individuals, groups, corporations and other entities, as well as agents acting under their authority. The obligation includes, *inter alia*, adopting the necessary and effective legislative and other measures, for example, to restrain third parties from denying equal access to social security schemes operated by them or by others and imposing unreasonable eligibility conditions; arbitrarily or unreasonably interfering with self-help or customary or traditional arrangements for social security that are consistent with the right to social security; and failing to pay legally required contributions for employees or other beneficiaries into the social security system."

10. On the extraterritorial application of the Covenant, see, among others, Coomans (2004, pp. 183–199) and Künnemann (2004, pp. 201–231).

11. CESCR, General Comment 14, §39: "To comply with their international obligations in relation to article 12, States parties have to respect the enjoyment of the right to health in other countries, and to prevent third parties from violating the right in other countries, if they are able to influence these third parties by way of legal or political means, in accordance with the Charter of the United Nations and applicable international law."

12. CESCR, General Comment 15, §31 to 33: "31. To comply with their international obligations in relation to the right to water, States parties have to respect the enjoyment of the right in other countries. International cooperation requires States parties to refrain from actions that interfere, directly or indirectly, with the enjoyment of the right to water in other countries. Any activities undertaken within the State party's jurisdiction should not deprive

another country of the ability to realize the right to water for persons in its jurisdiction. 32. States parties should refrain at all times from imposing embargoes or similar measures, that prevent the supply of water, as well as goods and services essential for securing the right to water. Water should never be used as an instrument of political and economic pressure. In this regard, the Committee recalls its position, stated in its General Comment No. 8 (1997), on the relationship between economic sanctions and respect for economic, social and cultural rights. 33. Steps should be taken by States parties to prevent their own citizens and companies from violating the right to water of individuals and communities in other countries. Where States parties can take steps to influence other third parties to respect the right, through legal or political means, such steps should be taken in accordance with the Charter of the United Nations and applicable international law."

13. CESCR, General Comment 18, §30: "To comply with their international obligations in relation to article 6, States parties should endeavor to promote the right to work in other countries."

14. See, among others, Dennis (2005, p. 123), Künnemann (2004, p. 228), Meron (1995, p. 78). For a different view, see McGoldrick (2004, p. 47).

15. I. C. J., *Legal Consequences of the Construction of a Wall in the Occupied Palestinian Territory*, Advisory Opinion, I. C. J. Reports 2004, p. 136, §109 and 111. The complete reasoning of the Court is the following: "108. The scope of application of the International Covenant on Civil and Political Rights is defined by Article 2, paragraph 1, thereof, which provides: 'Each State Party to the present Covenant undertakes to respect and to ensure to all individuals within its territory and subject to its jurisdiction the rights recognized in the present Covenant, without distinction of any kind, such as race, colour, sex, language, religion, political or other opinion, national or social origin, property, birth or other status.' This provision can be interpreted as covering only individuals who are both present within a State's territory and subject to that State's jurisdiction. It can also be construed as covering both individuals present within a State's territory and those outside that territory but subject to that State's jurisdiction. The Court will thus seek to determine the meaning to be given to this text. 109. The Court would observe that, while the jurisdiction of States is primarily territorial, it may sometimes be exercised outside the national territory. Considering the object and purpose of the International Covenant on Civil and Political Rights, it would seem natural that, even when such is the case, States parties to the Covenant should be bound to comply with its provisions. The constant practice of the Human Rights Committee is consistent with this. Thus, the Committee has found the Covenant applicable where the State exercises its jurisdiction on foreign territory. It has ruled on the legality of acts by Uruguay in cases of arrests carried out by Uruguayan agents in Brazil or Argentina (case No. 52/79, Lopez Burgos v. Uruguay; case No. 56/79, Lilian Celiberti de Casariego v. Uruguay). It decided to the same effect in the case of the confiscation of a passport by a Uruguayan consulate in Germany (case No. 106/81, Montero v. Uruguay). The *travaux préparatoires* of the Covenant confirm the Committee's interpretation of Article 2 of that instrument. These show that, in adopting the wording chosen, the drafters of the Covenant did not intend to allow States to escape from their obligations when they exercise jurisdiction outside their

national territory. They only intended to prevent persons residing abroad from asserting, vis-à-vis their State of origin, rights that do not fall within the competence of that State, but of that of the State of residence (see the discussion of the preliminary draft in the Commission on Human Rights, E/CN.4/SR.194, para. 46; and United Nations, *Official Records of the General Assembly, Tenth Session, Annexes*, A/2929, Part II, Chap. V, para. 4 (1955)). 110. The Court takes note in this connection of the position taken by Israel, in relation to the applicability of the Covenant, in its communications to the Human Rights Committee, and of the view of the Committee. In 1998, Israel stated that, when preparing its report to the Committee, it had had to face the question 'whether individuals resident in the occupied territories were indeed subject to Israel's jurisdiction' for purposes of the application of the Covenant (CCPR/C/SR.1675, para. 21). Israel took the position that 'the Covenant and similar instruments did not apply directly to the current situation in the occupied territories' (CCPR/C/SR.1675, para. 27). The Committee, in its concluding observations after examination of the report, expressed concern at Israel's attitude and pointed 'to the long-standing presence of Israel in [the occupied] territories, Israel's ambiguous attitude towards their future status, as well as the exercise of effective jurisdiction by Israeli security forces therein' (CCPR/C/79/Add.93, para. 10). In 2003 in face of Israel's consistent position, to the effect that 'the Covenant does not apply beyond its own territory, notably in the West Bank and Gaza . . .', the Committee reached the following conclusion: 'in the current circumstances, the provisions of the Covenant apply to the benefit of the population of the Occupied Territories, for all conduct by the State party's authorities or agents in those territories that affect the enjoyment of rights enshrined in the Covenant and fall within the ambit of State responsibility of Israel under the principles of public international law' (CCPR/C0/78/1SR, para. 11). 111. In conclusion, the Court considers that the International Covenant on Civil and Political Rights is applicable in respect of acts done by a State in the exercise of its jurisdiction outside its own territory."

References

Coomans, F. (2004). Some remarks on the extraterritorial application of the International Covenant on Economic, Social and Cultural Rights. In F. Coomans and M. T. Kamminga (eds.), *Extraterritorial application of human rights treaties* (pp. 183–199). Antwerp & Oxford: Intersentia.

Dennis, M. J. (2005). Application of human rights treaties extraterritorially in times of armed conflict and military occupation. *The American Journal of International Law*, *99*(1), 119–141.

De Schutter, O. (2006). The challenge of imposing human rights norms on corporate actors. In O. De Schutter (eds.), *Transnational corporations and human rights* (pp. 1–39). Oxford & Portland Oregon: Hart Publishing.

Frydman, B. (2007). L'affaire total et ses enjeux. In Larcier (ed.), *Liber amicorum Paul Martens; L'humanisme dans la résolution des conflits. Utopie ou réalité?* (pp. 301–321). Brussels: Larcier.

Kamminga, M. T. (2003). Mensenrechtenschendingen door multinationale ondernemingen: Wat val ter juridisch tegen te doen. In E. Brems and P. Vanden Heede (eds.), *Bedrijven en mensenrechten: verantwoordelijkheid en aansprakelijkheid* (pp. 9–19). Antwerp: Maklu.

Künnemann, R. (2004). Extraterritorial application of the International Covenant on Economic, Social and Cultural Rights. In F. Coomans and M. T. Kamminga (eds.), *Extraterritorial application of Human rights treaties* (pp. 201–231). Antwerp & Oxford: Intersentia.

Lawson, R. (2004). Life after Bankovic: On the extraterritorial application of the European Convention on Human Rights. In F. Coomans and M. T. Kamminga (eds.), *Extraterritorial application of human rights treaties* (pp. 83–123). Antwerp & Oxford: Intersentia.

McGoldrick, D. (2004). Extraterritorial application of the International Covenant on Civil and Political Rights. In F. Coomans and M. T. Kamminga (eds.), *Extraterritorial application of human Rights Treaties* (pp. 41–72). Antwerp & Oxford: Intersentia.

Meeran, R. (1999). The unveiling of transnational corporations: A direct approach. In M. K. Addo (eds.), *Human rights standards and the responsibility of transnational corporations* (pp. 161–170). The Hague: Kluwer Law International.

Meron, T. (1995). Extraterritoriality of human rights treaties. *American Journal of International Law, 89*(1), 78–82.

Norberg, N. (2005). Entreprises multinationales et lois extraterritoriales: L'interaction entre le droit américain et le droit international. *Revue de Science Criminelle et de Droit Pénal Comparé, 4,* 739–745.

Sornarajah, M. (2001). Linking state responsibility for certain harms caused by corporate nationals abroad to civil recourse in the legal systems of home states. In C. Scott (eds.), *Torture as tort: comparative perspectives on the development of transnational human rights litigation* (pp. 491–512). Oxford & Portland Oregon: Hart Publishing.

Part III

Financial Flows, Human Rights, and the Global South

6
Do Official Development Aid and Foreign Direct Investment Promote Good Governance in Africa?

Adugna Lemi

Introduction

Africa needs capital inflows more than any other region in the world to support its development initiatives and provide its basic emergency needs. In its 2006 report, the Economic Commission for Africa reiterated that the continent needs capital in the form of foreign direct investment (FDI) and foreign aid. The report indicated that total official development aid (ODA) to Africa had recovered from a decline experienced between 1990 and 2000, in that in 2004 official development assistance increased to US$26.5 billion from US$15.7 billion in 2000. The report further stated that to achieve and sustain higher levels of GDP growth rates and to accelerate poverty reduction, Africa will need higher volumes of aid in the coming years. The flow of FDI was also encouraged given the meager levels that Africa usually receives compared to other developing regions (ECA, 2006).

If previous performance can serve as a guide, capital flows will continue to be limited for much of Africa. It is often argued that institutional and macroeconomic environments have something to do with why Africa receives so little capital compared to other regions (Asiedu, 2002). The presence of democratic institutions[1] and degree of good governance are considered important for attracting more and long-term-oriented foreign capital. Especially in the early stages of a country's developmental process, foreign investors are looking for political and social stability as well as functioning democratic institutions when thinking of investing in a host country. Thus, the role that democratic institutions, governance, and stability play in attracting foreign capital has been the focus of empirical works since the late 1990s (Asiedu, 2004, 2006; UNCTAD, 1998; World Bank, 2002, 2006). It has also been implied that corruption is a bottleneck impeding capital flows (Habib and Zurawicki, 2002). Further, it has been argued that the effectiveness of capital, especially foreign aid, in attaining its development objectives is limited by domestic economic policies (Burnside and Dollar, 2000) and the availability of working institutions and infrastructure needed for communications and production purposes (Arslanalp and Henry, 2006). Finally, Easterly (2003) questions the current state of foreign aid flows, arguing that effectiveness cannot be guaranteed due to the absence of complementary factors (i.e. institutions, policies, and infrastructure).

One issue ignored so far, in spite of unclear results, concerns the side effects (or rather the reverse effects) of capital inflows on democratic institutions in host countries. Given that most foreign aid donors, except for some Scandinavian countries, provide economic assistance with the intention of furthering their own national interests (Akram, 2003; Alesina and Dollar, 2000; Schraeder, Hook, and Taylor, 1998), unintended side effects should be expected in host countries. The belief that foreign capital inflows impose no influence on governance and democratic institutions is fading. Increasing evidence points to large multinational firms having a significant impact on small and economically weak states, such as those in Africa. Some studies also attempt to link capital flows, mostly foreign aid, to these unintended effects—namely, corruption, undemocratic regimes, and deterioration in the rule of law. The impact of foreign aid on corruption is well-documented (Alesina and Weder, 2002; Tavares, 2003). In opposition to critics of international aid who allege it leads to corruption, Tavares (2003) argues that such aid does the reverse, or decreases corruption. On the other hand, Alesina and Weder (2002) argue that aid increases corruption either because donors do not distinguish between corrupt and other governments when they provide official aid or because some governments use aid money to stay in power and hence use the money inappropriately. Brown (2005) further recognizes the impact of capital flows (in this case that of ODA) on democracy in Africa, confirming the possibility of capital flows undermining democracy.

In fact, the two major multilateral donor institutions, the International Monetary Fund and the World Bank, have made it clear that promoting good governance has been on their agendas since the 1990s (IMF, 1997; World Bank, 1994). However, both institutions' definitions of governance are not as broad as the idea of political governance that we use in this chapter. The IMF has made it known that it is "primarily concerned with macroeconomic stability, external viability, and orderly economic growth in member countries. Therefore, the IMF's involvement in governance should be limited to economic aspects of governance" (IMF, 1997, p. 3). The IMF has been trying to distance itself from direct political governance interventions as critics suggest it should not be involved in internal political issues, which are not the organization's mandate. The World Bank has gone further by directly funding governance reform. According to Harrison (2005), Sub-Saharan Africa (SSA) has experienced the most governance reforms under the Bank's funding initiatives. Even for the World Bank, however, governance is subsumed under the theme of "participatory development," which is defined as "a process by which people influence decisions that affect them" (Harrison, 2005, p. 243). With such a definition, significant political changes need not be realized with respect to governance in Africa. It seems that the belief of these two multilateral institutions is that economic progress will eventually lead to positive changes in political governance. As to whether this is true, one has to look into the actual impact of ODA flows and changes in governance in Sub-Saharan African countries.

In his 2004 book on globalization, Bhagwati (2004) asserts that there is a paradox as to how globalization (in his mind, the spread of economic prosperity and increased connectivity) affects democracy. He states that globalization promotes democracy through mass access to information technology and the subsequent loosening of control of traditionally hegemonic groups. The changes brought about by globalization make people into more independent actors with greater democratic aspirations in the political arena. On the other hand, he also states that globalization constrains democracy by limiting revenue sources (as countries liberalize trade and capital flows) and hence undermining spending on social programs, which would otherwise help promote democracy. From Bhagwati we can surmise that although globalization offers potential benefits for developing nations in the form of foreign loans or grants, the fact that it compromises the degree of autonomy of a country calls for special consideration in promoting globalization in its current form and pace of change.

Given their implications for human rights in Africa, the assertions of the world's largest multilateral institutions and Bhagwati's paradox need to be subjected to an empirical test. The purpose of this study, therefore, is to investigate the impact of capital flows on governance in Africa. Unlike previous studies that focus only on one form of capital flow (e.g. ODA) and only one indicator of governance (e.g. political free-dom indicators from Freedom House), this study considers the impacts of two types of capital flows on three different indicators of governance. The significance of this study for African countries should be readily apparent. The economic power of most African countries is relatively less compared to that of most transnational corporations (TNCs) and most donor countries. As both TNCs and donor countries often lever-age their influence to shape critical decisions in recipient countries, the independence of democratic institutions in a host country can poten-tially be adversely affected. As such, this chapter seeks to answer the following questions: How do capital flows influence a host country's governance institutions? Is there a difference between the effects of FDI and ODA? Do these capital flows have lag effects or only immedi-ate contemporaneous effects? The chapter is divided into three sections. The next section presents a review of previous studies. This is followed by a section presenting this study's data and methodology, a section showing and discussing the results, and the final section, in which a set of conclusions are offered.

Previous studies

Most previous studies focus on the effects of democratic institutions and/or political instability on FDI.[2] Nevertheless the results from these studies are inconclusive. The inconclusive nature of the direct effect of governance on FDI and the cautions placed on the interpretation of the results from previous studies call for a consideration of the causal-ity assumptions placed on these variables. In this regard, the influence of capital flows on democratic institutions has recently been attract-ing attention. As the effects of globalization are increasingly evident in developing countries, it is important to assess how democratiza-tion is being affected in such environments. Previous theoretical and empirical studies have attempted to assess the impact of globalization on democratic institutions. However, the studies have not reached a consensus as to the effect of globalization. The key globalization compo-nents considered in most of these studies have been flows of capital as well as goods and services. Li and Reuveny (2003) categorized the stud-ies into three groups. One category argued that globalization enhances democracy while the second group suggested the opposite; the third group, however, concluded that globalization does not affect demo-cratic institutions. To assess these conflicting findings, Li and Reuveny (2003) investigated the effect of four national aspects of globalization on democracy for 127 countries during the period 1970–96 by using a pooled time-series cross-sectional statistical model. They found that two out of the four national aspects of globalization, namely, trade openness and portfolio investment inflows, eroded prospects for democracy. On the other hand, the other two aspects of globalization, FDI and the spread of democratic ideas, positively affected democracy. Huntington (1991) confirmed the latter finding by asserting that global economic integration promotes the diffusion of democratic ideas, which in turn leads to domestic democratization.

Contrary to Li and Reuveny's (2003) findings, Rudra (2005), using a sample of 59 developing countries, reported that trade and capital flows will be associated with enhanced democratic rights if social groups receive sufficient compensation for their (potential and actual) losses. These findings challenge popular conceptions that globalization automatically guarantees greater political freedom. The study also claimed that it is invalid to assume that the expansion of democratic rights in the least developed countries (LDCs) necessarily preceded globalization.

On the other hand, other studies have questioned the assumptions regarding globalization's effects on domestic political institutions, calling for more theoretical work on the link between governance and globalization. Berger (2000), for instance, uses international trade theory to derive political models for observing the links between globalization and institutions. One of the most important predictions of these political models is that globalization lessens the power and sovereignty of individual nations. This prediction stems from two arguments, one being the notion that the magnitude and velocity of international economic exchanges erode the state's capabilities. The other argument is that the extension of market relations across national borders diminishes the citizen's attachment to national authority, leading to a decline in the legitimacy of central governments. Berger argues that the spread of neoliberal doctrines, an outcome of globalization, has reduced the legitimacy of state involvement in national economies as well as governments' abilities to shape or change market outcomes.

In the case of Africa, although the literature on the impact of globalization on domestic institutions is vast, a limited number of studies analyze the effect of capital flows on governance in the region. Even those studies that focus on Africa deal only with the role of foreign aid (Brautigam and Knack, 2004; Goldsmith, 2001; Knack and Rahman, 2007). A study by Goldsmith (2001) assessed how foreign aid influences statehood in Africa. The analysis failed to show a negative association between foreign aid and levels of democracy and economic freedom. His results supported a positive, but limited, relationship between aid and indicators of political rights and economic freedom. Could this modest contribution of foreign aid apply to other forms of capital flows as well?

It is important first to note some of the caveats of Goldsmith's study to improve on the results or to update it. Though providing valuable insights, Goldsmith lumps all sample countries in one estimation model without accounting for country-specific effects. The indicators used for democracy are political rights from Freedom House surveys and one other indicator that shows the prevalence of the rule of law and the enforcement of property rights. The latter indicator is available only for some of the sample countries and it is not available on a yearly basis.

Brautigam and Knack (2004) use quality of governance from the International Country Risk Group (ICRG) as an indicator to estimate the impact of foreign aid on governance. In contrast to Goldsmith, Brautigam and Knack conclude that the relationship between foreign aid and governance is negative. Knack and Rahman (2007) justify the negative association between foreign aid and governance in terms of donor fragmentation. Knack and Rahman's model predicts that "the number of administrators hired declines as the donors' share of other projects in the country increases and as the donors' concern for the success of other donors' projects increases" (p. 176). Our study attempts to resolve these conflicting results by using a different methodology and by adding FDI into the pack of capital flows.

In this chapter we attempt to improve on previous studies by using democracy and political freedom indicators on a yearly basis and more reliable estimation techniques to take into account country-specific effects and the heterogeneous nature of sample countries. In addition, the present study differs from Goldsmith's (2001) research in that the latter covers only foreign aid whereas this study examines two different components of capital flows, ODA and FDI. We also employ a larger sample, a more advanced methodology, and improved governance indicators to estimate governance models as a function of various components of capital flows. For the purpose of comparison, we have reproduced Goldsmith's regression results, which employ an instrumental variable estimation technique with lags for ODA, and Brautigam and Knack (2004)'s regression results. It is important to look into the major forms of capital flows to discern if there are differential effects of capital flows on governance. In the case of African economies especially, it is necessary to analyze the effects of these capital flow components not only due to the sheer size of their flow but also due to the recent surge in FDI in addition to ODA.

Data and methodology

Forty-four sample countries were drawn from Africa, based on the availability of data on FDI and ODA flows as well as data on indicators of governance and major economic development for the period between 1975 and 2002. These periods were chosen purely because of the availability of relevant data. Capital flow variables were drawn from the United Nations Conference on Trade and Development (UNCTAD)'s *Handbook of Statistics*, 2003. Economic development indicators that are used as control variables were obtained from the World Bank's World Development Indicators.

Three governance indicators are used in this study. The three indicators approximate the prevalence of democratic institutions and political rights in each host country. All three indicators involve rankings of countries based on surveys of stakeholders in each host country. Democracy (DEMOC), Autocracy (AUTOC),[3] and Polity (POLITY) indicators are obtained from datasets compiled by Marshall and Jaggers (2003), and data for political freedom (POLITICAL) indicators are obtained from the *Annual Surveys of Freedom House Country Ratings*. Brief descriptions, components, and ranges for each indicator are indicated in the data appendix. Table 6.1a in the appendix presents descriptive statistics of the three governance indicators and shows significant variations across countries of the region. Mean values of the variables for each country in the years 1975–2002 are presented in the table. The mean of the DEMOC variable, which ranges from 0 to 10, is close to 10 for Mauritius and close to 0 for the Democratic Republic of the Congo, Egypt, Gabon, Libya, Rwanda, and Swaziland.

Table 6.2a in the appendix provides mean values for the components of capital flows in the form of ODA and FDI as well as other official flows to Africa. ODA is an aid with more than a 25 per cent grant component whereas the other official flow is capital flow with less than a 25 per cent grant component. The ratio of FDI inflow to GDP ranges from over 22 per cent for the Central African Republic to less than 1 per cent for Nigeria, South Africa, Togo, and Egypt. The ratio of ODA to GDP also ranges from over 47 per cent for Guinea-Bissau to less than 1 per cent for Libya and Algeria. Ratios of other official flows are highest for Gabon (17.7 per cent) and lowest for Guinea (less than 1 per cent). The variation in some of the key variables for the sample countries confirms differences in history, culture, governance, and size, among other things. These differences imply heterogeneity in the sample.

This study pools the countries together to draw inferences for the region as a whole rather than for individual countries. There is an advantage to using a larger sample in that more observations are possible, and this helps us obtain more reliable and robust results. The panel nature of the pooled data also yields some modest benefits through allowing for interlinkage among countries on the continent. A challenge presents itself when analyzing heterogeneous countries through pooled data. As one can read from the descriptive tables, sample countries are heterogeneous, hence correction for group-wise heterogeneity of the data is warranted. A panel-heteroscedasticity test (i.e. log-likelihood test) is conducted to test for the presence of heteroscedasticity. The result of the test reveals the restrictive assumption of the same variance of heteroscedasticity across countries is in fact invalid; hence, we need to allow for group-wise variations in variances of the error terms in our estimation.

One way to minimize the effect of heterogeneity in the sample is to account for country characteristics. As indicated above, size, history,[4] location on the continent, income per capita, and infrastructure are among some of the key variables that characterize a country. Bhagwati (2004) also indicates two key variables as determinants of democracy in a global world: degree of communication and economic prosperity. As both of these variables are believed to be important for promoting democracy, we incorporate indicators for them in our models. The proxy indicators are the number of phone lines (both fixed and mobile) to represent the degree of communication and income per capita to represent economic prosperity. Greater per capita income and communication are expected to promote democracy, as these are the key economic progress indicators that form the building blocks of the democratic institutions of a country. In addition to these control variables, dummy variables were created as controls for subregions (southern, north-eastern, western and central Africa), decades (pre-1980, between 1980 and 1990, as well as post-1990), and colonial dummies (Britain, France, Portugal, and Belgium) for each sample country. Subregion dummies are intended to account for any contagion effects from the spread of democratic ideals in neighboring countries. Dummies for decades are used to account for any external shocks specific to each decade since the continent started to integrate into the world economy in the early 1980s. Colonial dummies control for aid flow due to previous relations between the donors and a host country.[5]

The other estimation issue that one faces—in addition to the issue of heterogeneity—is the possibility of endogeneity of key variables. Given the approach of previous studies that address the impact of democracy and democratic institutions on capital flows, it is not convincing to dismiss the two-way relationship of these two variables. Hence, using capital flow indicators in a democracy equation without accounting for endogeneity may yield biased results. In this study, it is believed that capital flow variables may be endogenous in the governance model since capital flows could be driven by a country's governance status. An appropriate estimation technique should be employed to address the issue.

The ideal approach would be to account for both estimation issues (endogeneity and heteroscedasticity) at the same time in a single estimation technique. Attempting to deal with both problems simultaneously, however, is rendered difficult[6] due to a larger observation requirement and computational difficulties. The approach employed in this study is to tackle each problem one at a time and compare them to see if there are any significant differences in the results. The first estimation technique adopted is the generalized least squares (GLS) estimation, which takes into account only the heteroscedastic nature of the data by allowing panel-wise heteroscedastic error terms (Greene, 2003). The second estimation approach is the instrumental variable (IV) technique to account for endogeneity of capital flow indicators in the governance models (Baltagi, 2001). The generic estimation equation has the following form:

$$Y_{it} = X_{it}\delta + Z_{it}\beta + \mu_i + v_{it}$$

Where Y_{it} is the dependent variable, X_{it} is a vector of capital flow variables included as covariates, Z_{it} is a vector of control variables, μ_i is a vector of country effects, and v_{it} is a vector error term.

In the GLS estimation, all explanatory variables (X_{it} and Z_{it}) are considered exogenous but the variance of the error term is assumed to vary across the panel (panel-wise heteroscedastic). In the instrumental variable (IV) estimation technique, capital flow variables (X_{it}) are considered as endogenous variables but the error term is assumed to be homoscedastic. For each governance indicator a separate estimation was conducted using both GLS and IV techniques.

In the IV estimation, one difficult issue is the selection of relevant instruments for the capital flow variables. The selection of instruments for IV models should be based on previous studies that establish the key determinants of capital flows. Although there are some studies that have identified key determinants for FDI in Africa (Asiedu, 2002; Lemi and Asefa, 2003), studies on the flow of ODA to Africa are few in number and limited in scope. Following Brautigam and Knack (2004), we have adopted the instruments used in their study to get predicted values for foreign aid. For FDI, we have used traditional determinants of FDI as instruments to get predicted values. As in Brautigam and Knack (2004), we have used initial population, infant mortality rate, initial GDP per capita, and dummy variables for colony as instruments for foreign aid. For FDI, we have used trade ratios (export plus import per GDP), initial GDP per capita, and dummy variables for colony as instruments.

Capital flow variables are first included in governance models as ratio of capital flow to GDP. Effectiveness of capital flow (especially foreign aid), however, becomes even more apparent if one takes account of the per capita capital flows instead of just the ratio to GDP. To see the robustness of the results, one should consider the alternative approach of measuring capital flows in per capita terms. In this study, separate estimations were run with capital flows in per capita terms. One other contention regarding the effectiveness of capital flow is to discern lag effects for capital flows. It is logical to expect that the effects of capital flows may be felt only after a year or more on the democratic institutions of a country. To investigate this contention, one-year, two-year, and three-year lags of the two capital flows were added in the above estimation equations to assess the delayed effects of capital flows on governance. This compensation for lag is especially important for countries in Africa where the market system changes slowly so that it is not always possible to witness the contemporaneous effects of capital flows, especially for FDI. To account for these effects and to see the robustness of the above results, lagged values of the capital flows—lag of ODA (LAGODA) and lag of FDI (LAGFDI)—were used together with the contemporary variables to test for the presence of lag effects. Equations with lagged capital flow variables were estimated using only the GLS estimation technique, not an IV estimation, to avoid the complication of using lagged variables in the instrumental variable estimation.

Results and discussion

For the purpose of comparison with Goldsmith (2001)'s results, Tables 6.1 and 6.2 report results that use the instrumental estimation technique without accounting for country effects and heteroscedasticity. Estimation results in Table 6.1 use democracy and

Table 6.1 Impacts of official government aid on governance: IV estimation without control for country effects and heteroscedasticity

	Democracy	Democracy extended[a]	Democracy subsample[b]	Polity	Polity extended[a]	Polity subsample[b]
Aid intensity	6.221***	9.307***	6.686***	2.695	8.937*	6.992*
	(4.111)	(5.278)	(3.892)	(0.765)	(2.535)	(2.079)
Initial democracy	0.574***	0.554***	0.677***			
	(10.718)	(10.254)	(13.784)			
Population growth	−0.030*	−0.002	−0.001	−0.042	0.015	0.038
	(−2.228)	(−0.113)	(−0.044)	(−1.493)	(0.438)	(0.735)
GDP growth rate	0.031***	0.014	0.005	0.043***	0.009	−0.020
	(8.839)	(1.751)	(0.370)	(7.660)	(0.760)	(−0.718)
Infrastructure		0.016**	0.030		0.030***	0.075*
		(3.104)	(1.824)		(3.844)	(2.237)
Initial polity				0.614***	0.604***	0.746***
				(12.919)	(12.672)	(16.092)
Constant	0.242	−0.316	−0.396	−0.587	−1.771**	−1.757*
	(1.726)	(−1.522)	(−1.446)	(−1.172)	(−3.095)	(−2.454)
Observations	687.000	667.000	508.000	687.000	667.000	508.000
Chi2	903.110	328.538	257.828	647.630	361.498	382.131

Note: *$P<0.10$, **$P<0.05$, ***$P<0.01$
[a]Extended model included infrastructure (telephone lines per 1000 people).
[b]The subsample estimation refers to the period 1975–95.

Table 6.2 Impacts of FDI on governance: IV estimation without control for country effects and heteroscedasticity

	Democracy	Democracy extended[a]	Democracy subsample[b]	Polity	Polity extended[a]	Polity subsample[b]
FDI inflow	-1.190	9.503**	9.524*	8.396	12.415*	0.049
	(-0.588)	(2.955)	(2.564)	(1.728)	(2.472)	(0.014)
Initial democracy	0.690***	0.339**	0.684***			
	(17.903)	(2.885)	(11.071)			
Population growth	-0.017	-0.017	0.002	-0.002	0.011	0.058
	(-1.353)	(-0.580)	(0.102)	(-0.058)	(0.245)	(1.478)
GDP growth rate	0.014***	0.045***	0.019	0.045***	0.044*	-0.051*
	(5.280)	(4.074)	(1.772)	(4.572)	(2.429)	(-3.036)
Infrastructure		-0.002	0.004		0.007	0.101**
		(-0.412)	(0.371)		(0.907)	(5.304)
Initial polity				0.514***	0.452***	0.782***
				(5.847)	(4.616)	(13.795)
Constant	1.343***	0.556*	0.126	-1.209	-2.036**	-1.480***
	(8.741)	(2.228)	(0.740)	(-1.490)	(-2.755)	(-3.762)
Observation	778.000	625.000	445.000	637.000	625.000	470.000
Chi2	1243.500	928.184	814.944	733.538	807.883	1374.580

Note: *P < 0.10, **P < 0.05, ***P < 0.01.
[a]The subsample estimation refers to the period 1975–95.
[b]Extended model included infrastructure (telephone lines per 1000 people).

polity as dependent variables to show the impacts of official development aid on these two governance indicators. Table 6.2 reports the instrumental estimation of the impact of FDI on governance. In fact, the tables report comparable results to that of Goldsmith (2001) and Brautigam and Knack (2004), although the control variables are not exactly the same. In both tables, the first three columns refer to different specifications using democracy as a governance indicator, whereas the last three columns refer to similar specifications but use polity as a governance indicator. The first and the fourth columns, labeled democracy and polity, use traditional explanatory and control variables, an approach similar to Brautigam and Knack (2004)'s estimations. The second and the fifth column extend these models by adding an infrastructure variable, as suggested by Bhagwati (2004), to approximate the degree of connectivity to the world. The third and the sixth columns limit the period of analysis pre-1995 to compare findings with Goldsmith (2001) and Brautigam and Knack (2004), who use pre-1995 or pre-1997 data for their analysis.

The results confirm that official development aid has positive and significant effects on governance in Africa. These results support Goldsmith's findings. They are also indicative that countries with higher income per capita experience higher levels of governance. Initial governance level also has positive contributions on the current level of governance in sample countries. For FDI, the results seem to support positive contributions from FDI on governance, especially in the extended model and for the subsample, although the results are not as marked for ODA. However, as we shall see below, some of the results for FDI may not hold as we allow for heteroscedasticity and control for country-specific effects.

Estimation results that show the contemporaneous effects of capital flows are presented in Table 6.3 (for the GLS estimation) and results that show the lag effects of capital flows on governance are reported in Table 6.4. In both estimations, some of the instrumental variables that have been used in the IV estimation are incorporated into these models. In addition, a third governance proxy (political rights from Freedom House) has also been added to show the robustness of the results. The fitness test for each model reveals the significance of each model. For the heteroscedasticity-corrected GLS and IV models, Wald tests (chi-square) show the significance of coefficients in all specifications. Results that use capital flows in per capita terms have similar findings and significance.[7] The results show that ODA has had a positive

Table 6.3 Impacts of official development aid and FDI on governance in Africa: results from panel-heteroscedastic model (GLS)

	Democracy	Polity	Polity right	Democracy	Polity	Polity right
Aid intensity	0.466 (1.017)	1.803* (1.864)	0.627* (1.869)		0.223 (0.541)	−0.020~ (−0.145)
FDI inflow				−0.048 (−0.241)	−0.001 (−0.047)	0.017*** (4.239)
GDP per capita	0.006 (0.624)	−0.033** (−2.132)	0.024** (5.802)	0.026*** (2.744)	0.015*** (4.163)	0.003*** (3.034)
Infrastructure	0.010*** (4.475)	0.023*** (5.571)	0.004*** (3.214)	0.006*** (3.212)		
Britain Colony	1.331*** (8.807)	2.725*** (9.780)	1.108*** (11.741)	1.631*** (10.383)	3.352*** (10.868)	1.033*** (11.023)
France Colony	0.333*** (2.980)	1.527*** (7.191)	0.178* (1.842)	0.289** (2.564)	1.607*** (6.942)	0.188* (1.954)
Portugal Colony	0.334** (2.426)	1.966*** (7.638)	−0.177* (−1.736)	0.226** (2.139)	1.643*** (7.621)	−0.225** (−2.241)
Between 1980 and 1990	−0.051 (−0.566)	0.146 (0.713)	−0.054 (−0.568)	−0.068 (−0.887)	0.144 (0.726)	−0.039 (−0.390)

Post-1990	0.742***	3.865***	0.456***	0.850***	3.956***	0.508***
	(7.757)	(17.437)	(4.739)	(10.452)	(19.013)	(5.090)
Western Africa	−1.350***	−2.030***	−0.618***	−1.920***	−3.205***	−0.595***
	(−6.173)	(−4.673)	(−4.480)	(−8.477)	(−7.186)	(−4.190)
Central Africa	−1.647***	−3.231***	−1.114***	−2.268***	−4.319***	−1.138***
	(−8.855)	(−8.607)	(−11.178)	(−12.093)	(−11.316)	(−11.267)
North-East Africa	−2.050***	−4.118***	−0.946***	−2.818***	−5.668***	−1.006***
	(−10.538)	(−9.712)	(−7.149)	(−14.396)	(−13.527)	(−7.429)
Constant	1.297***	−5.740***	1.273***	1.876***	−4.501***	1.426***
	(6.079)	(−13.760)	(9.997)	(9.250)	(−10.885)	(11.425)
Observation	991.000	991.000	1043.000	992.000	992.000	1040.000
Chi2	556.263	1288.436	780.677	1104.052	1670.241	705.782
Log-likelihood	−1908.206	−2641.834	−1617.633	−1943.336	−2682.48	−1638.032

Note: $^*P < 0.10$, $^{**}P < 0.05$, $^{***}P < 0.01$.

Table 6.4 Impacts of official development aid and FDI with lags on governance in Africa: Results from panel-heteroscedastic model (GLS)

	Democracy	Polity	Polity right	Democracy	Polity	Polity right
Aid intensity	0.446	0.127	0.288			
	(0.496)	(0.062)	(0.423)			
One-year lag of ODA	−0.569	−2.314	−0.467			
	(−0.581)	(−0.920)	(−0.563)			
Two-year lag of ODA		0.041	0.159			
		(0.016)	(0.191)			
Three-year lag of ODA	1.760**	7.209***	1.299*			
	(2.456)	(3.536)	(1.891)			
FDI inflow				−0.167	−0.301	0.055
				(−0.820)	(−0.655)	(0.346)
One-year lag of FDI				0.469*	1.286**	0.229
				(1.883)	(2.289)	(1.408)
Two-year lag of FDI					1.292**	0.137
					(2.320)	(0.893)
Three-year lag of FDI				0.284	1.107*	0.160
				(1.153)	(1.824)	(0.932)
GDP per capita	0.017	−0.008	0.028***	0.024**	−0.005	0.022***
	(1.515)	(−0.414)	(5.841)	(2.190)	(−0.295)	(5.095)
Infrastructure	0.011***	0.026***	0.005***	0.007***	0.016***	0.003***
	(5.063)	(6.221)	(3.993)	(3.812)	(4.449)	(2.986)
Britain Colony	1.349***	2.539***	1.105***	1.798***	3.674***	1.178***
	(8.012)	(8.766)	(10.688)	(10.137)	(10.006)	(10.313)

France Colony	0.459***	1.423***	0.189*	0.340***	1.619***	0.250**
	(3.398)	(5.903)	(1.826)	(2.806)	(5.969)	(2.302)
Portugal Colony	0.490***	2.178***	−0.044	0.316***	1.623***	0.042
	(3.148)	(8.187)	(−0.381)	(2.779)	(6.037)	(0.250)
Between 1980 and 1990	−0.115	−0.066	−0.310**	−0.161	0.253	−0.259
	(−0.977)	(−0.232)	(−2.238)	(−1.078)	(0.677)	(−1.522)
Post-1990	0.657***	3.371***	0.138	0.601***	3.613***	0.076
	(5.294)	(10.810)	(0.971)	(3.964)	(9.628)	(0.450)
Western Africa	−1.226***	−1.511***	−0.593***	−2.094***	−3.408***	−0.767***
	(−5.211)	(−3.263)	(−4.136)	(−8.160)	(−6.558)	(−4.584)
Central Africa	−1.512***	−2.839***	−1.135***	−2.394***	−4.528***	−1.330***
	(−7.597)	(−7.098)	(−10.625)	(−11.194)	(−9.873)	(−10.791)
North-East Africa	−2.038***	−3.622***	−0.930***	−3.041***	−5.919***	−1.316***
	(−9.962)	(−8.032)	(−6.504)	(−13.631)	(−12.037)	(−7.866)
Constant	0.956***	−6.360***	1.437***	2.112***	−4.142***	1.810***
	(3.812)	(−12.972)	(8.542)	(8.210)	(−7.372)	(9.532)
Observation	879.000	879.000	932.000	782.000	734.000	778.000
Chi2	544.489	1213.071	718.336	864.864	1148.378	533.889
Log-likelihood	−1718.634	−2350.259	−1451.771	−1445.992	−1991.215	−1239.958

Note: *$P < 0.10$, **$P < 0.05$, ***$P < 0.01$.

and significant, albeit limited, effect on polity and political rights in Africa during the period in question.

For the case of FDI, there is no significant contemporaneous effects for all specifications on all indicators of governance (see Table 6.3). This result implies that the immediate effects of FDI are difficult to detect since the flow of FDI is market-based and hence time is needed to notice the effects on democratic institutions. It is often argued that FDI investors may not necessarily require functioning political and democratic institutions before they decide to invest in a host country as long as a host country is stable. For that matter, only business- and security-related government institutions may affect the performance of FDI directly. Therefore, FDI investors may consider pushing for improvements of some of the branches of democratic institutions once they secure investment permits and start operations in a host country.

Some of the control variables—income per capita, communication indicator, colony dummies, regional dummies, and decade dummies—have the expected signs (Table 6.3). Income per capita has significant positive effects on the political rights within a country, but it has negative and significant effects on polity, which is a combination of democratic institutions and autocracy. If one looks into the component of each of these governance indicators, political rights include components that highlight individual freedom and participation, unlike the other two indicators, which focus mainly on the functionality of governance institutions. People in countries with higher income tend to demand more participation in governance. Those countries in Africa with high per capita incomes are countries with skewed income distribution, where the elites dominating the political system may resist the openness of political institutions (i.e. democracy and polity); however, they may be willing to allow freedom of choice and speech (i.e. political rights). Oil- and mineral-rich countries have high incomes per capita but their political institutions may not function well, at least compared to countries in other parts of the world with comparable incomes per capita. As stated in Bhagwati (2004), economic development or prosperity leads people to demand more freedoms after they secure their economic stability. This may not be true in the case of Africa where most income is concentrated in the hands of elites who have or have had links with the government. These elites may not want to change the status quo, apart from some minor changes in opening up freedom of speech and choice that may not significantly alter the existing functionality of government institutions.

Communications, approximated by the number of fixed and mainline telephones, has had positive and significant effects on all governance indicators. This result is consistent with Bhagwati's (2004) assertion that higher levels of communication within a country and the connection of a country to the rest of the world help promote democracy. The other control variables have consistent effects. The results imply that being in the western, north-eastern and central part of the continent, compared to being in the southern part of the continent, helps countries promote democracy. It seems that there is a neighboring country contagion or demonstration effect, where countries in politically unstable neighborhoods have the same fate with regard to undemocratic institutions. The other control variables are dummies for colonies, which reveal that countries colonized by Britain (and to some extent France) were in a better position to have democratic institutions compared to those countries colonized by Belgium. The results also confirm that the 1990s were a decade when the continent witnessed good governance in comparison to the 1980s. This may support the notion of the spread of democratic ideas in recent decades.

One can, therefore, conclude that for the case of Africa what matters most is not just higher income levels and better communication facilities, which are the necessary conditions for functioning democratic institutions, but also influence from neighboring countries (through contagion effects) and history, especially colonial history (and its inherited institutions). These factors, together with official development aid, are key variables that one needs to examine carefully to promote democracy and political rights on the continent. The regional effects are apparent in the current situation that one can witness in the eastern and western parts of the continent. In West Africa, the political crisis in Liberia has spread to the neighboring nations of Ivory Coast and Sierra Leone; in East Africa, the tribal conflicts in Somalia have affected neighboring Ethiopia and Eritrea. This could be either due to rebel groups that were harbored in neighboring countries or the result of regional conflicts over resources/boundaries not clearly demarcated during the scramble for Africa and the colonial era.

To investigate the lag effects of FDI and ODA on governance, we included lags of these capital flows in our governance equations (see Table 6.4). Lag effects also confirmed that ODA has significant and positive effects on governance in Africa. When we used ODA both in levels and the lags, the level effects became weak but positive signs were still maintained. Once we included lag effects for FDI in our model, the one-year and two-year lags had positive and significant effects on governance in Africa. These results confirm the contention that it takes time for FDI to have noticeable effects on governance in Africa. It is also important to note that, even with lags, FDI has no significant impact on political rights. As stated above, political rights scores include individual freedom and choice components, which are not major issues of concern for FDI investors. For ODA, on the other hand, the impact is positive not only for democracy indicators but also for political rights as donors often gauge progress in democratic institutions through political rights, which are often measured by the degree of individuals' freedom of expression and political views and choices.

Conclusions

The impacts of ODA and FDI on governance in Africa were empirically tested in this study. We have argued that both ODA and FDI can influence governance reform in African states given the dependence of these countries on foreign capital (ODA and FDI) to cover a significant share of their annual official budget. The economic size of host countries is another factor related to capital flow influence, with economically weak states in Africa more influenced by capital inflows. The question that we ask in this chapter is how these two forms of capital flows impact governance in Africa. Do the donors (through ODA) or the investors (through FDI) have some agenda that targets the governance of a nation-state? If they follow their national interest (ODA) and profit-maximization interest (FDI) agendas, which are often the case, what are the side effects on the functioning of governance in the recipient countries?

The results reveal that, unlike pessimistic views on the role of ODA, aid does promote good governance in Africa. For three different indicators of governance in Africa, we found that ODA promotes good governance (i.e. improves democratic institutions and political rights) in a host country. This result is consistent with that of Goldsmith (2001). Although weak, the lag effects from ODA have some positive effects on governance; it is expected that if there is consistent aid flow the process of good governance may deepen well into later years by improving the performance of governance institutions in African states.

For FDI, one has to look into the objectives of investors who engage in cross-border investments. The objective function is to maximize profits for the company and affiliate firms in each host country, and hence investors may not be interested in engaging themselves in overall governance issues. Investors of FDI may be concerned with the functioning of business- and security-related institutions but not the political governance of a host country per se. The empirical result confirms that there is no significant impact from FDI flows on any of the three governance indicators. However, investors may demand smooth functioning of the country's democratic institutions to make their day-to-day activities easier in the country. Institutional efficiency or compliance may become an issue to investors once they start operations in the country of their investment destination. Therefore, it is only after a year or two that FDI investors demand, and in fact push for, improved performance of local institutions.

The implications of other control variables reveal that promoting democracy in African states is not just about increasing income and providing communication facilities, and it is also not about promoting good governance in just one country in a region where neighboring countries are in disarray. It takes a region to promote sustainable democratic institutions in a region. One also has to account for the institutional framework inherited from the colonial past to see if the nation's institutions are in accord with participatory democratic institutions in African states.

From the approaches of the two major multilateral institutions—the World Bank and IMF—it seems that pursuing good economic governance can eventually lead to good political governance. Donors beyond these institutions also play a significant role, especially those donors who provide aid directly for governance reform. In 2001–2, the major donors to Africa were the US, the European Commission, the International Development Agency (IDA), and France. Each of these countries or groups accounts for over 10 per cent of total aid from all donors; and together they account for over 50 per cent of aid from all donors. Of the total aid money from these donors, 54 per cent goes to social infrastructure and services, which includes funding for government and society (OECD, 2005). Coupling the direct involvement of these donors in the governance and democratic process of African states and the role of the IMF and the World Bank in promoting good economic governance, it is not surprising that ODA has had positive and significant impacts on governance in Africa. However, if one considers ODA only from the perspective of bilateral donors who have not explicitly committed themselves to the promotion of democratic institutions, are significant and positive effects from capital flows still likely? Is there any role to play in terms of a democratization effect for the IMF and the

World Bank, who pursue governance only from an economic perspective? Future studies need to distinguish between those who promote only good governance from an economic perspective and those who promote democratic institutions, and investigate if the same results are manifested through each type of overseas development assistance.

Acknowledgments

I would like to thank participants of the 32nd annual conference of the Eastern Economic Association and the 4th annual conference of the Asia Association for Global Studies for their suggestions. I would also like to thank Professor Sisay Asefa and Dr. Blen Solomon for their comments and suggestions on an earlier version of this chapter.

Appendix: Data

[Note: Capital flow and official development aid data were obtained from *UNCTAD, Handbook of Statistics*, CD-ROM, 2003.]

Official Development Aid/Assistance (ODA): Grants or loans to developing countries that are undertaken by the official sector, with the promotion of economic development and welfare as the main objective, at concessional financial terms (if a loan, having a grant element of at least 25 per cent).

Other Official Flows (OOF): Transactions by the official sector with developing countries. OOF are flows that do not meet the conditions for eligibility as official development assistance or official aid because they are not primarily aimed at development, or because they involve a grant of less than 25 per cent.

Foreign Direct Investment (FDI): A private investment made to acquire or add to a lasting interest in an enterprise in a country on the Development Assistance Committee List of aid recipients. "Lasting interest" implies a long-term relationship where the direct investor has a significant influence on the management of the enterprise, reflected by ownership of at least 10 per cent of the shares, or equivalent voting power or other means of control. In practice it is recorded as the change in the net worth of a subsidiary in a recipient country to the parent company.

Imports: Imports of goods and services in millions of dollars.

Exports: Exports of goods and services in millions of dollars.

[Note: Other development indicators are obtained from World Bank, *World Development Indicators*, 2003.]

GDP: Gross domestic product of a host country (constant 2000 US dollars).

GDP per capita (GDPPC): GDP per capita (constant 2000 US dollars).

Telephone mainlines per thousand people (TELEML): includes fixed and mobile phone lines.

[Note: Governance/Democracy indicators were obtained from datasets compiled by Marshall and Jaggers (2003) and Freedom House's *Annual Survey of Freedom Country Ratings* (1972–73 to 2002–03).]

Democracy: Democracy Score (DEMOC)—general openness of political institutions. The 11-point Democracy scale is constructed additively. This indicator of the degree of institutionalized democracy rates ranges from 0 to 10 (0 = low, 10 = high). Democracy is conceived as three essential, interdependent elements. One is the presence of institutions and procedures through which citizens can express effective preferences about alternative policies and leaders. Two is the existence of institutionalized constraints on the exercise of power over the executive. Three is the guarantee of civil liberties to all citizens in the daily lives and in acts of political participation. Data obtained from Marshall and Jaggers (2003).

Autocracy: Autocracy Score (AUTOC)—general closedness of political institutions. It is defined in terms of the presence of a distinctive set of political characteristics. Autocracies sharply restrict or suppress competitive political participation. Chief executives are chosen in a regularized process of selection within the political elite, and once in office they exercise power with few institutional constraints. The 11-point Autocracy scale is constructed additively. This indicator of degree of institutionalized autocracy rates ranges from 0 to 10 (0 = low, 10 = high). This is the opposite of democracy. Data obtained from Marshall and Jaggers (2003).

Polity: Combined Polity Score (POLITY)—Computed by subtracting AUTOC from DEMOC; range = −10 to 10 (−10 = high autocracy; 10 = high democracy). Data obtained from Marshall and Jaggers (2003).

Political freedom (POLITICAL): The ratings process is based on a checklist of ten political rights questions. The questions are grouped into three categories: electoral process, political pluralism and participation, and functioning of government. Rating ranges from 0 to 7 (0 = high freedom, 7 = low freedom). To make the indicator consistent with the other democracy indicators, this variable has been recoded to make that 7 indicates high political right and 0 indicates low political right. The higher the numeric values, the higher the freedom. Data obtained from the Freedom House Survey.

Other constructed control variables

Regional dummies:

> *Western Africa*: dummy for western African countries
> *Northern and Eastern Africa*: dummy for northern and eastern African countries
> *Southern African*: dummy for southern African countries
> *Central Africa*: dummy for central African countries

Colony Dummies:

> *Britain*: dummy for countries colonized by Britain
> *France*: dummy for countries colonized by France
> *Portugal*: dummy for countries colonized by Portugal
> *Belgium*: dummy for countries colonized by Belgium

Decade Dummies:

> *Pre-1980*: dummy for the years before 1981
> *1980s and 1990s*: dummy for the years between 1980 and 1990
> *Post-1990*: dummy for the years after 1990

Export Dummies:

> *Fuel exporters*: dummies for fuel exporters
> *Metal exporters*: dummies for metal and other mineral exporters

Table 6.1a   Mean of governance indicators by country: 1975–2002

No	Country	DEMOC	AUTOC	POLITY[a]	POLITICAL
1	Algeria	0.393	6.714	−6.321	1.036
2	Angola	0.273	6.182	−5.909	0.429
3	Benin	2.667	3.889	−1.222	2.107
4	Botswana	7.786	0.000	7.786	5.143
5	Burkina Faso	0.593	5.037	−4.444	1.714
6	Burundi	0.136	6.136	−6.000	0.357
7	Cameroon	0.393	6.786	−6.393	0.750
8	Central Africa	1.786	4.429	−2.643	1.500
9	Chad	0.350	5.000	−4.650	0.571
10	Congo, Dem. Rep.	0.000	8.882	−8.882	0.964

11	Congo, Rep.	1.111	6.000	−4.889	0.464
12	Ivory Coast	0.385	7.500	−7.115	1.143
13	Egypt, Arab Rep.	0.000	6.036	−6.036	1.679
14	Ethiopia	1.000	5.625	−4.625	0.929
15	Gabon	0.000	6.778	−6.778	1.571
16	Gambia, The	5.107	1.786	3.321	3.321
17	Ghana	1.731	4.077	−2.346	2.071
18	Guinea	0.286	5.929	−5.643	0.464
19	Guinea-Bissau	1.346	5.269	−3.923	1.750
20	Kenya	0.643	5.679	−5.036	1.429
21	Lesotho	2.000	5.250	−3.250	2.286
22	Libya	0.000	7.000	−7.000	0.429
23	Madagascar	3.259	3.556	−0.296	3.000
24	Malawi	2.179	6.143	−3.964	1.857
25	Mali	2.630	4.148	−1.519	2.000
26	Mauritania	0.000	6.571	−6.571	0.571
27	Mauritius	9.750	0.000	9.750	5.286
28	Morocco	0.000	7.500	−7.500	2.536
29	Mozambique	1.929	5.036	−3.107	1.679
30	Namibia	6.000	0.000	6.000	4.857
31	Niger	1.778	4.815	−3.037	1.000
32	Nigeria	2.154	4.346	−2.192	1.929
33	Rwanda	0.000	6.444	−6.444	0.571
34	Senegal	2.429	3.107	−0.679	3.143
35	Sierra Leone	0.435	6.261	−5.826	1.786
36	South Africa	7.692	1.885	5.808	3.286
37	Sudan	0.889	6.296	−5.407	0.929
38	Swaziland	0.000	9.643	−9.643	1.357
39	Tanzania	0.679	5.536	−4.857	1.429
40	Togo	0.385	5.462	−5.077	0.750
41	Tunisia	0.357	6.179	−5.821	1.286
42	Uganda	0.769	4.692	−3.923	1.679
43	Zambia	1.821	5.643	−3.821	2.357
44	Zimbabwe	2.148	4.407	−2.259	1.964
	Total	1.756	5.129	−3.373	1.722

Note: DEMOC (institutional democracy), AUTOC (institutional autocracy), and POLITICAL (political right).
[a] Polity is computed as Democ—Autoc.

Table 6.2a Mean values (in millions of dollars) of FDI, ODA, and other official flows: 1975–2002

No.	Country	FDIINF	TODAOA	TOOF	RFDIINF	RTODAOA	RTOOF
1	Algeria	134.540	212.959	376.152	0.003	0.005	0.092
2	Angola	165.537	199.115	18.196	0.029	0.031	0.037
3	Benin	154.547	169.393	6.822	0.082	0.110	0.052
4	Botswana	85.725	96.700	7.319	0.026	0.050	0.043
5	Burkina Faso	110.288	291.070	1.142	0.053	0.160	0.011
6	Burundi	113.303	150.993	0.392	0.176	0.218	0.010
7	Cameroon	140.267	340.630	82.326	0.018	0.047	0.118
8	Central African	204.493	125.300	0.996	0.226	0.156	0.013
9	Chad	108.231	168.226	0.313	0.092	0.151	0.002
10	Congo, Dem. Rep.	85.139	338.533	136.374	0.016	0.050	0.181
11	Congo, Rep.	126.364	126.496	47.041	0.044	0.051	0.194
12	Ivory Coast	100.107	434.248	99.522	0.011	0.049	0.132
13	Egypt, Arab Rep.	54.321	2126.522	287.885	0.000	0.041	0.055
14	Ethiopia	294.216	613.926	4.981	0.057	0.152	0.015
15	Gabon	36.227	74.589	67.085	0.005	0.019	0.177
16	Gambia, The	80.624	58.522	0.989	0.094	0.207	0.047
17	Ghana	14.429	415.796	12.041	-0.001	0.118	0.039
18	Guinea	9.452	215.226	0.237	0.015	0.133	0.001
19	Guinea-Bissau	39.499	84.681	0.571	0.197	0.478	0.035
20	Kenya	80.062	539.633	-0.741	0.009	0.068	0.023
21	Lesotho	61.340	89.500	7.758	0.094	0.170	0.121
22	Libya	47.512	9.552	11.147	0.001	0.001	0.015
23	Madagascar	73.594	290.033	23.263	0.021	0.091	0.080
24	Malawi	62.546	301.604	2.696	0.041	0.233	0.040

25	Mali	97.610	332.382	3.437	0.041	0.195	0.023
26	Mauritania	79.566	210.441	8.244	0.086	0.333	0.169
27	Mauritius	58.453	39.744	2.707	0.018	0.018	0.028
28	Morocco	45.616	598.593	220.633	0.002	0.026	0.103
29	Mozambique	65.260	630.030	39.342	0.017	0.314	0.130
30	Namibia	22.124	119.165	2.380	0.003	0.042	0.008
31	Niger	26.100	258.222	-1.307	0.016	0.171	0.003
32	Nigeria	21.830	135.519	204.648	0.001	0.004	0.084
33	Rwanda	5.857	267.889	1.500	0.003	0.190	0.010
34	Senegal	77.104	451.641	25.144	0.029	0.147	0.100
35	Sierra Leone	61.790	108.259	1.659	0.072	0.131	0.012
36	South Africa	52.176	421.222	181.000	0.000	0.003	0.015
37	Sudan	89.992	542.222	52.078	0.013	0.081	0.091
38	Swaziland	93.222	37.330	3.433	0.132	0.048	0.069
39	Tanzania	124.360	798.726	17.030	0.028	0.137	-0.013
40	Togo	158.504	122.919	9.678	0.150	0.122	0.109
41	Tunisia	120.651	235.548	163.022	0.009	0.022	0.134
42	Uganda	89.228	405.867	0.256	0.041	0.138	0.013
43	Zambia	132.558	499.311	17.515	0.043	0.169	0.069
44	Zimbabwe	119.388	261.326	31.411	0.020	0.045	0.057
	Total	88.608	317.126	48.995	0.047	0.119	0.067

Note: FDIINF (FDI inflows), TODAOA (total official development aid), TOOF (total other official flows), RFDIINF (ratio of FDI inflow to GDP), RTODAOA (ratio of ODA to GDP), RTOOF (ratio of OOF to GDP). Variables in levels are in millions of dollars.

Notes

1. In this study, democratic institutions and governance are used interchangeably. Both of them are used to refer to a well-behaved and functioning government that has institutions that follow the rule of law and protect its business entities and citizens.
2. For instance, see studies by Li and Resnick (2003), and Lemi and Asefa (2003). Li and Resnick (2003) develop a theoretical model to investigate the effects of domestic institutions on FDI. They conclude that institutions affect FDI in a very complex manner. The complexity of the effect of institutions on FDI stems from the fact that functioning democratic institutions have a positive effect on FDI inflows because good institutions are associated with improved property rights. However, they also find that democracy also reduces flow of FDI since these institutions close loopholes that often benefit large corporations. Similarly, Lemi and Asefa (2003), focusing on African states, address the same issue and show that there is a differential effect of governance on different FDI industries due to the nature, size, and objectives of the FDI firms that enter African economies.
3. Estimation results that use AUTOC are not reported in this chapter to save space, but are available from the author.
4. For the importance of the latter, see Acemoglu, Johnson, and Robinson (2001), who demonstrate the role colonial history plays in affecting economic growth.
5. For previous use of some of these control variables, see studies by Alesina and Dollar (2000), Tavares (2003), and Alesina and Weder (2002).
6. There is robust GMM estimation that accounts for both endogeneity and heteroscedasticity at the same time, as indicated in Wooldridge (2002).
7. Results are not reported in this chapter to save space, but are available on request.

References

Acemoglu, D., Johnson, S., and Robinson, J. A. (2001). The colonial origins of comparative development: An empirical investigation. *American Economic Review*, *91*(5), 1369–1401.

Akram, T. (2003). The international foreign aid regime: Who gets foreign aid and how much? *Applied Economics*, *35*(11), 1351–1356.

Alesina, A., and Dollar, D. (2000). Who gives foreign aid to whom and why? *Journal of Economic Growth*, *5*(1), 33–63.

Alesina, A., and Weder, B. (2002). Do corrupt governments receive less foreign aid? *The American Economic Review*, *92*(4), 1126–1137.

Arslanalp, S., and Henry, P. B. (2006). Policy watch: Debt relief. *Journal of Economic Perspectives*, *20*(1), 207–220.

Asiedu, E. (2002). On the determinants of foreign direct investment to developing countries: Is Africa different? *World Development*, *30*(1), 107–119.

Asiedu, E. (2004). Policy reform and foreign direct investment to Africa: Absolute progress but relative decline. *Development Policy Review*, *22*(1), 41–48.

Asiedu, E. (2006). Foreign direct investment in Africa: The role of government policy, institutions and political instability. *World Economy*, *29*(1), 63–77.

Baltagi, B. H. (2001). *Econometric analysis of panel data* (2nd edn). New York: John Wiley & Sons.

Berger, S. (2000). Globalization and politics. *Annual Review of Political Science, 3*(1), 43–62.

Bhagwati, J. (2004). *In defense of globalization.* Cary, NC: Oxford University Press.

Brautigam, D. A., and Knack, S. (2004). Foreign aid, institutions, governance in sub-Saharan Africa. *Economic Development and Cultural Change, 52*(2), 255–285.

Brown, S. (2005). Foreign aid and democracy promotion: Lessons from Africa. *The European Journal of Development Research, 17*(2), 179–198.

Burnside, C., and Dollar, D. (2000). Aid, policies, and growth. *American Economic Review, 90*(4), 847–868.

Easterly, W. (2003). Can foreign aid buy growth? *Journal of Economic Perspectives, 17*(3), 23–48.

Economic Commission for Africa (2006). *Economic report on Africa 2006: Capital flows and development financing in Africa.* Addis Ababa: Economic Commission for Africa.

Goldsmith, A. (2001). Foreign aid and statehood in Africa. *International Organization, 55*(1), 123–148.

Greene, W. H. (2003). *Econometric Analysis* (5th edn). Upper Saddle River, NJ: Prentice-Hall.

Habib, M., and Zurawicki, L. (2002). Corruption and foreign direct investment. *Journal of International Business Studies, 33*(2), 291–307.

Harrison, G. (2005). The World Bank, governance and theories of political action in Africa. *British Journal of Politics and International Relations, 7*(2), 240–260.

Huntington, S. P. (1991). *The third wave: Democratization in the late twentieth century.* Norman, OK: University of Oklahoma Press.

International Monetary Fund (IMF) (1997). *Good governance: The IMF's role.* IMF Staff paper, Washington, DC.

Knack, S., and Rahman, A. (2007). Donor fragmentation and bureaucratic quality in aid recipients. *Journal of Development Economics, 83,* 176–197.

Lemi, A. and Asefa, S. (2003). Foreign direct investment and uncertainty: Empirical evidence from Africa. *African Finance Journal, 5*(I), 36–67.

Li, Q., and Resnick, A. (2003). Reversal of fortunes: Democratic institutions and foreign direct inflows to developing countries. *International Organization, 57*(1), 175–211.

Li, Q., and Reuveny, R. (2003). Economic globalization and democracy: An empirical analysis. *British Journal of Political Science, 33,* 29–54.

Marshall, M. G., and Jaggers, K. (2003). *Polity IV Project: Political regime characteristics and transitions, 1800–2002.* College Park, MD: Center for International Development and Conflict Management at the University of Maryland.

OECD (2005). *Investment for African development: Making it happen.* NEPAD/OECD investment initiative roundtable presentation, Uganda.

Rudra, N. (2005). Globalization and the strengthening of democracy in the developing world. *American Journal of Political Science, 49*(4), 704–730.

Schraeder, P. J., Hook, S. W., and Taylor, B. (1998). Clarifying the foreign aid puzzle: A comparison of American, Japanese, French, and Swedish aid flows. *World Politics, 50*(2), 294–323.

Tavares, J. (2003). Does foreign aid corrupt? *Economics Letters, 79,* 99–106.

UNCTAD (1998). *World investment report 1998: Trends and determinants*. United Nations, New York and Geneva.

Wooldridge, J. M. (2002). Econometric analysis of cross section and panel data. Cambridge, MA: MIT Press.

World Bank (1994). *Governance: The World Bank's experience*. Washington, DC.

World Bank (2002). *Global development finance 2002: Financing the poorest countries*. Washington, DC.

World Bank (2006). *Global development finance 2006: The development potential of surging capital flows*. Washington, DC.

7
The "Creditors in Competition": Chávez and the Bank of the South versus the IMF

Rab Paterson

Introduction: birth of the debt beast

The Allied powers held a meeting at Bretton Woods, New Hampshire, as World War II was drawing to a close in 1944. This was mainly at the insistence of the United States and Britain and was for the purpose of deciding the postwar economic infrastructure of the world. The conference was attended by representatives of many nations, but as an omen of things to come most non-Western nations had but marginal input into the plans and policies formulated (Black, 2001). From this conference two international organizations came into being: the International Monetary Fund (IMF), which was to provide short-term loans to countries struggling to avoid defaulting on loans or causing deflation to make the payments, and the International Bank for Reconstruction andint Development (better known as the World Bank), which was to help finance the reconstruction of postwar Europe and aid the economic development of former colonies as they gained their independence. Commissions on global financial issues at Bretton Woods were chaired by the United States and the United Kingdom and resulted in the creation of these two organizations; the organizations themselves were set up to favor the interests of the developed world with a European always heading the IMF and a US citizen always heading the World Bank. All signatory nations agreed to peg their currencies to the US dollar with the dollar pegged to gold, and rates were declared changeable only in extreme situations. This arrangement became known as the Bretton Woods system, and it lasted until the US government temporarily took the dollar off the gold standard in 1971, mainly in response to the costs of the Vietnam War at a time of increased domestic spending in the United States. A decline of US gold stocks caused by many nations exchanging their dollar reserves for gold was another factor in the demise of the Bretton Woods system. Therefore, from 1973 currency exchange rates varied as there was no longer a standard exchange mechanism and an earlier attempted repair of the old system had failed.

This Bretton Woods system did oversee a period of economic growth throughout much of the world in the postwar period with many newly independent colonies in Asia and Africa having a period of relatively successful economic growth and some even outperforming the developed world (Chang, 2008, pp. 26–29). However, the 1970s proved to be the start of a different story for these nations as well as for many other semi-periphery and periphery states located mainly in the Global South. The economic woes that fully exploded in the 1980s cannot be attributed to any one factor, as a variety of factors helped to undo earlier economic growth and development. First of all, Western commercial banks were happy to lend huge sums of money to developing nations given the economic growth they had just experienced, and this they did without much care as to the type of governments doing the actual borrowing, or what their rulers did with the money once it was in their hands. Walter Wriston, Citicorp's chairman of the time, famously said "A country does not go bankrupt," thereby downplaying the importance and character of the leaders borrowing in the name of their countries (as cited in Nossiter, 1987, p. 6). This was the start of the developing world's "Odious Debt," as it has since come to be known. By the early 1980s the world's poorest nations were in debt to Western commercial banks to the tune of US$7 billion (Bello, Cunningham, and Rau, 1994).

The oil shocks of the 1970s were a factor in this, as rising oil prices contributed to place the poorer nations in serious financial trouble. This is ironic as the Western developed nations, not the poorer nations, were the targets of the Organization of the Petroleum Exporting Countries' (OPEC) oil price hikes. However, most poorer nations did not have oil resources, nor did they have stockpiles of strategic petroleum reserves like those of their developed counterparts to see them through the crisis. As a result, they had to import oil at the new higher cost without any corresponding increase in their earnings from export commodities to offset fuel costs. The fact that Western consumers paid more for these products from poorer nations did not mean that the poorer nations got more money for their products. The higher costs resulted from oil-producing nations passing on higher prices to oil companies, which in turn passed on these higher costs to shipping companies, which then passed them on to importers who passed them on to consumers.

The poorer nations that supplied the goods and raw materials to the prosperous nations could not pass on high prices as the oil majors did, and this caused their balance of trade to suffer as a result. Paying for expensive imports such as fuel and medicines left them short of money to repay their commercial bank loans.

Another major factor in setting up the then-called "Third World" for an economic fall was economic liberalism. The non-aligned countries had experienced economic growth throughout the 1960s and 1970s, mainly as a result of Cold War tensions. The prosperous West gave some economic and trade leeway to such nations to avoid driving them into the arms and trade blocs of their communist rivals as part of the US containment strategy, but some of the South's demands were seen as excessive by the wealthy nations. For example, the desire for a Special United Nations Fund for Development (SUNFED) was headed off by the creation of the less powerful International Development Agency (IDA) (Bello, Cunningham, and Rau, 1994, p. 11). The IDA was under the control of the US World Bank in contrast to the more open SUNFED, which would have been under the auspices and therefore the control of the more democratic United Nations. However, loans initially enabled the South to grow economically at the time, as the alternative was seen as having the potential to drive these nations into the arms of the communists. So the Third World was able to borrow even more money from the IMF, World Bank, and IDA during this time, and borrowing from the World Bank alone went from an average of US$2.7 billion per annum in the early 1970s to around US$12 billion in the early 1980s (Bello, Cunningham, and Rau, 1994, p. 13).

Unfortunately these good economic times did not survive the coming of the Reagan administration (1981–9), which brought with it the "Reagan Rollback" (Bello, Cunningham, and Rau, 1994, p. 18). Here the effect was indeed deliberate as the South was viewed in a more hostile way by Reagan and his supporters. Although previous lending to the Third World was relatively successful at staving off a mass transition to communism, the expected financial windfalls for Western elites from the Third World did not materialize on the whole—such benefits went to local elites instead as a result of their markets being closed to Western competition. This was seen most clearly in Japan from the 1950s to 1970s. Although Japan was not technically in the Third World, economically it had a lot in common with such nations until the Korean War boom in the early 1950s. Its notoriously closed markets even now are not fully open despite its entry to the WTO and the openness that this is supposed to signal. However, by the late 1970s Japan was no longer a poor nation and was therefore immune to economic and financial attacks via the IMF or World Bank to try to open and dominate its markets. Hypocritically most of the Western developed nations had climbed to their wealthy economic positions by practicing exactly those kinds of closed-market policies in the past, policies they were now denying to developing nations (Chang, 2008, p. 17). Closed-market economies in the Third World now, however, came under attack, and those nations were not as resilient as Japan when economic and financial attacks began in the early 1980s.

Much has been written about the political psyche of the Reagan administration; basically Reagan and his followers rejected Keynesian philosophies in favor of Milton Friedman's free market economics. As such, Reagan began by attacking and rolling back any gains made by the domestic left since Franklin D. Roosevelt's New Deal of the Great Depression. In addition to smashing unions, this also entailed cutting government spending on healthcare benefits, unemployment insurance, education, and other social safety net programs. IMF and World Bank loans to the Third World were similarly targeted by the Reagan regime, and these attacks came in the form of tying aid to furthering US interests and stopping loans to borrowers that did not co-operate (Bello, Cunningham, and Rau, 1994, pp. 18–31). Also the goals tended to be free-market-oriented ones, hardly a surprise given the economic orientation of the Friedman-influenced Reagan team (Klein, 2008). This resulted in the United States cutting its contributions to the IDA by US$300 million in 1982, a move that led to other members of the prosperous North doing the same (Bello, Cunningham, and Rau, 1994, p. 26). More important were the US moves to set up structural adjustment loans (SALs) at the World Bank, the forerunners of the infamous structural adjustment programs (SAPs) that were to come in the mid-to late 1980s.

The SALs forced borrowers to adjust their economic policies before they could get any loans. These adjustments took the form of cutting government spending on social programs that greatly benefited the poor, cutting wages across the board, reducing or removing entirely any protectionist restrictions on imports, privatizing state-owned enterprises (SOEs), allowing foreign investment and ownership of key sectors of the economy including the SOEs, and even the devaluation of currency in some cases. Even an acceptance of these conditions was not enough to guarantee the loan—the borrower nations had to allow the IMF and/or World Bank staff full access to ensure the implementation of these measures (Bello, Cunningham, and Rau, 1994, p. 27). This process transferred economic sovereignty from the state to foreign lending institutions; needless to say, these SALs were not popular with borrower nations and few nations accepted them until the debt crisis of the 1980s left many nations with no choice.

This debt crisis also had its roots partly in US policies under Reagan. In 1981 the Federal Reserve (a private banking institution with little or no government oversight despite its name) under Chairman Paul Volcker increased US interest rates to 21 per cent and kept them near this level for much of the 1980s. And Third World countries ran deeper into debt (Klein, 2008, p. 159). This debt forced many to accept the poisoned chalice of SALs. Adding to this injustice was the Odious Debt incurred when Western commercial banks lent money to dictators knowing full well that the people of the borrowing nations would see little or none of the money, except when it was spent on security forces used to repress them. If and when the people in such places managed to free themselves from totalitarian rule, they still found themselves shackled to repaying loans made to their former oppressors. Indeed, the banks had few qualms demanding full repayment for loans they made to authoritarian leaders who had spent heavily on military hardware and enriched themselves and their supporters. Table 7.1 shows the extent of these loans in four major Latin American borrower nations of the period.

Table 7.1 Loans to Latin American nations (in US$ billions)

	Argentina	**Brazil**	**Chile**	**Uruguay**
Pre-military rule	7.9	3	5	0.5
Post-military rule	45	103	41	5

Source: (Klein, 2008, pp. 156–158).

The "moral hazard" implicit in this arrangement was the fact that power brokers at the IMF, World Bank, and even from within the US government shared interlocking chairmanships and were members of boards of directors of other corporations and banks (Domhoff, 2005). These elite bankers knew they had a very good chance of getting their money back no matter what happened within the borrowing nations. After all, if these debtor nations needed more money, the IMF and World Bank were the only sources of credit for poor nations at this time.

Furthermore, the people in power at the IMF and World Bank also had a shared interest in seeing the commercial banks get their money back. If the commercial banks failed, they all stood to lose financially due to interlocking personal and financial relationships. This would have produced a negative impact on the economies of the banks' host nations, host nations that had most of the power at the IMF and World Bank due to the unequal voting rights. IMF voting rights are granted according to the size of the economies of members, not the one-nation one-vote that a more democratic system would require. As a result, the United States has around 17 per cent of the votes, Japan controls 6 per cent, and the combined European nations make up around 30 per cent. This adds up to democratic inequality on a grand scale, something that even the IMF has recently addressed by pledging to redistribute voting rights (Blustein, 2006, p. A14). Nevertheless, the US government said it would only accept a small cut in its voting power, and China complained that its voting power did not reflect its true status in the world economy. While China had no pretensions of being democratic, it seemed the United States as a self-titled promoter of democracy was contradicting its own professed high standards.

The bottom line for the poor in their time of waning political freedoms and growing economic need was to pay their debts regardless of the banks' culpability in lending the money without care for the risk. This lead to the IMF and World Bank lending ever greater sums of money (at interest of course) to the Third World and displacing the commercial lenders who began to reduce their exposure in the poorer regions. By the time the 1980s were ending, the Cold War was also drawing to a close, and after it actually ended there was no longer any need for Western neoliberal elites to be conciliatory with nations in the developing world. That was when the situation deteriorated for developing nations and former Soviet Bloc borrowers as they found their economic difficulties and situations worsening even as the rich Western nations got richer (Chossudovsky, 2003; Klein, 2008; Stiglitz 2002). It is worth noting that the poor living in the wealthy nations also fared badly, just like their poor counterparts in the developing world (Krugman, 2006).

Chávez regaining the left's past losses in Latin America

These economic woes were particularly devastating in Latin America, located as it is within America's "Backyard" and not the "Core" (Wallerstein, 2004). At the peak of lending activities, 81 per cent of all IMF loans went to Latin America along with all the SALs and SAPs that accompanied these loans. By 2007 that figure was only 1 per cent, a sure sign that democratically elected regional leaders were finally getting out from under the IMF's rule. This dramatic about-turn in Latin American economics came about when Hugo Chávez entered the scene.

Hugo Rafael Chávez Frias was born in 1954, joined the army as a teenager, but was influenced through personal study and early life experiences to embrace Bolivarianism and other left-wing doctrines. He rose through the ranks of the military to lieutenant colonel, was decorated several times, and set up the Revolutionary Bolivarian Movement 200 (MBR200) in 1983 on the 200th anniversary of Simón Bolívar's birth. At this time Venezuela was under the right-wing rule of Luis Herrera Campins and was in the process of moving to the more politically moderate presidency of Jaime Lusinchi. However, external borrowing was rife in both presidencies as indeed it was throughout the region for the reasons described earlier. This borrowing continued throughout their terms and into the second presidential term of the next president, Carlos Andrés Pérez, even though he had campaigned on an anti-IMF, anti-neoliberal economics platform. Shortly after winning the presidency for the second time, Pérez signed a major loan deal with the IMF in return for imposing neoliberal type policies on the country, the very thing voters had elected him to avoid. The protests against this led to his sending in the National Guard, and hundreds of civilians died when troops opened fire on protestors during the Caracazo protests in Caracas (Andrade, 2004). It was this massacre that allegedly prompted Chávez to start plotting his 1992 coup attempt.

The coup was a failure, but Chávez became a hero figure to the poor through his attempt to stand up for them. The next year Pérez was forced to step down by the Supreme Court for a variety of dubious semi-legal activities, and his eventual long-term successor (after a series of presidents that each lasted a few months only), Caldera, was forced to pardon Chávez as a result of popular protests. Once freed, Chávez revived the MBR200 and renamed it the Fifth Republic Movement (MVR). He then started political campaigning along Bolivarian lines and finally came to power in Venezuela in December 1998 when he won the election on an anti-IMF and anti-globalization platform. He received 57 per cent of the popular vote, which was a landslide in practical terms given the fragmented nature of Venezuela politics (Trinkunas and McCoy, 1999).

After taking control in February of the following year Chávez set about instituting policies that went under the name of Plan Bolívar 2000. The beneficiaries of this Plan were the poor underclass as the Plan called for the utilization of 40,000 military personnel to distribute vaccinations and food, as well as building roads to poor outlying areas. Furthermore, the Plan called for low-cost housing for the poor to be built, and the availability of education to be increased. At this time Chávez's rhetoric was largely ignored by the United States as then-ambassador

John Maisto advocated a "soft-line" approach, feeling that Chávez would eventually abandon Bolivarian principles for the same pragmatic reasons that drove many other Latin American leaders to the right after winning power (Ellner, 2005). Indeed, many of Chávez's proposed policies did stall in the National Assembly, resulting in Chávez creating a new Constitutional Assembly after 72 per cent of the electorate voted for it in a landslide referendum victory (McGirk, 1999). Chávez's party gained 95 per cent of the seats, and the poor continued to vote for him when he also won the 2000 election with around 60 per cent of the vote, an increase from the previous last election (Neumann and McCoy, 2001).

By 2001 Chávez had also stopped the privatizations of the social security system and the oil industry and other industrial concerns. Further reforms passed by Chávez gave the state greater control over the oil industry, accompanied by land reform legislation and other measures to benefit the poor majority of Venezuelans. In return, they voted for him consistently. Chávez then became the fifth Venezuelan president to pass the Enabling Act to clear political "logjams." This constitutional Act allows the president to rule by decree for 18 months. However, it does have limitations. Decrees passed under the act must be passed by the Supreme Court; they cannot go against the letter or spirit of the constitution or be used to deprive people of property. Such decrees can only be used in areas pre-set by the assembly, and any law passed by it can be later revoked by public referendum or from within the assembly (Wilpert, 2007). These limitations and constitutional permission did not stop many mainstream mass media outlets from painting it as yet another example of Chávez's dictatorial style of rule, conveniently forgetting his many democratic electoral victories and the previous usage of this act by other Venezuelan presidents—those earlier instances being totally ignored by the same media outlets.

After passing this act, Chávez enacted more laws to benefit the poor, including the Land Law, which gave poor landless people the right to use land to grow food if that land was not being used (Guevara, 2005). He also established a free healthcare and immunization plan, later expanded in 2005 and called the Barrio Adentro, which contributed greatly to lowering infant mortality rates. He also enabled universal university education irrespective of financial means (UNICEF, 2005). Finally, he set about trying to democratize the leadership of the major unions in Venezuela (Neumann and McCoy, 2001, p. 73).

These reforms did not pass unchallenged. In late 2001 a large general strike was called for by reactionary union leaders with the support of management and elites but failed to get widespread support from the majority of the population, mainly the working class and the poor, who benefited from Chávez's reforms. These reforms included universal medical care and a free adult literacy program modeled on that of Cuba; this enabled previously illiterate people to gain the ability to read and write and thus vote for the first time, a move that added many new pro-Chávez voters to the electoral rolls. This unpopular "management strike" was organized against Chávez by senior managers from the state-run petroleum company, who were duly fired for their role in the strike. Compared with many previous right-wing Latin American governments, which had murdered, kidnapped, and otherwise abused political opponents in large numbers (Klein, 2008), Chávez was mild in his treatment of those who broke the law by opposing his policies. Once again, this comparison was omitted in much of the media coverage of the time.

Over the next few months the more affluent sections of Venezuelan society became increasingly hostile to Chávez and his policies while the poorer sections became more supportive. In early April 2002, union leaders again called for another general strike against Chávez and his policies. This call was given huge airplay on all the privately owned TV and radio channels, channels owned by the same powerful interests threatened by Chávez and his reforms. Given the work by Bakan (2005) on corporations and how they operate this was hardly surprising. A selection of the broadcasts of those TV stations in the preceding months and years provides a good understanding of just how strongly they opposed Chávez: news and public affairs shows lampooned him by using impersonators and called for him to be committed to a mental institution. They presented computer-generated images of him wearing Nazi uniforms, implied he was behind gunrunning to Colombian guerrillas, and made numerous other false but damaging slurs (Bartley and O'Brian, 2002; Palacios, 2003; Pilger and Martin, 2007). Guests on such shows all revealed anti-Chávez views, as did their "man in the street" interviews. Very rarely were there any contrasting views broadcast to offer journalistic balance. Not surprisingly, therefore, those media channels were all strongly supportive of the strike and its accompanying protest march (Palacios, 2003). Radio Caracas Television (RCTV), part of the Empresas 1BC group, and headed by Marcel Granier, was one of the most supportive of the strike. Furthermore, the strike was the catalyst that led to the short-lived coup that briefly ousted Chávez, and again RCTV and other privately owned Venezuelan media played a special and pivotal role in this (Andrade, 2004).

There is no doubt that some privately owned media groups in Venezuela are virulently opposed to Chávez, or that they participated in the coup of 11 April 2002. In the days immediately before the coup, four of the major private TV channels (including RCTV) canceled their regular programs and instead aired anti-Chávez speeches urging people to take to the streets in the upcoming protest march and strike (Lendman, 2007a). General Nestor Gonzales even went on television to demand that Chávez resign or be removed (Bartley and O'Brian, 2002). On the day after the coup, private television stations in Venezuela were ecstatic with headlines of "mission accomplished," saying the coup was completed without firing a shot (Bartley and O'Brian, 2002; Palacios, 2003; Pilger and Martin, 2007). Tellingly, the US government under George W. Bush was the only nation in the world to congratulate President Carmona and was implicated in the coup as stories emerged about US military involvement (Campbell, 2002). Furthermore, Carmona used the offices of the privately owned Venevision as a control center during the period immediately before the coup, attempting to take control of the country (Lendman, 2007a). He was ousted less than two days later as hundreds of thousands of angry Venezuelans besieged the presidential palace in Mira Flores demanding the return of Chávez.

When the Venezuelan National Assembly held an enquiry after Chávez was returned to power, RCTV managers testified that they were ordered to withhold any accurate information on Chávez and his officials from the media. Indeed, one broadcaster incorrectly claimed that Chávez had resigned when this was not the case, and RCTV broadcast old movies and cartoons to avoid showing any news of pro-Chávez demonstrations. The private channels even refused to carry news for some time after his subsequent return to power. News of this was broadcast by the state-run TV station, Channel 8, only after pro-Chávez people retook the station from the anti-Chávez protestors who had seized it during the coup (Bartley and O'Brian, 2002; Lendman, 2007a).

There were no mass arrests or retaliatory attacks against the coup plotters in the wake of Chávez's return. According to Chávez, it was his intention to help try and diffuse a still very tense situation. Whatever the reason for the leniency, the local private media were not punished for their role in attempting to thwart the democratic will of the Venezuelan people, and perhaps it was for that reason that they felt secure enough to try to oust Chávez again by supporting or perhaps even organizing a strike by employees of the state-run oil company, Petróleos de Venezuela, S.A. (PDVSA). Chávez weathered this economic storm and afterwards refused to renew the public license of one of the worst media offenders, RCTV, when their lease expired. For this he was accused of censorship even though the station was still able to broadcast on cable and satellite despite being involved in political plotting (Blackmore and Bunscombe, 2007). The reality of this situation has been documented very well elsewhere (Lendman, 2007a), as has the hostility of the mainstream mass media to those viewed as ideological "threats" like Chávez (Herman and Chomsky, 1994), and also US elites' past hostility to such perceived "threats" (Blum, 2000).

Chávez then set up still more programs focused on improving public education after the strike ended, a move that won him further support among the poor. Meanwhile, the rich became even more estranged from him, resorting to a variety of tactics including a failed recall referendum (Chávez won a convincing 59 per cent of the vote), a scheme by right-wing elements in Venezuela to import Colombian mercenaries (BBC, 2004), and a strike by Venezuelan doctors fueled by their loss of income due to Cuban doctors treating people for free under Chávez's health-care reforms. The fact that Venezuelan doctors were asked to participate in the program and refused to take part long before the Cuban doctors were brought in was conveniently omitted from the complaints. Chávez broadened his Bolivarian Revolution horizons economically as he promised to set up another free medical school like the one Cuba currently manages to train an extra 100,000 doctors for the region (Whitney, 2005).

He also set up a PetroCaribe initiative to share affordable oil with poor Caribbean nations at a time when the invasion of Iraq sent oil prices soaring, a move that ironically gave Venezuela the oil sales to fund many programs for the poor. The plan gives them 185,700 barrels a day with 30 per cent of the payment held for 15 years, and a low interest on the deferred payment of a base 2 per cent linked to world oil prices; it also gives low-cost loans and the ability to pay for the oil in goods and services (Howe, 2006). Most of the Caribbean nations quickly signed on to the PetroCaribe initiative, seeing it as an economic lifeline (Williams, 2005), but oil-rich Trinidad and Tobago was one of only two Caribbean nations that did not sign up, which was surprising given the history of IMF intervention in their affairs (Klein, 2008, pp. 260–262). The other was Barbados, which heavily relies on US tourism for its economy.

This bartering of oil for services is particularly threatening to the United States as most of the world's oil sales are carried out in US dollars in New York, and in London. Iraq started selling its oil for euros, which soared as the dollar plummeted. This made the vast dollar foreign-reserve holdings surplus to requirements, and central banks quickly diversified into euros. If the surplus dollars came back to the US en masse, then massive inflation would be the result. Not surprisingly, the US invaded Iraq (under a number of pretexts) and changed Iraqi oil sales back to dollars to try and stave this off (Clark, 2005); however, this oil bartering is not the only reason for US interest in Venezuela. Besides holding large reserves of oil, Venezuela also has one of the largest reserves of tar sands or shale oil as it is sometimes known (Quinn, 2005). In oil industry circles, the term "peak oil" refers to the almost universally accepted theory that global oil production will peak in the next decade and then decrease, slowly at first and more dramatically later. (See the chart in Appendix 1 for a graphical view of those nations that have already peaked; Venezuela, Iran, Iraq, and Saudi Arabia are all absent from this graph as they have not peaked yet.) Therefore, any oil-possessing nation (Venezuela is fifth globally in terms of reserves) that has yet to "peak" and that also has an alternative source of oil (Venezuela is first in terms of reserves of extra heavy crude—the shale oil or tar sands) will be in a very strong position economically and politically. In view of this it is clear that the oil-hungry United States is not keen on seeing Venezuela run along Bolivarian principles.

Given Chávez's cheap, no-strings-attached loans (unlike IMF SAPs), the IMF is not pleased with Chávez either. Venezuela has lent billions to other Latin American nations since Chávez came to power, especially those governed by other leftists discontented with the IMF. This focused lending to support people-friendly projects is also influencing US policies in the region by forcing a competition for hearts and minds. As Chávez expands accessible state-funded medical care programs throughout the region, the US has had to adopt similar polices by using military vessels to dispense medical treatment to sick locals to bolster its tarnished image in the region to compete with Venezuela. However, this is not enough to counter Chávez and the amount of funding he has provided. An example of this was the flooding in Bolivia in 2007. The US gave US$1.5 million while Chávez donated US$15 million and dispatched Venezuelan rescue teams to provide assistance. While the US is trying to compete in this arena, the IMF does not even get involved in such matters at all, meaning it is further being marginalized in the region by Chávez.

Furthermore, the Chávez government has paid off Venezuela's IMF and World Bank loans, refused to borrow more, and encouraged other Latin American governments to do likewise. As much of Latin America has taken a left turn over the last few years (Argentina, Bolivia, Brazil,

Chile, Ecuador, Guatemala, Nicaragua, Panama, Paraguay, and Uruguay have all joined Venezuela and Cuba on the left), many of these newly formed leftist governments have followed Chávez's lead in dealing with the IMF and World Bank, something that is hardly surprising given the two organizations' history in the region (Klein, 2008; Perkins, 2004). Bolivia, under President Morales, went even further than Chávez by expelling World Bank representatives from Bolivia for interfering in domestic policymaking (Lendman, 2007b). Chávez has used the increase in Venezuela's wealth from rising oil prices to further his low-cost loans throughout the region (Global Exchange, 2007), leading to a downturn in overall IMF lending to Latin America. Recent IMF statements show that they have less money to lend than before, and at a time of recession the richer Western nations (except for Japan, which seems to have escaped the worst of the recent financial crisis) are not in any great position to contribute more (IMF, 2009).

The clash of the creditors

Hugo Chávez has lent money throughout the region, a move made possible by high oil prices. Some analysts have argued that he cannot continue these loans on the same scale as before with the recent drop in oil prices. That might be true if the loans all came from oil profits, but Chávez has reformed the way the government acquires revenue from the state-owned oil company via royalties rather than taxes on revenues, and this has actually increased government revenue irrespective of oil prices. Furthermore, Chávez has lobbied the OPEC hard to get members to stick to their quotas to keep prices from dropping (Wilpert, 2003). These actions have made it more likely that Venezuela's lending programs can weather any temporary drop in oil prices, and this current drop in oil prices will in all likelihood be a temporary one given the looming peak-oil scenario's effect on supply and demand.

Chávez's plans for the future also need to be examined. In the past he has made loans on an ad hoc basis without any overarching international economic framework or institutions to work with. Largely this was brought about by contingency as the alternative was better-established neoliberal institutions such as the World Bank or IMF. When the leaders of the left-leaning Latin American nations started paying attention to Chávez's ideas for the creation of a Latin American political and economic union—the Bolivarian Alternative for the Americas (ALBA)—as an alternative to the Free Trade Area of the Americas (FTAA), they worked together and stalled plans to set up the FTAA. To date

ALBA has six members with the possibility of Ecuador joining sometime in the near future as promised by President Correa. In addition to ALBA, Mercosur (Mercado Común del Sur or "Southern Common Market" in English) has shown interest in this economic arena as over half of its members rejected the FTAA treaty at the trade summit in 2005. Venezuela has applied to join Mercosur and is in the process of having its application ratified by member states. Then there is the Andean Community, which has Bolivia, Colombia, Ecuador, and Peru as full members, with Argentina, Brazil, Paraguay, and Uruguay as associate members. Chávez has promised to take Venezuela back into the group. There are a number of groups in the Latin American Caribbean region that cooperate on a variety of economic and trade-related issues. What was missing was a formalized group specifically set up to provide financing to poorer members. This led to the latest part of Chávez's plans to spread the Bolivarian Revolution's Bank of the South, which has the potential to put the IMF totally out of business in the region.

Chávez proposed the Bank as a rival to the IMF and World Bank in South America, and an exploratory meeting was held in Quito, Ecuador, in April 2007. Argentina, Brazil, Bolivia, Colombia (surprisingly given its ties to US neoliberalism), Ecuador, Paraguay, Uruguay, and of course Venezuela, all participated. However, when another meeting was scheduled in Rio de Janeiro, Brazil, in October 2007, Colombia dropped out but very surprisingly asked for membership afterwards. This meeting in Brazil led to the formal creation of the bank on 9 December 2007 and its headquarters was set up in Caracas, Venezuela; however, actual voting rights and finalization of its policies remain uncompleted and many of the members still need to ratify their membership with their electorate and/or assemblies (Almeida, 2008).

Although not yet fully operational, the Bank of the South shows great promise. When it does start making loans it has the potential to be another nail in the IMF's coffin. Not surprisingly, the IMF opposes any such rival taking shape, as demonstrated during the Asian Financial Crisis of 1997 when the IMF blocked Japan's plans to create an Asian Monetary Fund to bail out Asian nations at the time; the benefits of the bailouts would have accrued to Japan alone and not to the other rich IMF members (De Los Reyes and Bello, n.d., p. 2). So the powers behind the IMF are not likely to be keen on the Bank of the South, as it will hurt their power and profits.

Nor is the IMF the only financial organization that will be hurt by the Bank of the South. At present much of Latin America's currency reserves are held at private US banks, and with the intricacies of fractional reserve banking these deposits enable the banks to lend even more money they do not have and thereby increase revenue and profits accordingly. However, Chávez has said that Venezuela will put 10 per cent of its reserves into the Bank of the South and many other Latin American nations are likely to follow suit (Bretton Woods Project, 2007). The many areas in which the Bank of the South can compete with the IMF and hold the moral high ground are covered elsewhere (Toussaint, 2007), but needless to say the IMF and its wealthy backers are deeply worried about the trend being set by the Bank of the South, especially if it encourages similar actions in other regions.

Actions against the IMF are being encouraged around the globe. Davison Budhoo is an economist from Grenada who worked for the IMF until 1988 when he resigned because of what he called its increasingly genocidal policies and its manipulation of data to achieve its ends (Klein, 2008). He and many others have been advocating a different way for years (Danaher, 1994). Many of these alternatives, such as Muhammad Yunus' Grameen Bank, do actually benefit people rather than the powerful, but they are not really intruding on the IMF's sphere of influence, and this is where the Bank of the South is different. It will offer a real alternative to the IMF for poor nations, directly operating in areas that were formerly the domain of the IMF. If it is successful other regional imitators may also spring into existence, an eventuality the IMF and it supporters do not want to see happen.

Conclusion

Neoliberal economic policies promoted by the IMF since the 1970s have left a terrible legacy in Latin America. As a result the IMF is not looked on with any great favor by the majority of those who live in the region. Unfortunately for the IMF, democracy springs from majority rule, and that majority has finally been able to oppose the neoliberal economic policies of the IMF in deed as well as word. Hugo Chávez is at the forefront of this anti-IMF, anti-neoliberal, and anti-globalization movement, and he is using Venezuela's oil wealth and resources to further this cause.

These sentiments are leading to success in Latin America despite the recent drop in oil prices. The effect of economic supply and demand on oil prices for the long term combined with Chávez's reforms of Venezuela's oil industry in the short term would seem to indicate that there will be no shortage of money to fund his Bolivarian Revolution now or in the foreseeable future. This spells big trouble for the IMF, which has already seen its loans to Latin America go from 81 per cent of its portfolio to 1 per cent in recent years, largely as a result of the leftward swing in Latin America politics and the effects of this swing on regional borrowing from the IMF.

If the Bank of the South firmly establishes itself and starts dispensing loans it could sound the death knell for the IMF and its neoliberal economic policies in Latin America. If this happens, then the example being set could encourage other regions of the developing world to set up similar banks to aid their economic growth and further diminish the influence of the IMF. Then the debt beast that has enriched the North at the expense of the South will hopefully be slain once and for all, and economic development can finally be something that is available to all nations.

Appendix 1

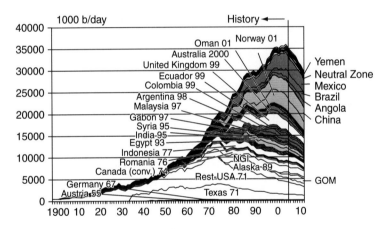

Source: Industry database, 2003 (IHS 2003)
OGJ, 9 Feb 2004 (Jan–Nov 2003).

References

Alvares de Azevedo e Almeida, T. (27 May 2008). Still on the drawing board: The Banco del Sur a half year later. *Council on Hemispheric Affairs*. Retrieved 25 February 2009, from http://www.coha.org/2008/05/still-on-the-drawing-board-the-banco-del-sur-a-half-year-later/.

Andrade, M. (director) (2004). *Venezuela Bolivariana: People and struggle of the Fourth World War*. [Motion Picture]. Venezuela: Calley Media.

Bakan, J. (2005). *The corporation: The pathological pursuit of profit and power*. New York: Free Press.

Bartley, K., and O'Brian, D. (directors) (2002). *The Revolution will not be televised.* [Documentary]. UK: British Venezuela Solidarity Campaign.

BBC (2004). Colombian plotters face charges. *BBC News Online.* Retrieved 25 February 2009 from http://news.bbc.co.uk/2/hi/americas/3840087.stm.

Bello, W., Cunningham, S., and Rau, B. (1994). *Dark victory: The United States, structural adjustment and global poverty.* Manila: Freedom from Debt Coalition Press.

Black, S. (producer/director) (2001). *Life and debt.* [Documentary]. Jamaica: Tuff Gong Pictures Production.

Blackmore, L., and Bunscombe, A. (10 May 2007). Chavez accused of censorship over threat to close TV station. *The Independent.* Retrieved 25 February 2009 from http://www.independent.co.uk/news/world/americas/chavez-accused-of-censorship-over-threat-to-close-tv-station-448187.html.

Blum, W. (2000). *Rogue state: A guide to the world's only superpower.* Monroe, ME: Common Courage Press.

Blustein, P. (23 April 2006). China's rise prompts IMF to reallocate voting power. *The Washington Post.* Retrieved 1 March 2009, from http://www.washingtonpost.com/wp-dyn/content/article/2006/04/22/AR2006042201246.html.

Bretton Woods Project (2 April 2007). Bank of the South to challenge IMF or IDB? Retrieved 14 March 2007, from http://www.brettonwoodsproject.org/art-552120.

Campbell, D. (2002). American navy helped Venezuelan coup. *The Guardian.* Retrieved 9 February 2009, from http://www.guardian.co.uk/world/2002/apr/29/venezuela.duncancampbell.

Chang, H.-J. (2008). *Bad Samaritans: The guilty secrets of rich nations and the threat to global prosperity.* London: Random House.

Chossudovsky, M. (2003) *The Globalization of poverty and the New World Order.* Ontario: Global Outlook.

Clark, W. (2 August 2005). Petrodollar warfare: Dollars, Euros and the upcoming Iranian Oil Bourse. *Energy Bulletin.* Retrieved 23 February 2009, from http://www.energybulletin.net/node/7707.

Danaher, K. (ed.) (1994). *50 years is enough: The case against the World Bank and the International Monetary Fund.* Cambridge, MA: South End Press.

De Los Reyes, J., and Bello, W. (n.d.). Can the IMF Be reformed? *Forums SocioEco.* Retrieved 14 March 2009, from http://www.forums.socioeco.org/d_read/intreg/IMF_delosreyes_bello.pdf.

Domhoff, G. W. (2005). *Who rules America?* New York: McGraw-Hill.

Ellner, S. (2005). Venezuela's "demonstration effect": Defying globalization's logic. North American Congress on Latin America (NACLA) from *Venezuela Analysis.* Retrieved 27 February 2009, from http://www.venezuelanalysis.com/articles.php?artno=1579.

Global Exchange (2007). Venezuela offers billions to countries in Latin America. Retrieved 14 March 2009, from http://www.globalexchange.org/countries/americas/venezuela/4949.html.

Guevara, A. (2005). *Chavez, Venezuela and the new Latin America: An interview with Hugo Chavez.* New York: Ocean Press.

Herman, E. S., and Chomsky, N. (1994). *Manufacturing consent: The political economy of the mass media.* London: Vintage.

188   *Financial Flows, Human Rights, and the Global South*

Howe, D. (13 March 2006). Urban life: Darcus Howe senses a power shift. *New Statesman*. Retrieved 24 February 2009, from http://www.newstatesman.com/200603130016.
International Monetary Fund (IMF) (19 February 2009). IMF gains new funding, puts focus on bank clean up. IMF website. Retrieved 1 March 2009, from http://www.imf.org/external/about/histend.htm.
Klein, N. (2008). *The shock doctrine*. London: Penguin.
Krugman, P. (30 November 2006). The great wealth transfer. *Rolling Stone*. Retrieved 1 March 2009, from http://www.rollingstone.com/politics/story/12699486/paul_krugman_on_the_great_wealth_transfer.
Lendman, S. (25 January 2007a). RCTV and its acts of sedition. *Venezuela Analysis*. Retrieved 25 February 2009, from http://www.venezuelanalysis.com/analysis/2192.
Lendman, S. (29 October 2007b). The Bank of the South. *Global Research*. Retrieved 1 March 2009, from http://www.globalresearch.ca/index.php?context=va&aid=7207.
McGirk, T. (December 1999). Hugo Chávez Frías. *Time Magazine*. Retrieved 26 February 2009, from http://www.time.com/time/europe/magazine/1999/1227/chavez.html.
Neumann, L., and McCoy, J. (February 2001). Observing political change in Venezuela: The Bolivarian constitution and 2000 elections. *The Carter Center*. Retrieved 25 February 2009, from http://www.cartercenter.org/documents/297.pdf.
Nossiter, B. (1987). *The global struggle for more*. New York: Harper and Row.
Palacios, A. (director) (2003). *Llaguno Bridge: Keys to a massacre* [Documentary]. Global Exchange.
Perkins, J. (2004). *Confessions of an economic hitman*. San Francisco: Berrett-Koehler Publishers Inc.
Pilger, J., and Martin, C. (directors) (2007). *The war on democracy* [Documentary]. Lions Gate Home Entertainment.
Quinn, T. (16 July 2005). Turning tar sands into oil. *Energy Bulletin*. Retrieved 27 February 2009, from http://www.energybulletin.net/node/7331.
Stiglitz, J. (2002). *Globalization and its discontents*. London: Penguin.
Toussaint, E. (2007). *Bank of the South: An alternative to the IMF-World Bank*. Mumbai: Vikas Adhyayan Kendra.
Trinkunas, H., and McCoy, J. (1999). Observation of the 1998 Venezuelan elections: A report of the council of freely elected heads of government. *The Carter Center*. Retrieved 1 March 2009, from http://www.cartercenter.org/documents/1151.pdf.
UNICEF (January–March 2005). Venezuela's Barrio Adentro: A model of universal primary healthcare. *Immunization Plus Quarterly eNewsletter*. Retrieved 23 February 2009, from http://www.unicef.org/french/infobycountry/files/IPlusQuarterlyeNewsletterJanMarch2005.pdf.
Wallerstein, E. (2004). *World systems analysis: An introduction*. Durham, NC: Duke University Press.
Whitney, Jr, W. T. (1 September 2005). Cuba graduates doctors from over 20 Nations. *People's Weekly World*. Retrieved 24 February 2009, from http://www.pww.org/article/articleprint/7636/.

Williams, C. J. (13 September 2005). Chavez extends an oil-rich hand to neighbors. *Los Angeles Times.* Retrieved 24 February 2009, from http://articles. latimes.com/2005/sep/13/world/fg-petrocaribe13.

Wilpert, G. (30 August 2003). The economics, culture and politics of oil in Venezuela. *Venezuela Analysis.* Retrieved 24 February 2009, from http://www. venezuelanalysis.com/analysis/74.

Wilpert, G. (6 February 2007). Venezuela's enabling law could also enable the opposition. *Venezuela Analysis.* Retrieved 24 February 2009, from http://www. venezuelanalysis.com/analysis/2213.

Part IV
Genocide in Global Perspective

8

The Role of Globalization in the Causes, Consequences, Prevention, and Punishment of Genocide

Maureen S. Hiebert

Introduction

Humanitarian intervention aside, genocide is usually identified with the internal dynamics of a society rather than globalization. Most studies on the causes and processes of genocide link the outbreak of genocidal violence to domestic factors such as a history of ethnic, racial, or class divisions between groups in society, radical exclusionary ideology, instability (political, social, and/or economic), and the dehumanization and demonization of the victim group as a dangerous "enemy within." These factors and processes, however, are not strictly endogenous to societies. At least some factors such as societal divisions, radical ideology, and instability often find their origins in the wider global context, particularly in the case of genocides in the developing world. Colonialism brought to many parts of the Global South exclusionary conceptions of race, nationalism, political ideologies such as Marxism, economic exploitation, and various policies that pitted different societal groups against each other. In the post-colonial period many of these legacies of colonialism set the stage for state-directed attempts to exterminate entire groups of people. The more recent and more thoroughly globalized era has seen globalization contribute to the perpetration of genocide through an easily accessible arms trade in full view of a well informed but seemingly indifferent interconnected world.

Genocide has also shaped the globalized world in which we now live. Provided media organizations are sufficiently interested, new communications technology allows for the dissemination of information about acts of genocide to governments, intergovernmental organizations (IGOs), non-governmental organizations (NGOs), and ordinary people throughout the world. Our increasing ability to know about the perpetration of genocidal violence in real time even when it takes place in relatively remote parts of the world has given impetus to the emergence of an increasingly strong anti-genocide norm. This norm has motivated NGOs, both local and global, to contemplate the need to prevent and stop genocide as well as assist the victims. IGOs and states, who have been rightly criticized for failing to take heed of ample warnings of potential or actual genocides in the last few decades, are no longer in the position to credibly say that they do not know when or if genocide is occurring. Because of this knowledge of genocidal violence, states have largely agreed among themselves that genocide is an unpardonable act. The belief that genocide is *jus cogens*, a peremptory norm that prohibits genocidal policies under any and all circumstances, has also given rise to a robust body of international human rights and international criminal treaty and case law that has made the actual or attempted destruction of entire groups of people simply because of who they are not only immoral but illegal—the ultimate "crime of crimes" under international law. International criminal tribunals and the permanent International Criminal Court (ICC) have been created to try individuals accused of committing genocide and other atrocity crimes.

In the analysis that follows several linkages between genocide, globalization, and, to an extent, development will be explored. It must be stressed that these linkages are not directly causal in nature. Genocide is simply too complex a phenomenon to be the result of one or only a few variables. Globalization is instead a dynamic modern context within which genocide has and continues to happen. Further, in the modern era, genocides have been perpetrated during periods of both low global connectedness (e.g. the Armenian genocide during World War I, the Nazi Holocaust during World War II, and one of the cases explored in this chapter, the Cambodian genocide from 1975 to 1979) and high global connectedness (e.g. Bosnia, Darfur, and the second case in this chapter, the Rwandan genocide in 1994). As such, it cannot be argued that globalization "causes" genocide. Rather, the argument is that it is the indirect effect of an earlier colonial form of globalization in concert with largely domestic factors that have in the long run contributed to the perpetration of genocidal violence in the developing world. In the contemporary more thoroughly globalized world, globalization, either as a phenomenon or a process, does not cause genocide either, but it does provide the capacity to make genocidal violence possible, even for poor states, through the international arms trade. Genocide itself, meanwhile, affects the globalized world by exporting the negative consequences of genocide beyond national borders in the form of refugee flows and insecurity. At the same time globalization facilitates the free flow of information about genocidal violence that in turn shapes norms against gross human rights abuses and enhances the will to punish those who perpetrate such crimes, and possibly to intervene and stop them from happening.

If the linkages between genocide and globalization are varied and at times tenuous, the linkages between genocide, development, and globalization are even more so. One could argue, following the arguments of anti-globalization scholars and activists, that economic globalization is tantamount to the exploitation of much of the developing world, and that this exploitation, coupled with draconian adjustment policies demanded by the world's development assistance institutions, create dire economic circumstances that seriously impair the economic and social rights of millions of people, and that these circumstances in turn fuel intergroup conflicts and even genocide. While a *prima facia* case of this kind may be made in the cases of Darfur or Rwanda, it would likely be quite difficult to establish with concrete empirical evidence such a direct causal chain of events. And in other historical cases such as the Holocaust during the global economic chaos of World War II, or isolationist Cambodia in South-East Asia after the US withdrawal from Vietnam in 1975, or more recently in Bosnia, which remained relatively untouched by the vagaries of economic globalization after the collapse of communism, globalization and its possible relationship to a lack of development cannot explain the implementation of genocidal policies by the state or other actors. Moreover, genocide has occurred in both less developed (e.g. Cambodia, Rwanda, Darfur) and relatively more developed (e.g. Nazi-occupied Europe) societies. It is also important to note that in the current globalized era there are undoubtedly several societies in the Global South that have ended up getting the short end of the economic globalization stick, but mercifully the vast majority of them have not experienced genocidal violence. While it is tempting to blame globalization for all of the world's evils, genocide is one sin for which globalization is not exclusively responsible.

Definitional issues

Before beginning the analysis a few brief comments are in order about how globalization, human rights, and genocide will be defined in this chapter. As the introduction implies, globalization is conceptualized here as both a condition (globalism) and a historical process (Van Der Bly, 2005, p. 881). As a condition, globalization describes a situation of significant and increasing interconnectedness across time and space. As a process, globalization is seen here as a specifically modern process that is qualitatively new but that has its roots in earlier processes of the sixteenth to nineteenth centuries—namely, the spread of trade among the great powers and European colonialism in the Americas, Asia, and Africa. As Van Der Bly (2005) notes, such a view of globalization does not suggest that globalization as we experience it now is simply a different form of something that has been around for a long time. Rather, globalization is a relatively new phenomenon that is qualitatively different from what has come before; however, globalization has nonetheless grown out of earlier global processes and conditions, like colonialism, which have set the stage for the development of the globalized world of today. Globalization in this chapter is also taken to be multidimensional rather than unidimensional. Unidimensional views of globalization see globalization typically as driven by and consisting primarily of economic connections across societies around the globe. The multidimensional view of globalization used here sees globalization as a complex web of economic, social, cultural, and legal connections and influences around the world.

Following Helen Fein's (2007) typology, human rights are defined and categorized here into three kinds of rights. The most fundamental human rights, the violations of which constitute the most serious human rights abuses, are what Fein calls "life integrity rights." These rights are distinguished from the two other categories of rights: civil and political rights and "subsistence rights," such as access to food and other economic and social rights (Fein, 2007, p. 5). For Fein, life integrity rights include the right to life, the right to "personal inviolability" (the right not to be hurt), the right to be free of fear of arbitrary seizure, detention, and punishment, freedom of one's body and labor, the right to free movement without discrimination, and the right to procreate and cohabit with one's family. Genocide, as a systematic form of direct and indirect causing of mass death intended to bring about the destruction of a group in whole or in part, based on the real or perceived identity of the members of the group, constitutes the most egregious violation of life integrity rights; that is, the right both as an individual and as a member of a racial, ethnic, religious, national, political, socioeconomic, or other group to continue to physically exist. This definition of genocide goes beyond the legal definition of the crime of genocide codified in the 1948 United Nations Convention on the Prevention and

Punishment of the Crime of Genocide (UNCPPCG) by including political and socioeconomic groups, and potentially other groups as well. Broadening the definition recognizes that the exclusive list of groups named in Article I of the UNCPPCG was more the result of a political compromise rather than based on sound analyses about the actual "mutability" or "primordial" nature of human groups (Kuper, 1981, pp. 19–39), and that genocidal violence has been perpetrated against political and socioeconomic groups as well as against ethnic, racial, national, and religious groups (Chalk and Jonassohn, 1990, pp. 25–26). Indeed, genocide has and can be perpetrated against any group, real or imagined, that has been constructed by the perpetrator (Chalk and Jonassohn, 1990, p. 23) as an overwhelmingly powerful mortal "enemy within" that must be exterminated in order to save a nation, race, or revolution from "certain" destruction (Hiebert, 2008, pp. 11–13).

Setting the stage for genocide: colonialism and the spread of modern ideas

The advent of European colonialism in the Americas and later in Asia and Africa not only brought with it genocidal violence perpetrated by supposedly superior colonizers against supposedly inferior indigenous populations sitting on valuable land and resources, it also sowed the seeds of exterminationist policies that would be conceived and executed years later by independent states in the post-colonial period against segments of their own populations. These legacies of colonialism were uniquely modern European ideas such as "race," "nation," and "class" as well as exploitative and discriminatory practices. Such ideas and practices, while intimately tied to the colonial project, played largely an indirect role in laying the groundwork for the genocides of the post-independence period by establishing a latent potential for the physical destruction of groups made manifest by more proximate and specifically local triggers for genocidal violence.

The concepts of nation, race, and class that originated in Europe and spread around the world with colonialism represented uniquely "modern ways of understanding and organizing human difference" (Weitz, 2003, p. 17). Although the pre-modern world divided groups into different categories who often did terrible things to each other because of real and perceived group identities, it was not until the modern era and the advent of categories like nation and race that group identities came to be seen as fixed, immutable, or "primordial." So conceived, human communities in the modern era became closed communities deemed to be characterized by commonly held histories, languages, cultures, religions, and, in the case of race, physical, intellectual, and even moral capacities, all encased in a relatively inflexible shell that separated and hierarchically ordered groups relative to one another. This, of course, was not the reality of intergroup relationships within and between societies at the time, or at any other time in human history, but this was how many political and intellectual elites in Europe (and later in other "developed" parts of the Global North) increasingly saw the world.

The concept of "nation" found its origin and lifeblood in the French and American revolutions in which membership in and fidelity to the nation became synonymous ideationally and politically with the revolution itself and citizenship in the new revolutionary political community. Although born alongside emancipatory concepts like democracy and rights, "nation" began as an exclusionary concept that left out ethnic and religious minorities, women, and, in the colonial world, slaves and indigenous populations (Levene, 2005, pp. 147–150). Limited conceptions of membership in the nation in the emerging democracies of Western Europe and North America in turn circumscribed the reach of both democracy and rights such that groups who were denied membership in the nation were also denied full participation in the democratic political community and access to rights granted by the community. By the early twentieth century appeals to membership in a national community by an emerging generation of indigenous leaders would inspire anti-colonial national liberation struggles in Asia and Africa, but in the post-independence period it would also fuel—as we will see in the Rwandan case—genocidal policies aimed at groups deemed to be foreign and hostile to the "real" national community.

It was, however, the rise of "race-thinking" and the conception of humanity as naturally divided into "superior" and "inferior" races that set the stage for some of the most destructive genocides of the twentieth century. The modern academic discipline of anthropology, along with the continuing secularization of modern European society, gave to the human body a different and ultimately dangerous meaning. Secularization and the influence of scientific thinking (Bartov, 1996, pp. 3–5; Rubenstein, 1975, p. 54) set the body free from Christian values that saw the body as ephemeral "to become a symbol of a different sort," as a "racialized" body that "now became the outer marker of inner worth, or of inner damnation," which could simultaneously be classified according to supposedly scientific principles just like plants, other animals, rocks, and fossils (Haas, 1999, p. 52; Weitz, 2003, pp. 26–27). Employing a perversion of Charles Darwin's theory of evolution, the

Social Darwinists of the nineteenth century further argued that races were fundamentally unequal, that races were defined by a specific set of intellectual and moral traits found among the members of the race, that race determined a people's destiny, that the decline of civilizations could be traced to "race-mixing," and that the only way to prevent such an unhappy demise was to engage in "purification through purges, an engineered process of weeding out unwanted traits and people to achieve a healthier and more accomplished race" (Weitz, 2003, pp. 34, 36). The tendency to see different "races" of people as inferior, polluting, and therefore dangerous was heavily influenced and reinforced by contact between Europeans and hitherto unknown human groups in the South whose physical appearance, customs, religions, and languages varied significantly from the European colonizers'. Added to this was the reality that Europeans regularly took ill in unfamiliar lands or succumbed to tropical diseases, thus further solidifying in their minds the notion that indigenous populations were not only racially inferior "savages," but the source of real biological contamination, disease, and even death (Weitz, 2003, p. 39).

The final concept that made its entry, albeit much more indirectly, into the South via colonialism, was class. While a modern European concept like nation and race, class was not an idea used by colonial officials themselves to understand the nature of colonial economic relationships. It became, however, a key concept for many anti-colonial national liberation movements, following the Russian Revolution in 1917. Karl Marx and Friedrich Engels' identification of class as based on prevailing modes of economic production and, more importantly, the location of the source of economic exploitation in class relationships grounded in the relations of economic production resonated with the anti-colonial leadership in several parts of Asia and Africa. Coupled with Vladimir Lenin's thesis that imperialism was the final stage of late capitalism, class analysis seemed to explain the economic rationale for colonialism, the reasons for what clearly appeared to be, from the perspective of the colonized, an exploitative economic relationship between the home countries and the colonies, as well as a prescription not only for terminating an intolerable situation and achieving independence, but also for the creation of a new, better, and more equitable society. However, different anti-colonial leaders took different lessons from European Marxists. Some, such as Julius Nyerere of Tanzania, emphasized equality and development while others, like China's Mao Zedong and the Vietnamese revolutionary leader Ho Chi Minh, adopted and refined strategies for fighting revolutionary warfare. As we shall see, the lessons learned from Marx, Mao, Lenin, and most importantly, Stalin, by the extremist and ultimately genocidal Khmer Rouge in Cambodia was that classes were, as with race, supposedly immutable identities. Certain classes were seen as naturally and eternally exploitative, as permanently outside of and hostile to the revolutionary struggle, and therefore in need of physical liquidation (Jackson, 1989, p. 241).

Cambodia

The genocide in Cambodia was perpetrated against several groups in Cambodian society by the ruling Khmer Rouge from April 1975 to early January 1979. The majority of victims were ethnic Khmers, the dominant ethnic group of which the Khmer Rouge themselves were members, in addition to the minority Vietnamese, Chinese, and mixed Sino-Khmer populations and the Muslim Chams. Most of the Khmer victims were slated for elimination because of their socioeconomic class identity as middle-class urbanites from the capital Phnom Penh and other cities and towns. Similarly, in the latter years of Khmer Rouge rule thousands of Khmer Rouge cadres from within the ruling communist movement itself were also victimized because of their allegedly "hidden" counterrevolutionary class affiliations. The Vietnamese minority was almost completely exterminated during the genocide because of the supposed racial identity of the victims, while Khmers, many of them revolutionary cadres, who had lived and trained in Vietnam during the 1960s and early 1970s, were liquidated because they were seen as either closet Vietnamese ("Khmer bodies with Vietnamese minds," as the expression went) or as secret agents for Hanoi. Although the triggers for the genocide included a number of specifically local economic, political, and security crises of the 1960s and early 1970s that both preceded the genocide and facilitated the rise of the Khmer Rouge to power, the adoption by the Khmer Rouge of a radical exterminationist hybrid Maoist/Stalinist ideology in the 1950s, and the identification of the urban middle class (the so-called "new people"), suspect cadres, and the Vietnamese and other minorities as implacable enemies of the new revolutionary order requiring extermination, found their roots in the concepts of class and race, along with exclusionary colonial practices.

Relatively ethnically homogeneous, pre-colonial Cambodia was nonetheless an already hierarchically ordered society. At the top of a tripartite socioeconomic hierarchy sat the king and a very small group of court officials and their families, followed by a slightly larger group of merchants, many of whom were ethnic Chinese and Sino-Khmers, living in regional towns and villages, who acted as middlemen by purchasing and selling rice and other agricultural products cultivated by what was by far the largest and lowest rung in society, the peasantry. When the French established a protectorate in Cambodia in 1863 along with other possessions in Indochina (present-day Laos and Vietnam), colonial administrators relied on two groups to act as local officials for a poorly staffed and underfunded colonial administration. One was the urban-based ethically Khmer royal courtiers and the other was the Vietnamese minority. The former were recruited into the colonial administration because of their presence in the capital Phnom Penh and other regional centers, their experience with government administration, and the need to placate a small but hitherto powerful strata now displaced by the French. Aside from a similar presence in urban areas, the Vietnamese minority was tapped as a source of administrative manpower for a different reason. The Vietnamese in Cambodia's much more powerful neighbor to the east, Vietnam, long saw themselves as the region's natural masters—superior in intellect, vigor, and martial skill to Khmers. The French, having already colonized Vietnam, agreed, and came to regard the Vietnamese in Cambodia as racially superior to Cambodia's purportedly backward, slothful, fatalistic Buddhist Khmer peasantry who would not and could not be modernized, francophonized, or Christianized. Exclusionary colonial policies flowed from these ideas. Aside from paid employment in the colonial administration, young Vietnamese and urban Khmer elites destined for colonial service were offered a French rather than a traditional Buddhist education. By the twentieth century this privileged education included primary and secondary school in Cambodia's urban centers, and, for a select few, post-secondary education in France. Believing that the Vietnamese were more industrious and thus amenable to modern capitalist economic production, French rubber plantation owners also tended to hire Vietnamese wage laborers over Khmers.

The explicit privileging of these two groups created urban–rural, class-based, and racial antagonisms between the vast majority of Cambodia's rural peasant population and urban Khmers and the Vietnamese minority during the colonial period and beyond. Urban–rural antagonism was also fostered during the colonial period by the perception among the urban elite that the peasantry existed to support the growing prosperity in the cities. Many members of this elite simply took the peasantry who worked in agriculture, forestry, and the fisheries for granted (Chandler, 1991, p. 181). As the cities became more westernized and prosperous, "the city folk began to regard peasants, not just as people who were poorer or less refined, but, because of the agricultural slack season, as people who did not work hard enough" (Vickery, 1984, p. 24). Following independence urban elites also believed that it was entirely appropriate for the revenues generated from the sale of rice, other crops, and raw materials extracted from the countryside to be used to finance an increasingly luxurious urban lifestyle instead of reinvestment in the rural economy. Rampant corruption by government officials and army officers did little to diminish the offenders' sense of personal entitlement at the expense of others, including the peasantry (Vickery, 1984, p. 16). Ironically it was the post-secondary, post-graduate education in France available to urban Khmer elites like Khieu Samphan, Ieng Sary, Ieng Thirith (later Sary's wife), and Saloth Sar (later known as "Brother Number One," Pol Pot) that would introduce Marxist class analysis and Stalinist purge tactics to some of the core leaders of what would become the Khmer Rouge.

Immediately after their victory in 1975 following a six-year civil war against the anti-communist Lon Nol regime, the Khmer Rouge leadership of the newly renamed Democratic Kampuchea set out to radically transform Cambodia into a thoroughly egalitarian rural economy and society shorn of any private wealth, property, or even money. Convinced that the urban middle class was perpetually locked in a series of "life and death contradictions" with the revolutionarily pure "based people" (peasantry) in the countryside, the party, and the revolutionary army, the Khmer Rouge drew on the ideological concepts taught to them by their fellow French communist party members in the 1950s to fashion an exterminationist communist ideology that built the foundations for genocidal policies aimed at the urban "new people," suspect Khmer Rouge cadres, and the Chinese and Sino-Khmer merchant class. The clearly perceived but in actuality non-existent threat posed by supposedly powerful class enemies, regardless of their thorough defeat in the civil war and complete subjugation by the new regime, could only be met with a genocidal "final solution." Over the next three years the new people would be repeatedly deported on long death marches to often remote parts of the country, where they were deliberately denied adequate food, water, shelter, and medical care, or "invited to study with *Ankar*" (code for torture and summary execution). These clearly genocidal policies were intended both as a means of punishing the regime's class enemies for their earlier position at the top of the Cambodian socioeconomic hierarchy and as a method for ensuring that what was constructed as a hopelessly and inherently counterrevolutionary class could not live to destroy Democratic Kampuchea from within. At the same time, the small Chinese and Sino-Khmer minorities were similarly targeted during the genocide largely because of their class identity as urban merchants, traders, and creditors, while the Muslim Chams were victimized because of their supposedly divided loyalties between the revolution and Islam. The much larger Vietnamese minority was singled out for almost complete extermination as a previously privileged and supposedly dangerous racial enemy tied by blood to a powerful predatory regional power.

Rwanda

The Rwandan genocide stands as the most intensive outbreak of genocidal killing to date, measured by the number killed over a specific period of time. In only three months, from early April 1994 to early July of the same year, approximately 800,000 men, women, and children from the country's Tutsi minority were killed along with moderate majority Hutus who opposed the killing. Constituting about 10 per cent of the total population of Rwanda, the Tutsis were targeted for extermination because of their perceived membership in a separate and dangerous race that threatened the dominant position of the majority Hutus and a political regime based on what was called "Hutu Power" ideology. This ideology, which preached that Rwanda was the land of the Hutus and as such should be ruled by the majority Hutu population, found its origins in a particularly exclusionary conception of the nation. Meanwhile the identification of the Tutsi minority as a rival threatening "enemy within" rested on a racialized understanding of the two main populations that made up Rwandan society. Both the concepts of race and nation came to Rwanda through the identification of colonial Rwanda's populations by their Belgian colonial masters as members of different races who, because of alleged racial differences, were thought to be destined for different roles in the life in the colony, and later the independent nation of Rwanda. As with Cambodia, it was the ideational and policy legacies of colonialism that in part set the stage for the killing to come decades later.

When the first Europeans arrived in the region of Central Africa in what is now Rwanda they found three different groups of people, the majority of whom were farmers called Hutus, a smaller group of mostly pastoralists called Tutsis, and the Twas, a much smaller (physically and proportionally) pygmy population. To Europeans like the British explorer Hanning Speke and later the German (1890–1916) and Belgian (1923–59) colonizers, the two main groups not only seemed to carry out different roles in the local economy (although there were in fact Hutus who were pastoralists and Tutsis who were farmers), they also appeared to be physically different from each other. The Hutus were short and stocky with typical Bantu features while the Tutsi were tall and thin with fine facial features. From the colonizers' perspective Rwandan society seemed to be structured along European-like feudal lines with the minority Tutsis apparently sitting atop the economic, political, and social hierarchy. This was a gross oversimplification of the complexities of Rwandan economic and political culture and structure but it suited the race-thinking that was common among European colonizers at the time. If the Tutsis looked different and controlled the economic and political system, European commentators and colonial officials concluded that the Tutsis must originally be from somewhere else—most likely northern Africa, closer to "civilized" Europe—and therefore were a different, "superior race"(Prunier, 1995, pp. 5–8).

Whether the Tutsis really did originate outside of Central Africa and migrated over a lengthy period, or whether they were in fact indigenous to the region and constituted a socioeconomic category is not the main issue with respect to explaining the origins of the race-thinking that fueled the 1994 genocide. What is important is that German and Belgian colonial administrations constructed the Tutsis and Hutus as different and hierarchically ordered races. In making this distinction and then giving it the force of law, colonial ideas and practices constructed the Hutus as an indigenous race and the Tutsis (as well as the even more supposedly superior Europeans) as non-indigenous (Mamdani, 2001, pp. 26–27). Like the Vietnamese in French colonial Indochina, the Tutsis became a privileged minority, provided with a superior European education, and drafted into the colonial administration. And just to ensure that the Belgians could tell who was who, even though Hutus and Tutsis supposedly were from different racial groups and looked distinct from each other, members of each group (and the Twa) were issued identity cards that clearly indicated the racial identity of each card holder. This issuing of identity cards would survive into the post-colonial period and would be instrumental during the genocide in allowing the perpetrators to identify their victims.

The race-thinking of the Belgians also outlived the colonial period in the form of a particularly exclusionary racialized conception of the nation. Because the Belgians conceptualized Hutu and Tutsis as separate races, the former indigenous and the latter not, Hutu elites came to construct the Rwandan nation as a nation for the indigenous Hutus to the exclusion of what they believed was the unfairly privileged and "foreign" Tutsis. This understanding of the Rwandan nation was given impetus by the Belgian administration's decision to change policies in the late 1950s and begin politically and economically favoring the majority Hutu population as Belgium readied Rwanda for independence. The result once independence came in 1962 was that Hutu elites understood democracy to, in fact, be ethnic majority rule, and that membership in the political community was a racialized form of ethnic rather than civic citizenship in which most social and economic rights could only be claimed through membership in a "native," in this case Hutu, community (Mamdani, 2001, p. 29).

At the same time, the colonial practice of conceptualizing and treating Hutus and Tutsis as separate races eventually resulted in the creation of two separate racialized political communities across which, at least from the Hutu point of view, no common ground, and therefore identity, could be found. Even though the Hutu elite backed by the Hutu majority assumed the reins of power after independence, hatred and fear of the once favored Tutsi minority persisted, resulting in a series of pogroms in the early 1960s and again in the early 1970s that created a large exile community of Tutsis in Burundi, Zaire (present-day Democratic Republic of Congo), and, most importantly, Uganda. By 1994 the Tutsis had become for the Hutu political elite an inherently dangerous, threatening, and alien race lodged within the Hutu body politic, sustained and abetted by an armed and mobilized military force in Uganda (the Rwandan Patriotic Front), which given the chance would once again place the Tutsis atop the Rwandan political, economic, and social hierarchy at the expense of the native Hutus to whom the Rwandan nation properly belonged. For the Hutu Power regime such an overwhelming existential threat to the Hutu race and nation could only be neutralized once and for all through the wholesale, carefully planned and executed extermination of the Rwandan Tutsi population.

The perpetration of genocide in the global era: sovereignty, non-intervention, and the global arms trade

The rise of an increasingly interconnected globalized world might lead us to assume that genocide can no longer occur in secret, and that global actors such as states, IGOs, and NGOs armed with the proper knowledge will move to prevent or stop any genocidal destruction. While the former is for the most part true (think, for example, about the dissemination of information over the last several years by activists and NGOs about the atrocities in Darfur), the latter has been shown to be false, or at least thus far. While we might wish that global communications technology functions effectively as a tool to expose the despicable acts of *genocidaires*, and that such publicity forces genocidal elites to think twice, or leads to timely intervention by the outside world, neither of these outcomes can be credibly said to have actually happened. In short, globalization has not put a break on genocidal killing. Why?

The answer is twofold: knowledge is not always power and state sovereignty, the death of which has been loudly proclaimed by some globalization analysts, remains alive and well in our globalized world, in particular where genocide is concerned. With the possible exception of the NATO bombing campaign over Kosovo and Serbia in 1999 to protect Kosovar Albanians from ethnic cleansing at the hands of Serbia and local Serbian forces, one would be hard pressed to think of an example before or since of a genocide successfully deterred because of either the availability of information about the killing, or because states and IGOs were willing to undertake a concerted humanitarian operation to save civilians in another state. Indeed, if we look at the Cambodian and Rwandan cases we can see that globalization did not play a role in deterring or stopping the killing. Genocidal policies were just as easily conceived and implemented in Cambodia under almost complete international isolation as they were two decades later in Rwanda in full view of the world.

The Cambodian genocide began immediately after the Khmer Rouge took power, just two weeks before the last American helicopter lifted off from the roof of the US embassy in Saigon as North Vietnamese forces took the South Vietnamese capital. With the US forces gone after more than 15 years of direct and indirect intervention, and the rest of the world no longer interested in Indochina's role in the larger Cold War struggle between East and West, the genocide in Cambodia unfolded while the world was looking elsewhere. At the same time, the xenophobic and autarkic Khmer Rouge forced all foreign journalists, aid groups, and foreigners in general out of the country. In fact, from 1975 to early 1979 only three Western journalists were allowed into the country, and then under only very tight restrictions (Becker, 1998). News of what was happening only began to trickle out with refugees who managed to make their way to the Thai–Cambodian border with tales of horrors so incredible that they were not widely believed until after the genocide was over.

In Rwanda, by contrast, the planning for the genocide and the genocide itself was perpetrated while the world looked on. Although there were journalists from several countries and news organizations located either in Rwanda itself or elsewhere in the region, thus making the capacity to report timely and accurate information about the crisis a possibility in this case, several news organizations were more focused on South Africa's first multiracial elections in April 1994, or on the continued bloodletting in Bosnia (Melvern, 2004, p. 231). Further, journalists who were reporting from Rwanda frequently misunderstood and mischaracterized the outbreak of genocidal killing in April 1994 as merely traditional "tribal" violence, which they assumed was common in Sub-Saharan Africa (McNulty, 1999, pp. 275–277). Meanwhile, authorities in Washington, London, Ottawa, Brussels, and other international capitals were slow to recognize the scale and exterminatory intent of the killing in Rwanda, and, even once they did, they did not regard their own national interests to be at stake while at the same time they feared a repeat of the disastrous intervention in Somalia (Power, 2002, pp. 329–389). The major Western states that had the capacity to launch a concerted intervention to stop the genocide thus declined to intervene unilaterally or to change the UN mandate or bolster the capacity of Canadian Lieutenant-General Roméo Dallaire's beleaguered UN mission in Rwanda. Instead, the United Nations Security Council voted to reduce Dallaire's already small and under-resourced mission, following the murder and mutilation of ten Belgian peacekeepers, to a skeleton crew who were left with the impossible task of protecting as many Tutsis as they could while bearing witness to the unfettered crimes of the Hutu Power regime (Dallaire and Beardsley, 2003).

The Rwandan genocide is a cautionary tale, for it shows us that just because the capacity exists to globally disseminate information about genocidal killing, this does not mean that the media will necessarily seize the opportunity to tell the story or get the story right, or even that the world will listen and then act. Getting the story wrong is no minor criticism since doing so can lead policymakers in would-be intervening states and IGOs to misinterpret the meaning and extent of atrocities being committed, although, to be fair, states do have at their disposal their own sources of intelligence and capacity for analyzing such information. Of course, mainstream media is not the only source of public information in the global era. Ordinary people with the right kinds of personal communications technology can email, text, blog, tweet, or use social networking sites to alert the world to abuses committed by state or other armed groups, as was the case during student protests in recent years in Myanmar (Burma) and Iran. But, even in these cases, external intervention was not forthcoming despite the availability of some very compelling firsthand accounts of atrocities.

In the case of the Myanmar regime specifically, the state showed itself capable after only a few days of protests of severing the link technology provided anti-regime protesters to the outside world. Finally, while it is true that some genocidal regimes like the Nazis took pains to dispatch their victims away from prying eyes, others like the Rwandan Hutu Power regime were happy to use radio broadcasts to induce ordinary Hutus to do their "work" and slaughter their Tutsi neighbors in public, and to direct the army and Interahamwe militia to set up roadblocks so that Tutsis could be apprehended and openly murdered. Currently the regime in Sudan appears to be content to continue to victimize the Fur, Masalit, and Zaghawa minorities in Darfur despite widespread reporting of atrocities by high-profile Western journalists like Nicholas Kristof of the *New York Times* and celebrities like George Clooney. The use of real-time satellite images showing the perpetration of atrocities as they happen on websites run by human rights groups, or the public indictment of President Omar al-Bashir on charges of war crimes, crimes against humanity, and genocide by the ICC, are similarly reported with little result.

Just as globalization has failed to successfully transform the international community from bystanders whose inaction facilitates genocidal destruction to rescuers willing to sacrifice blood and treasure to save imperilled groups, globalization has also helped provide the physical means of destruction needed to kill large numbers of people through access to a burgeoning small arms market. This was not a factor in the Cambodian genocide because of the economic isolation of the regime, but it was most definitely a factor in Rwanda. Despite dire economic circumstances and a serious erosion of public services, the Rwandan government began to dramatically increase military spending in the early 1990s just prior to the genocide. Deals for small arms and ammunition were struck with the governments of France and Egypt, the latter culminating in a series of deals from 1990 to 1993 that included shipments of grenades, ammunition, mortars, assault rifles, rockets, rocket launchers, and land mines. During 1991–2 it is estimated that France sent Rwanda weapons valued at US$6 million; by 1993 that total was reduced to US$4 million, but an additional US$12 million in arms sales was brokered with the private French company, DYL (Melvern, 2004, pp. 57–58). At the same time the Rwandan army and the Interahamwe militia also began acquiring other more ordinary tools—farm implements—that they planned to use themselves while also providing them to ordinary Hutu Rwandans in order for them to strike down their Tutsi neighbors. In 1993 the Rwandan government began importing unusually large quantities of machetes and other agricultural tools including razor blades, nails, hoes, axes, screwdrivers, scythes, saws, spades, knives, pliers, hammers, and shears—all largely from China under eligible import licences. A total of US$4.6 million was spent on agricultural tools in 1993, enough new machetes, as journalist Linda Melvern points out, for one out of every three adult males in the country (Melvern, 2004, p. 56). All of these sales of small arms and machetes from governments and private companies were perfectly legal, a stark example of how the free flow of products around a globalized world came to facilitate the near destruction of an entire group of human beings.

The impact of genocide on a globalized world: refugees, security, norms, laws, and prevention

We have seen thus far that even though genocide is not a causal outcome of globalization, genocide is indirectly linked to the global context within which genocidal destruction takes place. This final section will deal with how the occurrence of genocide has shaped globalization on a number of fronts. On the negative side, genocide produces regional and international refugee flows that in turn breed a whole new series of humanitarian crises that the world community must respond to. Genocide also exports insecurity and communal conflicts beyond the borders of states where genocide has been perpetrated. On the more positive side of the ledger, repeated outbreaks of genocidal killing have contributed to the formulation of an increasingly accepted anti-genocide norm, the codification of international and domestic laws criminalizing genocide and other atrocity crimes, and the creation of international tribunals and a permanent international court to prosecute and punish those alleged to have committed such crimes.

Refugees, humanitarian crises, and insecurity

As genocides unfold, or in their immediate aftermath, victims and sometimes perpetrators flee within the country or across international borders. Victims become internally displaced persons (IDPs) or refugees in a bid to save themselves during the killing or later after the genocide is over to resettle and recover elsewhere if they are unable or unwilling to return home. Perpetrators may take flight in an attempt to evade justice and possible reprisals by their former victims, particularly when a genocidal regime has been removed from power and the perpetrators no longer enjoy the protection of the state. Refugee flows triggered by genocide can lead to the massive displacement of vulnerable populations either within the state affected or regionally as refugees flee across national borders to neighboring states, and possibly internationally as a smaller number of refugees seek asylum in Europe, North America, or elsewhere. With this movement of desperate people comes the need to deal with a number of humanitarian and security considerations not only on the part of the societies affected, but also on behalf of regional neighbors and other states and non-state actors in the international system.

IDPs or refugees who flee genocidal destruction are in dire straits, requiring humanitarian assistance to provide the most basic necessities of life: water, food, shelter, and security, as well as mechanisms for determining the fate of loved ones and facilitating family reunification. Providing in-country humanitarian assistance to genocide victims while the killing is ongoing is particularly challenging since the victims are often individually or collectively isolated, and are surrounded by hostile forces bent on the victims' destruction. Although global humanitarian NGOs may be more than willing to assist the victims as genocide unfolds, their ability to enter the territory of a state engaged in the genocidal destruction of a specific group, or to operate in areas where victim groups are clustered, is almost nil. During the genocide in Cambodia, for example, international relief agencies were completely absent from the scene since the Khmer Rouge regime prohibited the presence of all foreigners in the country. In Rwanda humanitarian NGOs such as Médecins Sans Frontières (Doctors without Borders) were operating in the country, but at reduced capacity due to the high level of insecurity generated by the genocide and the ongoing civil war. As such, relief agencies were only able to operate in limited areas, mostly the cities, leaving large numbers of the genocide's victims and survivors beyond the reach of assistance. Even in cases like the Darfur region of Sudan in which humanitarian agencies have been able to set up IDP camps, these camps continue to be subject to frequent attacks by armed groups, governmental and otherwise ("Situation in Darfur Camp," 2010). The task is somewhat easier once the killing is over and NGOs and other relief agencies can enter the country and set up proper IDP camps for those affected. This is not only because the killing has stopped and the situation is more secure, but also because the regime that has been perpetrating genocidal violence is often no longer in power. This was the case in both Cambodia and Rwanda, with the Khmer Rouge and Hutu Power regimes removed from power by the Vietnamese army operating with rebel Khmer Rouge forces and the Rwandan Patriotic Front respectively.

The real global impact of genocide occurs, however, when the killing produces a flow of significant numbers of people across international borders as refugees. Although Westerners often assume that refugees from man-made and natural disasters come in large numbers straight to North America or Europe to settle permanently, the reality is that the vast majority of refugees produced by crises, including genocidal violence, end up in neighboring countries. With the exception of the former Yugoslavia in the 1990s, all post-World War II genocides have occurred in the developing world, and as such, many states that receive refugees in the aftermath of genocide are ill-equipped to deal with the influx of large numbers of destitute and traumatized survivors, or former perpetrators keen to save themselves and, in some cases, bent on returning to power. If the recipient state is willing, establishing refugee camps under the auspices of the United Nations High Commission for Refugees (UNHCR), while a major logistical undertaking, is feasible. Further, the international community, both IGOs and NGOs alike, have a solid track record of providing effective and timely assistance in the initial period after refugees begin to cross regional borders in significant numbers. The task cannot be underestimated. Although refugees from the Cambodian genocide did not begin to trickle out of the country into Thailand until years into the Khmer Rouge's rule, only increasing significantly after the regime was removed from power, the people needing assistance were in poor physical and psychological condition once they reached the Thai–Cambodian border. The scale of the disaster inside Cambodia was not immediately apparent, nor was the number of people who would eventually flee the country, but over time the UNHCR and other agencies like the Red Cross were able to meet the needs of Cambodian refugees. In the Rwandan case, the genocidal killings occasioned the exodus of some Tutsi victims of the genocide, but interestingly a much larger proportion of Hutu Rwandans, many of whom were active participants in the genocide, also left. Unlike the Cambodian case, in which refugees fled over only one international border (into Thailand), refugees from Rwanda streamed into Zaire (shortly thereafter to be renamed the Democratic Republic of Congo), Uganda, and Tanzania, thus requiring a response from several host governments and operations by international relief organizations in a number of different states. To make matters worse, a virulent cholera epidemic broke out in the refugee camps in eastern Zaire's Goma region that eventually killed upwards of 300,000 mostly Hutu refugees. Relief agencies were, over time, able to treat those sickened by the epidemic and stop the spread of disease, but it was a major undertaking and one overshadowed by the possibility that the epidemic could spread beyond the camps. The recent Will to Intervene Project produced by Concordia University in Montreal has identified the possibility of epidemics and global pandemics originating in refugee camps in the aftermath of genocide and other atrocity crimes as a major and very real threat to global health and security (W2I, 2010). The refugee camps in Zaire also had a negative effect on the local economy in Goma, pushing up the cost of housing while at the same time reducing the cost of labor as Rwandan refugees tended to take up agricultural and domestic service jobs for lower pay than the local Congolese (Halvorsen, 1999, p. 311).

In the long term, refugee camps can become problematic not only for the refugees living in them, but also for the regional hosts and the international community. The camps themselves can become semi-permanent when refugees cannot or will not return home, or settle permanently either in the host society or elsewhere. The camps then become home to a large population whose physical survival has been secured but who require long-term support including more robust housing, continuing primary healthcare, education, and security, among other issues. While the provision of such services is well-intentioned, critics of the current refugee assistance model argue that it ultimately undermines the dignity and health of refugees over the long run (Wigley, 2006, pp. 159–185). Meanwhile, host societies are typically unwilling to provide the resources needed to maintain refugee camps over a lengthy period of time or access to the land on which camps have been constructed. At the same time, international organizations like the UNHCR and other relief agencies become overstretched as they are asked to continue maintaining camps over years or even decades while simultaneously confronting new refugee crises around the world. The refugee camps on the Thai–Cambodian border, for example, remained in place from the late 1970s until they were finally closed two decades later in the early 1990s, when the occupants were finally resettled either in Thailand or abroad, or repatriated back to Cambodia in the case of those who could not be resettled elsewhere. Wishing to avoid a repeat of the experience in South-East Asia with the prolonged presence of refugee camps in Thailand, and similar camps in Hong Kong, Malaysia, and Indonesia that housed Vietnamese "boat people," the UN decided to close the post-Rwanda genocide refugee camps in several Central African countries only a few years after the genocide was over, mostly relying on refugees being repatriated to Rwanda. In Cambodia repatriation meant that genocide survivors returned to live among their torturers while in Rwanda it was, generally speaking, the reverse, with perpetrators returning to live among the surviving remnant of Rwanda's Tutsi population.

Another problem produced by refugee camps across international borders is insecurity. In the camps, security challenges in post-genocide situations are created by the existence of former perpetrators in the camps. These people often enter the camps undetected, posing as refugees, and are later able to exert their influence inside the camps with the assistance of others like them. Some, as in the case of both the Khmer Rouge and elements of the Rwandan Hutu Power army and Interahamwe militia, are organized, armed, and able to manipulate the economics of the camps to their advantage. In both of these cases former perpetrators were able to dominate the camps by intimidating refugees and using the threat or actual use of violence to gain greater access to housing, food, and other resources. In the Rwandan context, the international community chose to close several camps in Zaire/DRC in 1996 once it became apparent that they had for all practical purposes been taken over by armed perpetrators of the genocide, and that the perpetrators were using the resources available to them in the camp to build the capacity to return to Rwanda to challenge the new Rwandan Patriotic Front (RPF) government (Gourevitch, 1998, pp. 269–271). The anonymity of large refugee camps can, and did in the Rwandan case, also serve as a safe haven of sorts for perpetrators evading justice in post-atrocity situations. Meanwhile, host police, security, and/or military forces, which under the international refugee regime are responsible for safety and security in the camps, may not only fail to do this job well, they may take advance of the chaos in the refugee camps and the vulnerability of the refugees to enrich themselves. This was the role played by the Congolese security forces in the camps in the Goma region of Zaire/DRC (Halvorsen, 1999, p. 311).

Finally, refugee flows in the aftermath of genocide can create more traditional security challenges. As both victims and perpetrators flee the site of genocidal violence and end up living together again across international borders, they potentially displace the violence to a new location. This is even more problematic when the influx of refugees from a particular ethnic group or groups flows into a host state, changing the local ethnic balance. Communal tensions in host societies, which might otherwise have remained dormant, can be inflamed by the presence of often unwanted refugee populations in societies that are already dealing with resource scarcity (Halvorsen, 1999, p. 309). This is precisely what happened in Zaire/DRC after the genocide in Rwanda.

The displacement of refugees in the aftermath of genocide and conflict can also shift the conflict across international borders. When the People's Army of Vietnam invaded Cambodia from December 1978 to January 1979, thousands of Cambodians poured over the border into Thailand to escape the fighting and the Khmer Rouge. Given the Cold War context within which Vietnam's invasion took place, the refugee camps on the Thai–Cambodian border became a literal battleground between East and West with hundreds of thousands of refugees living in camps on either side of the border amid fighting between Western-supported anti-communist rebel groups and the Khmer Rouge. And while the UN provided adequate support for refugees in the camps, Thai authorities did not effectively secure the camps, thus allowing all armed groups to exploit the refugees and resources available in the camps to pursue their own goals (Kenyon Lischer, 2005, p. 3).

The surviving remnants of atrocities can also sometimes use their new homes in neighboring countries to organize themselves for a return, sometimes through force of arms, to their home countries. The Rwandan Patriotic Front originated in the ranks of the rebel army of Yoweri Museveni (who is now president) in Uganda years after Rwandan Tutsis fled Rwanda from the violence of 1959, 1972, and 1975. After the genocide, surviving elements of the Hutu Power regime's armed forces and the Interahamwe made their way to eastern Zaire/DRC, where they began to organize themselves, first inside the refugee camps and later along the Rwandan border to one day cross it and retake power in the Rwandan capital of Kigali. The rise of armed Hutu forces in Zaire/DRC eventually led to a catastrophic multinational war in the DRC, which pitted the armed forces of Rwanda and Uganda and allied ethnic Tutsi armed groups operating in the DRC against the Congolese regime and its regional allies (including Zimbabwe and the Hutu Power forces) in a conflict that is estimated to have caused the death of approximately 4 million people. Even now that the war is over, several armed groups (some of them ethnic Tutsis from Rwanda and some from the DRC) are locked in a low-level and seemingly intractable conflict with Hutu forces and other opportunistic local armed groups vying for control over valuable mineral resources. The conflict has also recently seen the entry of the Ugandan-based Lord's Resistance Army, which is believed to be responsible for a series of massacres and the forced abduction into their forces of hundreds of civilians in the eastern DRC. Nearly 20 years after the genocide in Rwanda, the Great Lakes region of Africa and the DRC in particular is living and dying with the consequences of the attempted extermination of Rwanda's Tutsi population in 1994. This example vividly demonstrates that genocide is not only an outrageous assault on targeted groups within a specific society, but it can also create in its wake very real threats to international peace and security elsewhere.

Norms, prevention, laws, and legal institutions

The consequences of outbreaks of genocidal destruction globally are not uniformly negative, though it is obvious that genocide's more "positive" impacts are hardly worth the price. The first of such outcomes deals with the development of global norms. Repeated occurrences of genocide worldwide since the Holocaust have led most states and other actors in the global system to believe that the intentional physical destruction of whole groups of people is a profoundly immoral act deserving of condemnation and punishment. Along with slavery and torture, genocide is now widely seen in international legal circles to be *jus cogens*, or a peremptory norm, an act that is so morally wrong that it cannot be justified under any circumstances during either war or peace. The hope is that the emergence of a global anti-genocide norm will prevent genocidal violence by delegitimizing such violence by states or other actors and making those who commit atrocious acts pariahs in the international system (Akhavan, 2001, p. 12). Fearful of being cut off in an increasingly globalized world, would-be *genocidaires*, it is assumed, will avoid the most destructive of policies in favor of less drastic measures. This is a perfectly sensible argument and one with which most of us would very much like to agree.

The problem is that it is very hard to empirically prove whether or not political or military elites who have planned genocide in the past were in the end successfully deterred by emerging norms against genocidal policies and/or the fear of global isolation should such policies be pursued. There is, however, abundant evidence that genocidal elites are more than willing to risk international disapprobation, or, more frequently, that genocidal elites correctly calculate that the world will not be morally outraged enough to stop genocidal killing or exact serious consequences against those who do the terrible deed. While planning the destruction of Poland's elite at the beginning of World War II, Hitler famously quipped that the Nazi regime need not fear international opinion since "no one, after all, remembers the Armenians," a reference to the Ottoman Empire's destruction of the Armenian minority in Anatolia during World War I. Similarly the Hutu Power regime correctly calculated that foreign governments and the UN would not intervene seriously to stop the genocide against the Tutsis. The murder of ten Belgian peacekeepers was perpetrated specifically to test such a theory. Further, it is likely that although genocidal elites are rational actors in the sense that they think that genocidal policies are reasonable responses to perceived problems and threats, they are rarely if ever swayed by moral disapprobation or threats of isolation or punishment from international or other external actors. The threat they perceive (erroneously) to be posed by the continued physical existence of the victim group, even despite the victim group's objective powerlessness, is so overwhelming that genocide is seen as the only possible and rational policy option. All other considerations are beside the point (Hiebert, 2008, pp. 6–13).

That elites contemplating genocide are unlikely to be deterred by an emergent anti-genocide norm does not mean the norm is irrelevant. The apparent global consensus between states, NGOs, human rights activists, scholars, and many ordinary people around the world that genocide and other atrocity crimes are moral wrongs can still serve as a useful deterrent to genocide even if would-be *genocidaires* are unlikely to be moved by it themselves. The real role played by the emerging anti-genocide norm in today's globalized world is to serve as the normative foundation for the Responsibility to Protect (R2P) doctrine adopted by the UN system at the turn of the millennium. The norm reinforces that because genocide is so profoundly immoral the international community has a moral obligation to intervene to stop it and other atrocity crimes when the state affected cannot or will not act to stop the violence. Whether states and other actors will in fact move from accepting that genocide is morally wrong to acting to prevent the perpetration of this moral wrong is another matter. There is a real gap between what the anti-genocide norm tells international actors they should do and what they actually do. Some commentators, such as the authors of the Will to Intervene Project, who have taken a sober look at the record of the United States and Canada in a successful case of genocide prevention (Kosovo) and one spectacular case of international failure (Rwanda), have concluded that while moral appeals to international responsibility are not without their merits, strategies for encouraging genocide prevention and intervention by governments to stop atrocities should lean less on moral suasion and appeal more to the national and rational self-interest of the most powerful states in the global system (W2I, 2010).

The codification of international human rights law (IHL) and international criminal law (ICL) has been another much broader outcome of genocidal destruction. In the aftermath of the many civilian human rights abuses perpetrated in both theaters of war during World War II (and of course the Holocaust), the international community moved, over the decades that followed, to establish in law a set of core human rights owed to all individuals by all states. The use of IHL to define and uphold individual human rights constituted a significant change in the relationship between states and populations under their control. Historically, the rights of individuals were not protected by states and there were no international instruments available to force states to do so. In the nineteenth century a limited number of international treaties were signed to abolish slavery and to protect workers, for example, but it was not until the post-World War II period that IHL was employed to define and uphold the rights of all individuals *qua* individuals rather than as members of specific groups (Cassese, 2005, p. 376). As such, IHL has established a legal regime that clearly outlines the rights of individuals and the obligation of states to provide for and respect human rights. Starting with the United Nations Declaration of Human Rights in 1948, which is a statement of principles rather than a legally binding treaty, individual human rights were defined with greater specificity and clarity in subsequent treaties. These treaties include the 1966 Covenants on Political and Social Rights and Economic, Social and Cultural Rights; the International Convention on the Elimination of All Forms of Racial Discrimination (1965); the Convention on the Elimination of All Forms of Discrimination against Women (1979); the Convention on the Rights of the Child (1989); and two additional protocols concerning the sale of children, child prostitution, and child pornography (2000). In addition, there are treaties protecting the rights of migrant workers (1990) and various regional human rights conventions beginning with the European Convention on Human Rights (1950).

The connection between genocide and the development of IHL is not as direct, though, as that between genocide and ICL. In the aftermath of the Holocaust, which was itself preceded by the genocide perpetrated by German military forces against the Herero in South West Africa (1904–1907) and the Armenians by the Ottoman Empire during World War I, the international community said "never again." Having lost his family to the Holocaust, the Polish-American jurist Raphael Lemkin coined the term "genocide" in 1944 to define a "new" crime in international law that criminalized an "old scourge" in human history. In 1948, member states of the United Nations negotiated a genocide convention advocated by Lemkin that formally criminalized genocide under international criminal law. The crime of genocide joined a small set of international crimes that included war crimes established in the Hague

Conventions (1899 and 1907) and the Geneva Conventions (1864, 1906, 1929, 1949), crimes against peace (i.e. waging aggressive war), and crimes against humanity, the latter two of which were codified in the London Charter of the International Military Tribunal, commonly known as the Nuremberg Trials, at the end of World War II. The International Criminal Tribunals for the Former Yugoslavia (ICTY) and Rwanda (ICTR), and the legal statutes that underpin them, were similarly direct responses to the genocides and other crimes committed in the Balkans and Rwanda in the 1990s and further refined, in both treaty and case law, key principles and practices in international criminal law. Foundational to all international criminal law and institutions is the principle—originally found in all domestic criminal law—that international crimes are moral wrongs committed against the global community. Those who commit international crimes are *hostis humani generis* or "enemies of all humanity" who have committed significant moral wrongs against not only their victims, but the entire human community.

Beyond identifying atrocities as moral wrongs, the criminalization of acts like genocide was intended to bring an end to impunity. Prior to the Nuremberg Trials, the victimization of military personnel and civilians by armies or states was not punished save by summary judgement usually at the hands of the victor. Civilian and military leaders who ordered atrocities were seldom subject to any sort of penalty for their actions, largely because they could at that time legitimately and legally claim that their actions were the "acts of state" while subordinates could claim that they were following "superior orders." While states always had the capacity to try their own leaders or soldiers for committing atrocities, actual practice up to and including World War I confirmed that states rarely if ever sought justice for victims or meted out punishment to one of their own. The codification of genocide and other atrocities as international crimes following World War II was explicitly intended to ensure that those who perpetrated such acts could no longer get away with murder. The chief prosecutor at Nuremberg, Robert H. Jackson, proclaimed in his opening address to the court the hope that the law could end impunity and thereby facilitate deterrence, asserting that "the wrongs which we seek to condemn and punish have been so calculated, so malignant, and so devastating that civilization cannot tolerate their being ignored because it cannot survive their being repeated." Emphasizing that the law must apply to all, particularly those in authority who plan and order the perpetration of atrocity crimes, Jackson added that "the common sense of mankind demands that law shall not stop with the punishment of petty crimes by little people. It must also reach men who possess themselves of great power and make deliberate and concerted use of it to set in motion evils which leave no home in the world untouched" (International Military Tribunal, 1947, p. 98).

The criminalization of atrocities also established the principle of individual criminal responsibility. As with domestic crimes, international criminal law has adopted the liberal legal principle that crimes can only be committed by individuals, from the most senior leaders, to rank-and-file soldiers, to civil servants, to ordinary civilians. As such, international crimes are not crimes "of state" for which no one individual leader or group of leaders can be tried and punished. And while low-level perpetrators who actually do the killing in genocide are often following the orders of some kind of superior authority, they similarly cannot claim that they do not bear individual criminal responsibilities for their actions. Nonetheless, ICL emphasizes that civilian and military commanders bear the most responsibility for atrocity crimes.

Tribunals, particularly the ICTY/R, as well as the International Criminal Court (ICC), were also created to assist with conflict resolution and peace-building. By adopting a liberal legal order in which individuals are assigned individual criminal responsibility, proponents of the creation of the ICTY in 1993 while the war in Bosnia was still ongoing, for example, hoped that the exercise of trying individuals for atrocity crimes would displace both guilt and punishment for such crimes from whole groups to specific individuals. In so doing, intercommunal conflicts like that in the former Yugoslavia, in which genocide and other atrocities are perpetrated, could be more easily brought to an end if populations on all sides could be assured that those most responsible for committing heinous acts would be made to account and pay for their crimes, thereby bringing the cycle of communal revenge to an end (Akhavan, 2001, p. 7). It is worth noting, however, that the most serious atrocity crimes, including the siege of Sarajevo and the genocide at Srebrenica in 1994, occurred after the ICTY began operating, and that the negotiations of the 1995 Dayton Peace Accord ending the war referred only a handful of times in passing to the role of the ICTY in ending the conflict.

International criminal prosecution may also, in a very practical way, hasten the end of a conflict by removing indicted and captured war criminals from the scene. Whether in pre-trial detention, on trial, or behind bars post-sentencing, senior civilian and military leaders can neither continue their murderous role in the perpetration of atrocities, nor obstruct the path to peace. It is hoped that by removing the most radical and probably most guilty leaders, more moderate forces can come to the fore and end the bloodshed. Critics of this perspective suggest that the threat of prosecution for war crimes and atrocities, be it domestically or internationally, may cause leaders implicated in such acts to resist at all costs ending a conflict, or spur on the perpetration of gross human rights abuses. It is feared that abusive leaders, like Robert Mugabe of Zimbabwe who might otherwise have given up power by now, cling to it hoping to stave off indictment by a domestic or international tribunal, or avoid making peace and thus avoid arrest and extradition to the ICC, as in the case of Sudan's already indicted president, Omar al-Bashir.

Conclusion

The connection between globalization and genocide is multiple and varied. Although not a direct cause of genocide, globalization in the form of modern, potentially dangerous exclusionary ideas, were first spread around the globe via colonialism. Coupled with the implementation of discriminatory practices by colonial administrations, ideas such as race, nation, and class helped set the stage for the genocides perpetrated in the developing world in the twentieth and twenty-first centuries. More recently, globalization has also facilitated genocide by creating an easily accessible legal arms market. Paradoxically, global communications technology and practices now ensure that the world can know relatively quickly and in some detail about genocides that are underway or being planned, but this has failed in many cases to move international organizations, states, and other would-be interveners to stop the killing. At the same time, however, greater access to knowledge about the occurrence of genocide has generated an anti-genocide norm that is now accepted worldwide. This norm tells us that genocide is not only morally wrong, it is an illegitimate policy that states should not engage in, and that the international community has a moral responsibility to prevent and stop it once such policies are put into action. Globalization has helped us, on the one hand, to identify and comprehend a significant moral wrong and our moral obligations to the global human community to stop it; however, on the other hand, globalization has seemingly been unable to overcome the entrenched principle of sovereignty and the attachment of individual states to their own national interest. In short, thanks in part to globalization we know what we should do, but regrettably, remain unwilling to do it. Other effects of genocide on globalization have been much more tangible, but again rather varied. These range from the negative problem of refugee flows and exported humanitarian crises and insecurity in the regions surrounding the sites of genocidal violence, to the creation of an increasingly robust international human rights regime and an international criminal legal order replete with laws outlawing genocide, war crimes, crimes against humanity, and torture, to the construction of ad hoc tribunals and now a permanent international court to prosecute those suspected of gross human rights abuses. Given the complexity of genocide and globalization, it is no surprise that the interrelationship between these two processes should be equally as complex, varied, and sometimes paradoxical.

References

Akhavan, P. (2001). Beyond impunity: Can international criminal justice prevent future atrocities? *The American Journal of International Law, 95*(7), 7–25.

Bartov, O. (1996). *Murder in our midst: The Holocaust, industrial killing and representation.* Oxford: Oxford University Press.

Becker, E. (1998). *When the war was over: Cambodia and the Khmer Rouge revolution.* New York: Public Affairs.

Cassese, A. (2005). *International law* (2nd edn). Oxford: Oxford University Press.

Chalk, F., and Jonassohn, K. (1990). *The history and sociology of genocide: Analyses and case studies.* New Haven: Yale University Press.

Chandler, D. P. (1991). *The tragedy of Cambodian history: Politics, war, and revolution since 1945.* New Haven: Yale University Press.

Dallaire, R., and Beardsley, B. (2003). *Shake hands with the devil: The failure of humanity in Rwanda.* Toronto: Random House Canada.

Fein, H. (2007). *Slavery, terror, genocide.* Boulder: Paradigm Publishers.

Gourevitch, P. (1998). *We wish to inform you that tomorrow we will be killed with our families: Stories from Rwanda.* New York: Picador USA.

Haas, P. J. (1999). Science and the determination of the good. In J. K. Roth (ed.), *Ethics after the Holocaust: Perspectives, critiques, and responses* (pp. 49–59). St. Paul, MN: Paragon House.

Halvorsen, K. (1999). Protection and humanitarian assistance in the refugee camps in Zaire: The problem of security. In H. Adelman and A. Suhrke (eds.), *The path of a genocide: the Rwanda crisis from Uganda to Zaire* (pp. 307–320). New Brunswick: Transaction Publishers.

Hiebert, M. S. (2008). The "three switches" of identity construction in genocide: The Nazi final solution and the Cambodian killing fields. *Genocide Studies and Prevention, 3*(1), 5–29.

International Military Tribunal (1947). *Trial of the major war criminals before the international military tribunal* (vol. 1). Nuremberg: International Military Tribunal.

Jackson, K. D. (1989). Intellectual origins of the Khmer Rouge. In K. D. Jackson (ed.), *Cambodia, 1975–1978: Rendezvous with death* (pp. 241–268). Princeton: Princeton University Press.

Kenyon Lischer, S. (2005). *Dangerous sanctuaries: Refugee camps, civil war, and the dilemma of humanitarian aid.* Ithaca: Cornell University Press.

Kuper, L. (1981). *Genocide: Its political use in the twentieth century.* New Haven: Yale University Press.

Levene, M. (2005). *Genocide in the age of the nation-state, Vol. II: The rise of the West and the coming of genocide*. London: I. B. Taurus.

Mamdani, M. (2001). *When victims become killers: Colonialism, nativism, and the genocide in Rwanda*. Princeton: Princeton University Press.

McNulty, M. (1999). Media Ethnicization and the international response to war and genocide in Rwanda. In T. Allen and J. Seaton (eds.), *The media of conflict: War reporting and representation of ethnic violence* (pp. 268–286). New York: Zed Books.

Melvern, L. (2004). *Conspiracy to murder: The Rwandan genocide*. London: Verso.

Power, S. (2002). *"A problem from hell": America and the age of genocide*. New York: Basic Books.

Prunier, G. (1995). *The Rwanda crisis: History of a genocide*. New York: Columbia University Press.

Rubenstein, R. L. (1975). *The cunning of history: The Holocaust and the American future*. New York: Harper Torchbooks.

Situation in Darfur camp for displaced persons tense and insecure. (12 September 2010). *United Nations Daily News*. Retrieved 12 September 2010, from http://www.un.org/news.

Van Der Bly, M. C. (2005). Globalization: A triumph of ambiguity. *Current Sociology, 53*(6), 875–893.

Vickery, M. (1984). *Cambodia: 1975–1982*. Boston: South End Press.

Weitz, E. D. (2003). *A century of genocide: Utopias of race and nation*. Princeton: Princeton University Press.

Will to Intervene Project (W2I) (2010). *Will to Intervene. Mobilizing the will to intervene: Leadership and action to prevent mass atrocities*. Montreal: Montreal Institute for Genocide and Human Rights Studies.

9
Confronting "Linguistic Genocide": Language Repression in Kurdistan

Evangelos Voulgarakis, Bei Dawei

Introduction

Language, along with ethnicity or religion, is widely regarded as a core aspect of personal and group identity. Just as it would be monstrous to force someone to renounce their religion, and absurd to expect them to change ethnicity, so too must an individual's language receive respect, we are told, lest its oppressors stand complicit as the moral equivalent of Nazis. Yet compromises do occur—new languages are learned, old ones are neglected, conversions take place, and even ethnicity is subject to a certain amount of renegotiation and contextualization. In the case of language change, it can be difficult to disentangle the effects of political coercion, socioeconomic pressure, and the practical need for everyday communication. It is also difficult to decide what level of accommodation a state or society can reasonably demand of its people, or they of it.

In developed countries, language policy has evolved under the influence of European nationalism, which has traditionally assumed a common language to be one of the ideal characteristics of a nation. The persistence of regional or minority languages, as well as changes in national borders, has long posed a challenge to would-be nation-states. Responses have ranged from suppression (as in revolutionary France), to a variety of territorially based compromises (as in Belgium, Quebec, or South Tyrol), to the embrace of pro-diversity rhetoric (exemplified by the European Union), with the practical linguistic needs of travelers and immigrants made the subject of ad hoc accommodations. Developing countries show much the same range of responses. Turkey favors the French model of a centralized, officially monolingual state, while India and South Africa recognize more than a dozen official languages each (but in practice relegate most of them to regional use). Key differences include the role of the European languages of the former colonial powers as *linguae francae*, something which some developing countries have embraced and others have sought to rectify, as well as the relatively unstable and unsettled political situation of many of those countries.

We might expect to find language rights violations concentrated in the developing world, where human rights in general tend to be least respected. A peculiarity of the literature on language rights, however, is that as often as not the countries that it targets are relatively progressive ones with strong traditions of democracy and human rights. A number of writers use terms like "linguistic genocide" or "linguicide" (we shall treat them as synonyms) for policies that encourage language shift or language death. Kurdish scholar/activist Amir Hassanpour (2000) traces this rather emotive wording to one Jaroslav B. Rudnyckyj, whose *Language Rights and Linguicide* was published in 1967, but credits its popularization to the ubiquitous Tove Skutnabb-Kangas and her husband, Robert Phillipson, beginning with an entry in *The Encyclopedia of Language and Linguistics* (1994). While linguistic genocide need not involve the biological death of any human beings (in point of fact, the most common complaints seem to target children's education, and after that, the influence of mass media), proponents of the concept by no means consider themselves to be speaking hyperbolically.

It is a point of continuing debate whether "genocide" necessarily involves mass murder, or whether attempts merely to disband or assimilate an identity group—without killing its people—might also qualify. An extra-linguistic example would be the "Lost Generations" of aboriginal children taken from their parents by (often well-intentioned) agents of the Australian government. Skutnabb-Kangas (2000, pp. 533–535, 2006, pp. 277–287) appeals to the UN Convention on the Prosecution and Punishment of the Crime of Genocide (E793, 1948), Article II(e), which forbids "forcibly transferring children of the group to another group." Assimilationist educational policies, she asserts, have this effect. Article II(b) of the same Convention forbids "causing serious bodily or mental harm to members of the group." Skutnabb-Kangas produces studies to argue that the denial of mother-tongue education qualifies as "serious... mental harm." However, her legal determinations have never been tested in court, and they assume rights that governments and supranational bodies have pointedly avoided acknowledging. For example, a draft of the Convention included an Article III, which would have specifically addressed the issues of language and cultural rights; this was rejected by the UN and not included in the final text (Skutnabb-Kangas,

2000, p. 316). The UN Declaration on the Rights of Persons Belonging to National or Ethnic, Religious and Linguistic Minorities (1992) calls for states to take "appropriate measures" to protect language "wherever possible"; Skutnabb-Kangas (2006, pp. 275–276) rightly points out the watered-down language of this and other similar documents.

To the extent that the concept of "linguistic genocide" is at all legitimate or useful—we are not convinced that it is—the experience of the Kurds would surely qualify as a preeminent example. A 2010 Listverse article, "10 Modern Cases of Linguistic Genocide," ranks it as number one in importance, presumably based on the size of the affected population and the severity of the repression. (Its author, "Askalon," excludes from consideration all cases in which a language has suffered primarily as a by-product of the annihilation of its speakers.) Skutnabb-Kangas often discusses Turkey's policies toward the Kurdish language and identity,[1] most notably (with Sertaç Bucak) in "Killing a Mother Tongue—How the Kurds are Deprived of Linguistic Human Rights" (in Skutnabb-Kangas and Bucak, 1995, pp. 347–370), which, in combination with the testimony of Hassanpour and other writers, persuade as to the facts of repression. While we note recent improvements in Turkey, that country has far to go before its human rights situation can be considered as meeting the standards of the European Union (notwithstanding similar failings on the part of several EU members, such as Greece). Iran and Syria are frankly dictatorial, as was Iraq under Saddam Hussein. Although present-day Iraq hardly lacks for abuses, the position of the Kurds has obviously improved, to the point that they are more likely to number among the perpetrators, rather than the victims, of ethnic cleansing. This brings up a delicate point—that the Kurds, no less than their neighbors, have committed acts of *actual* genocide. A century ago, for example, they sided with the Turks against the Armenians out of Muslim solidarity, only to find themselves betrayed by the new Turkish nationalism. Of course, hardly any of the guilty parties are alive today, and the extent to which states, religions, or ethnic solidarities may be held responsible for the crimes of their presumed ancestors, leaders, or compatriots is a difficult philosophical and political issue. This unavoidable vagueness of group identity turns out to pose a major difficulty with the concept of linguistic genocide.

Language rights

Discussion of language rights involves us in several spheres of discourse. One is ethics, the philosophical study of what is morally right or wrong. Laypeople whose exposure to ethics comes primarily through its application to professions like medicine, business, or law may fail to appreciate the degree to which almost any ethical statement that might be proposed would become a matter of controversy in this philosophical subdiscipline. Philosophers approach issues such as language rights through the lens of various rival ethical theories, ancient and modern, typically without ever reaching agreement. Their conclusions can be famously counterintuitive, and regularly broach the possibility that the entire subject amounts to nothing more than vain projections. However, more practical approaches are common as well, as illustrated by the burgeoning literature on the ethics of secession.

A second sphere is law. As philosophical ethicists are wont to remind us, whether something is legal is an entirely different question from whether it is moral—it is entirely possible, indeed routine, to have unjust laws. Not only the likes of Nazi Germany, but even such liberal regimes as the UN, with its Universal Declaration of Human Rights, may be suspected of fundamental unfairness, or at least of falling short of the ideal. Furthermore, not everything that is right or wrong ought necessarily to be made a matter of legislation. Regardless of what conclusions may be reached by academic writers, the resolution of legal questions ultimately lies with lawyers, courts, and governments whose principles are not always consistent. Nevertheless bodies of law (such as the decisions of the US Supreme Court) are sometimes made the objects of philosophical analysis. Skutnabb-Kangas' interpretations, mentioned above, may perhaps be read in this light.

A third sphere is that of politics. Despite some overlap with the spheres of ethics and law, politics are more about choice, opinion, and preference than any attempt to behave according to overarching, neutral principles. Ethicists (*qua* ethicists) rarely consider budgetary matters, as politicians constantly do, and would be puzzled by suggestions to the effect that rights might fluctuate according to how well the economy is doing, or the vicissitudes of public opinion. It makes a difference whether linguistic accommodations are a matter of right or a negotiable policy, subject to competition with numerous other demands on resources. We may also find our divergent political cultures reflected in our contrary instincts, for example, to support language and other cultural phenomena with government funding, or else allow free competition to determine winners and losers, victims and survivors.

A fourth sphere is linguistics. Those linguists who warn of language extinction tend not to speak of "rights" per se, but focus on the welfare of languages and cultures rather than of their speakers and members.

One sometimes hears what we might call "ecological" rhetoric on the need for linguistic diversity, with language extinctions likened to species extinctions (see, for example, Skutnabb-Kangas, 2000, pp. ix, xxxi–xxxiii, 217–218).[2] Even if they turn out to have a common cause, the metaphor is flawed, since languages are not really bound together in a relationship of interdependence. Douglas A. Kibbee (2003) writes, "The non-equivalence of language and species has been recognized since linguistic debates in the 1860s and 1870s concerning the debate between historical linguistics and the theory of evolution.... A language is a behaviour, not a physical characteristic" (p. 51).

Here we should make special note of the academic ghetto called "interlinguistics," in which "rights" discourse does regularly appear. Participants conceive of their supposed field as concerned with communication between members of different speech communities ("the language problem"), and/or the suitability of certain artificial languages for solving this problem in a fairer and less burdensome way than, say, global English. With the first formulation, "interlinguists" arrogate to themselves the wider issue of sociolinguistics; the second reveals the cultic foundations of a network whose activities largely overlap with those of "Esperantology."[3]

Note the underlying assumption—by no means universally embraced—that language death is something bad. Salikoko S. Mufwene (2008) observes that

> the rhetoric has been less about the rights of speakers than about the rights of languages to survive (Skutnabb-Kangas, 2000) and, in much of the linguistics literature, about the benefits of linguistic diversity to the linguistics enterprise.... The literature has generally underscored the cultural impoverishment of the affected population—notwithstanding issues arising from such a static notion of "culture"—but little has been said about whether it has all been losses and no gains among the relevant populations who have somehow adapted to their changing socio-economic ecology. (p. 20)

National Review columnist John J. Miller (2002), writing for the *Wall Street Journal*, hails "a trend which is arguably worth celebrating: a growing number of people are speaking a smaller number of languages, meaning that age-old obstacles to communication are collapsing. Surely this is a good thing." Miller points out that "geographical isolation is an incubator of linguistic diversity," and scoffs at the notion that "a cure for cancer will one day find expression in an Amazonian dialect."

Rights of any sort are by no means "self-evident" (as the US Declaration of Independence blithely asserts) and, abstracted from the messy particulars of law, politics, and culture, discussion of them easily degenerates into mere opinion. Absent any means of proof or disproof, the most we may hope for is to formulate a coherent account, preferably one not too far removed from our ordinary moral intuitions. For example, rights imply duties. As tempting as it might be to claim that everyone has the right to receive an education in their own language, it would be inconsistent to do so without assigning to someone (probably the state) the duty of providing this. Another important principle is that "ought" implies "can"—that is, it is nonsensical to say that one has a duty to do something that one is in fact unable to do. Thus, if providing everyone with an education in their own language proves impractical (perhaps because there are too many languages), then it cannot be regarded as a duty. Unfortunately for ethical consistency, in real life what is possible or practical turns out to be rather fluid, and is usually a question of balance against competing desiderata.

With this in mind, let us briefly consider some of the *types* of language rights that one hears periodically proposed:

(1) *The right to use any desired language without interference.* Hardly any regimes impose complete bans on minority languages. Not even Turkey at its most anti-Kurdish, or Indonesia at its most anti-Chinese,[4] attempted to regulate languages spoken in the home. (After all, it is far simpler to organize massacres.) The roster of violators would expand considerably if we consider language restrictions in mass media, school, prison, or the workplace, as Skutnabb-Kangas urges. The aforementioned Article III of the Genocide Convention (the portion voted down) would have banned "Prohibiting the use of the language of the group in daily intercourse or in the schools, or the printing and circulation of publications in the language of the group" (Skutnabb-Kangas, 2006, p. 278). While it is easy to sympathize with those punished for speaking their native language in grade school (reports of schoolchildren being made to wear condemnatory signs around their necks are curiously widespread), prison officials have a legitimate security concern in monitoring communications, and the question of workplace rights is sufficiently murky to warrant caution.

Another issue arises from government manipulation of language development. This may include bans on certain intellectual works, or the enforcement of standards of script, grammar, and so on. For example, China supports the Uighur language of Xinjiang to a certain extent, but exercises control over its development for fear that the natural affinities of its speakers lie with other parts of Central Asia rather than China (Dwyer, 2005; Rudelson, 1997; Zhou, 2003). At the same time, a number of Arab governments maintain (rival) Arabic language committees, ostensibly in charge of standardizing usage. It is difficult to distinguish which projects should be considered as furthering language rights—rallying the community, so to speak—and which should be considered as illegitimate restrictions thereof.

(2) *The right to language equality—that is, for no language to be elevated over the others, thereby according unfair privileges to its speakers.* On this reading, services such as court translation or bilingual education should not be regarded as added expenses caused by the recognition of special rights for linguistic minorities, but as basic necessities to ensure that linguistic minorities receive what the majority already receives. Strict egalitarianism being impossible to implement (one might as well complain about the injustice of poverty), the question then becomes one of what degree of inequality is permissible. Few would dispute the desirability of common languages of communication; less obvious are the issues of which languages should be chosen, and what roles they should play. Esperanto and certain other artificial languages have produced endless promotional literature nominating themselves on the grounds that they are relatively neutral and easy to learn.

One issue is this: In which social spheres should this linguistic egalitarianism apply? For example, is the government expected to ensure equal access to employment? This seems implausible, as many jobs require the ability to communicate with outsiders. May governments forbid naming practices associated with linguistic minorities? Skutnabb-Kangas and Bucak (in Skutnabb-Kangas and Phillipson, 1995, p. 347) complain that Turkey refuses to register Kurdish personal or family names, and has unilaterally changed Kurdish place names. Yet surely it is asking too much for nations with alphabetic scripts to accommodate, say, Chinese characters, or the symbol formerly used by the pop singer Prince.

Another issue is whether some languages may be more deserving of accommodation than others. Common considerations include the size (and political clout) of minority-language populations, their claim to autochthony or indigenousness, and the configuration of recognized territorial boundaries. On these points Skutnabb-Kangas is difficult to interpret. On the one hand she seems to recognize the salience of territorial boundaries to language rights (2006, pp. 284–285) and the impracticality of providing education in an unlimited number of languages. For example, she and Phillipson (1995, pp. 94–95) praise the generous, but not open-ended, bilingual education policies of Finland and Poland. In the same essay (1995) a distinction is made between "*necessary* linguistic rights" and "*enrichment-oriented* language rights," specifying that only the former qualify as "inalienable, fundamental *linguistic* HUMAN *rights*" (p. 102; see also Skutnabb-Kangas, 2000, pp. 497–498). These apparently include the right to mother-tongue education (for all children, not only those belonging to largish national minorities). In fact, "Assimilationist subtractive education is genocidal" (Skutnabb-Kangas, 2006, p. 277). However, we can very easily envision a school district, in North America for example, where students represent dozens if not hundreds of immigrant communities with differing mother tongues. Even if sufficient funds were made available, it is by no means clear whether qualified teachers would appear as well. On the other hand, Skutnabb-Kangas (2006) informs us that Papua New Guinea, despite its poverty, has achieved a model policy of mother-tongue education covering some 470 out of 850 of local languages (p. 281). To this Miller (2002) retorts: "That's an odd thing to say about a country where 99 per cent of the people don't own a phone."

(3) *The right of a language to receive whatever support it needs in order to flourish, whether in the form of legal protections or government subsidies.* Skutnabb-Kangas (2006) cites a draft of a (non-governmental, activist-driven) Universal Declaration of Linguistic Rights, which proposed that "All language communities are entitled to have at their disposal all the human and material resources necessary to ensure that their language is present to the extent they desire at all levels of education within their territory," demands which even she concedes to be "completely unrealistic" (p. 273). The fatal difficulty, of course, is the requirement's open-endedness: What if a language "needs" services that a government cannot afford, or which contradict basic human freedoms?

Elsewhere, however, Skutnabb-Kangas (2000) calls for societies to "remove price tags from people" and their basic necessities, such as education and culture (p. xi). Alas, expenses are not so easily wished away, nor can states avoid painful budgetary questions simply by asserting expenditures to be morally necessary or of long-term benefit. On the subject of whether states can afford mother-language education, she writes with literal boldness that "The question...should rather be: can states afford not to implement MLE?" (2009, p. 12) One is reminded of a popular Indian bumper sticker that proclaims (usually in gaudy reflective lettering), "No money, no honey."

It is notable that state protections tend to pit languages and peoples against one another. For example, Quebec's language laws protect the status of French by restricting the use of English, among other languages, while Singapore's Speak Mandarin Campaign is intended to discourage the use of other Sinolects. Also the interests of a language (insofar as a language can be said to *have* interests) will not necessarily coincide with those of its speakers, or even of the language community. Joseph (2006) describes how an Albanian minority group in Italy, which has successfully maintained its distinct identity since the beginning of the fifteenth century, protested against government proposals to instruct their children in Albanian. The reason, according to Joseph, was that the group did not wish to be associated with the newer influx of Albanian immigrants that began arriving around 1991 (pp. 59–60).

(4) *The right of a language or cultural community to self-determination, including some degree of territorial autonomy.* Although the linguistic aspect is often difficult to untangle from ethno-political struggles, for examples we might point to Flemish separatism in Belgium as well as the Afrikaner *Volkstaat* movement in South Africa.[5] Here a considerable disconnect can be observed between liberal theoretical approaches, which tend to support such movements (or at least selected ones) insofar as they are consistent with a wider political balance, and real-world politics, in which governments are reluctant to give up power, whether for good reasons or bad. In particular, countries with a tradition of strong central governance (for example, Turkey and China) tend to resist localizing forces regarded as centrifugal.

The reader may well wonder whether language rights are thought to be held by individuals, language communities, or the languages themselves. Skutnabb-Kangas (2000) sees linguistic human rights as collective in nature, enabling linguistic minorities and indigenous people "to exist and reproduce themselves as distinct groups" (pp. 497–498). On the subject of people (or whole communities) who voluntarily abandon their native languages—typically for the sake of social advancement and/or economic gain—she sees this as a kind of false consciousness, which she proposes to correct through education. On the one hand she condemns economic coercion as a violation of human rights; on the other, she doubts whether the sacrifice of one's language really carries the promised benefits.

It is tempting to view languages, like religions, almost as living things coexisting with human beings in a kind of symbiosis, with each depending on the other for survival. This vaguely Talmudic line of thought, though not without a certain poetic quality, would essentially have us assign philosophical personhood to memes, behavior patterns, and/or cultural constructs. Counterintuitive conclusions are then hard to avoid. "The Lousy Linguist" (a blogger named Chris) puts it this way: "Imagine I argued that French teens should all be experts in the music of Édith Piaf and Jacques Brel, and if they didn't [fulfill this criteria], it was the equivalent of musical genocide."[6]

The notion of collective rights is difficult to articulate with any consistency. Which groups, if any, deserve protection? If language, why not religion? (Indeed, some states *do* protect religion, or at least certain religions, which raises important questions of selection.) How can we distinguish between a bona fide identity group and a subculture? Do traditional groups with deep historic connections to certain places deserve more consideration than those of recent manufacture? The inherent murkiness of group identity cautions against the assignment of rights on this basis. After all, the human population is not neatly divided like puzzle pieces. Rather, we typically belong to more than one identity group—some overlapping, some of them spin-offs of others—and display a certain amount of calculation in our choice of which to emphasize, or disaffiliate from. Skutnabb-Kangas (1995, p. 361) would have the state recognize whatever self-ascription we may report, but this arguably violates the free-association rights of identity groups (which are often intent on protecting their privileged access to certain funds or privileges).

A distinction must be drawn between language death and linguistic genocide. The former is likely to come about as the result of impersonal market forces, outside cultural influences, and/or well-meaning social policies. The latter is a deliberate attempt to destroy a language, or at least to eliminate it from a certain territory. After all, crimes against humanity cannot very well take place without criminals. Skutnabb-Kangas (2002) writes that "Languages are today being killed at a much faster pace than ever before in human history" (p. 45). In an endnote to the above (n. 2) we read:

> Using "killed" rather than "dying" or "disappearing" highlights the fact that it is neither natural (in the sense as for biological organisms) nor agentless for languages to disappear. And if there are agents responsible for/and/or contributing to the killing, then the scope for action may also be broader than if one thinks one is fighting against a natural development. Processes leading to linguistic assimilation and therefore often languages disappearing include linguistic genocide. Besides, all the verbs, *kill, disappear, die*, are equally metaphorical.

Yet the "agents" of language death typically include numerous people who lack murderous intent, sometimes including even the language's own speakers. One may rage against the corrosive effects of national politics, or global capitalism, but to label them "genocidal" overlooks the fact that no social system can avoid such pressures.

The Kurdish matter

So far we have been referring to "Kurdish" and "the Kurds" as if the meanings of these terms were perfectly clear. In fact the people known as Kurds are divided by language and dialect, nationality and political allegiance, and sometimes religion.[7] Like other peoples, their group identity has formed primarily in contrast to perceived outsiders, in relationships of alliance or enmity that have evolved considerably over time.

This is not the place to give a detailed account of the history or distribution of the Kurdish people. Suffice it to say that there seem to be some 30 million Kurds in the world, and that their traditional homeland straddles the mountainous regions of eastern Turkey, northern Syria, northern Iraq, and north-western Iran. Perhaps half of them speak some form of "Kurdish," which is not a standardized language so much as a cluster of related languages and dialects belonging mainly to the north-western Iranian group (and thus quite unrelated to Turkish, which is not Indo-European at all, but Altaic). Kurmanji is the major form used in Turkey, Syria, and in diaspora communities, while Soranî predominates in Iraq and Iran. They are mutually incomprehensible. The main grounds for regarding them as dialects rather than independent languages are their common origin and their shared role as symbols of Kurdish ethnic identity (Kreyenbroeck, 1992, p. 71). Jwaideh writes that

> Despite the fact that the [Soranî] group differs linguistically and religiously from the Kurmanji-speaking group, they believe themselves to be Kurds, and their Kurmanji neighbors do not contest this belief. [I]t is the concept universally held among members of the group that matters. (Jwaideh, 2006, p. 290)

Slightly less related are Gurani and Zaza, whose speakers usually consider themselves—and have been considered by other Kurdish groups—to be Kurds:

> Both Zaza and Gurani are normally identified as Kurds and regard themselves as such. From a purely historical and linguistic perspective, this is probably incorrect, but such considerations seem insignificant in comparison with the feelings of the people concerned. (Kreyenbroeck, 1992, p. 70)

Today Zaza speakers disagree on the issue of Zaza nationalism vis-à-vis a broader Kurdish identity. Hassanpour (2000) proposes that the supposed diversity among Kurdish dialects is a forced and deliberate development aimed at weakening Kurdish nationalistic claims.

Somewhat further afield, speakers of Luri languages (from the southwestern Iranian group, forming a linguistic continuum between Kurdish and Persian) were once considered Kurds, though this is no longer the case. Apparently the folk category of "Kurd" has been assigned as much from considerations of geography, lifestyle, and social organization as linguistic criteria. Specifically, Kurds were thought to be tribespeople, in contrast to mere non-tribal peasantry (van Bruinessen, 2006, pp. 25–26; see also Jwaideh, 2006, p. 291). Urbanization (and the consequent loss of tribal identities and lifestyles), coupled with exposure to the official state languages of Turkish, Persian, and Arabic, have "increased awareness of common Kurdishness among people of different regional origins in the same country, but, on the other hand, caused a widening cultural gap between the Kurds of Turkey, Iraq, and Iran" (van Bruinessen, 2006, p. 26).

Since mountain ranges make good, defensible borders, the Kurds (like the Pashtun) have seen their homeland contested and divided by various neighboring polities. The Ottoman Empire fought Safavid Persia and Czarist Russia over this region. Although boundaries fluctuated, until the empire's collapse the Ottomans managed to hold most of Kurdistan, apart from the Iranian province of that name. The 1920 Treaty of Sèvres called for a referendum aimed at establishing post-Ottoman Kurdistan (borders undefined, but centered on Mosul) as a British protectorate, alongside "Wilsonian Armenia." Events on the ground prevented either state from coming into existence, and the 1923 Treaty of Lausanne recognized the Republic of Turkey in something close to its present borders, with Syria and Iraq under French and British control, respectively. Subsequent Kurdish history has consisted of repression by all four states, interspersed with periods of relative liberalism, along with regular rebellions by leaders who fit the description of common warlords or mafia dons.

In Iran, Kurdish rebellions occurred periodically throughout the Qajar and Pahlavi dynasties, culminating in the 1946 establishment of the (extremely localized) Republic of Mahabad, which fell that same year. Although Kurds took part in the 1979 revolution, their leaders had no influence over the formulation of the new constitution, which was imposed upon them by force of arms. The political oppression that followed continues to this day, and has included regular executions. At the same time, non-political and non-religious expressions of Kurdish culture, including use of the Kurdish language, are said to be freer than in Turkey: "Most of the freedoms Turkish Kurds have been eager to spill blood over have been available in Iran for years; Iran constitutionally recognizes the Kurds' language and minority ethnic status, and there is no taboo against speaking Kurdish in public" (Wood, 2006, para. 7). The Party of the Free Life of Kurdistan (PJAK) wages guerrilla war against the Islamic Republic, apparently with covert US support, and maintains close ties with the Kurdish Workers Party (PKK) in Turkish Kurdistan.

In Syria, the newly independent Arab state adopted a hostile policy toward expressions of Kurdish identity (Zubaida, 2006, p. 108), and this continued without interruption under Ba'athist rule. Human Rights Watch has documented systematic discrimination against the Kurdish minority in Syria, including the arbitrary denial of citizenship to generations of Syria-born Kurds (Human Rights Watch Report, October 1996).

In Iraq, Britain supported the recommendations of the League of Nations regarding the need to promote the use of Kurdish in schools, and in local administration. This necessitated agreement among Kurdish groups on a standard form of Kurdish. Soranî was chosen, perhaps for its prominence around Suleymaniya, the capital of the short-lived Kurdish kingdom of Shaykh Mahmud Barzinji (see Kreyenbroeck, 1992). No such provisions were mentioned in the Anglo-Iraqi Treaty of 1935, which established Iraq's independence, and the attitude of successive Iraqi governments toward Kurdish language and culture alternated between periods of promotion and repression. Such shifts in policy must be understood in the context of internal and external political maneuvering among Iraqi Arab factions. In 1975 the Shah of Iran, who until then had been supporting the Iraqi Kurds, signed the Treaty of Algiers with Iraq's new Ba'athist regime. From then on, Baghdad's stance toward the Kurds was consistently hostile, culminating in (demographic as well as linguistic) "Arabization" campaigns and the al-Anfar massacres of the 1980s.

During the Persian Gulf War, the United States balked at attempting to invade and occupy Iraq proper, but did establish northern and southern "no-fly zones" aimed at denying air support to Iraqi forces intent on suppressing (US-encouraged) Kurdish and Shi'i Arab revolts. The result for Iraqi Kurdistan has been the establishment of de facto independent states centered on Erbil and Suleymaniya—the former under the Kurdish Democratic Party (led by Massoud Barzani), the latter under the Patriotic Union of Kurdistan (led by Jalal Talabani). The 2003 US invasion resulted in a Shi'ite-dominated Iraq with a weak central government, and the recognition of three Kurdish provinces as a self-governing "super-region" with rights over its own natural resources. The government of the Kurdistan region—formed as the result of systematic cooperation between the two Kurdish political parties mentioned above—faces conflict on two borders: to the north, between the PKK and the Turkish military, and to the south, with other Iraqi ethnic groups over the future of oil-rich Kirkuk, which the Kurds would like to annex to their confederation. For all its difficulties, the Kurdistan region is widely acknowledged to be the safest and most prosperous part of Iraq, and retains its de facto independence. Most young people there have avoided learning Arabic.

In Turkey, while Kemalist leaders at Lausanne were willing to acknowledge the existence of Kurds as a distinct group, by 1924 they could tolerate nothing except Turkish nationalism, hence the abolition of all Kurdish religious organizations, publications, and schools (McDowall,

1996, p. 191). Kurdish-language schools closed in 1924, and have never since been reopened. From 1925 until the 1930s the Kurds revolted a number of times, but always unsuccessfully. In 1932 a law came into effect legalizing forced resettlements of Kurds, whom the state now referred to as "mountain Turks" (Kreyenbroeck, 1992, p. 73). Several brief periods of relative liberalism have been followed by clampdowns. In 1950 Turkey had its first free general elections. The constitution of 1961 allowed freedom of expression and the press, and there appears to have been a surge of interest among the Kurds in their own cultural identity, including a number of publications in Kurmanji; however, Kreyenbroek (1992) reports that "most of these were banned soon after they appeared" (p. 74). Robert Phillipson writes that

> the assimilationist language policies persisted. The same year as the drafting of the "Liberal Constitution," a new law passed stating that the "foreign" village, city, and region names were to be replaced with Turkish ones. Numerous radio stations were set up in Kurdish towns, which together with the powerful central transmitters provided round-the clock programs in Turkish. In 1964, the state established boarding schools that aimed to physically separate Kurdish children from their homes and provide them with a Turkish education from early ages. (Cemiloglu, 2009, p. 35)

The constitution of 1982 (Law 2932) identified Turkish as the mother tongue of all Turkish citizens, thereby ruling out the possibility of mother-tongue education in any other language. The public use of Kurdish was banned, as was the "weakening of national feelings" (Section 143 of the penal code), on pain of ten years' imprisonment (Skutnabb-Kangas and Bucak, as cited in Skutnabb-Kangas and Phillipson, 1995, pp. 347–348). These bans were assisted through extrajudicial intimidation, torture, and disappearances, and were only lifted in the 2000s under pressure from the European Union. As of 2010, the ruling AK Party (Adalet ve Kalkınma Partisi, Justice and Development Party), a moderate religious party, is maneuvering to revise the 1982 constitution with an eye to satisfying the European Union, and lifting secularist restrictions on Sunni religious practice.

Another key development has been the rise of the Kurdish Workers Party (PKK) under Abdullah Öcalan. Having begun life in the 1970s as a communist student group, the PKK during the 1980s received paramilitary assistance from Syria and the Soviet Union, an arrangement that lasted until the end of the Cold War. The 1990s saw a turn to suicide bombings, and the 1999 capture of Öcalan (who then rather conveniently renounced violence) had no discernible influence on his comrades.

In 2004, the first (private) Kurdish schools were opened, only to close within a few months due to lack of demand (Fraser, 2005; Schleifer, 2005). Whether this was due to lack of interest or a reluctance to pay school fees is unclear. In any case, the incident raises the question of how central a role the Kurdish language plays in the preservation of the Kurdish culture. In many cases, issues of language and literary expression turn out to be political tools for the prosecution of ethnic disputes, rather than preexisting, fully developed expressions of an already unified, cohesive people. The suspicion naturally arises that given better interethnic relations, Kurds as a group would show less interest in expressions of their distinct group identity. For the sake of comparison, Zubaida (2006) reports that in 1970, in the wake of a truce between Iraqi Kurds and Arabs, "an interesting phenomenon was developed which was to be repeated elsewhere. Kurdish intellectuals from various parts of Iraq, who until then *had been fairly well integrated* into Arab intellectual life, started to become Kurdicised" (p. 110; italics added).

Van Bruinessen reports on the situation of Zaza migrant workers from Turkey working in Germany who, in the course of pressing for mother-tongue education for their children, faced the interesting problem of having Kurmanji as the only alternative to Turkish. "Some, in fact, did, as generations before them always had, learn Kurmanji as the *lingua franca* in their region" (van Bruinessen, 2006, p. 40). During the late 1980s, the Kurdish Institute in Paris reversed its decision to use both Kurmanji and Zaza in its literary journal, as "certain influential Kurdish nationalists were fiercely critical of the effort to develop Zaza as a written language. The arguments they used, for the sake of unity and progress, and to prevent enemies from breaking up the nation, were not unlike those with which Turkey had opposed the use of Kurdish" (van Bruinessen, 2006, p. 41). Thus the first Zaza journal to be published in the late 1980s was emphatically non-Kurdish.

Mehmet Uzun was a Kurdish resident of Sweden (having lived in that country for 25 years), and a trilingual writer. A member of the World Journalists' Union, and a former member of the board of directors of the Swedish Writers' Union, Uzun

> believe[d] that the only way to advance the Kurdish language is to create a Kurdish literary language. And to be able to create a literary language, the writer argues that all the barriers obstructing the free

transfer of language and thoughts should be removed. (Gozke, 2002, para. 3)

The notion that a trilingual literary professional, whose life experiences had been formed by many different cultures, might contribute to the quest for a "pure" Kurdish worldview is a startling one. And if such purity is not supportable, then how well does the theory of linguicide stand when its basic premise is the sacredness of the mother tongue as a unique expresser of a unique culture that must not be obscured or absorbed by international "killer" languages?

The history of the conflict between the Kurdish inhabitants of the region and non-Kurdish governments indicate that much more is at stake than language or even culture. In fact, Kurdish consciousness owes less to hoary antiquity than to Ottoman-era identity politics:

In the region, before the end of the nineteenth century, the written languages used for administrative, religious and even literary issues were the dominant ones, namely, Persian, Turkish and Arabic, not Kurdish, despite some literary activity. The issue of the Kurdish language did become prominent, however, with the development of issues of identity, *themselves the product of internal affairs of the Ottoman empire.* (Kreyenbroeck, 1992, p. 69, italics added)

Officials overseeing nation-building projects did, of course, ignore and repress Kurdish identity and it is difficult to conceive of any circumstances under which, for example, Turkish nationalism would ever willingly recognize non-Turkish elements in the society. Nevertheless the violence and rhetoric associated with secession movements make it obvious that repression has been aimed primarily at averting secessionism rather than non-Turkish ethnic identity, the latter being intolerable to the government only due to its connection to secessionism.

Paradoxically, perhaps, the strongest incentive for Kurdish groups to rally in solidarity for language rights has, of course, been the oppression that they have historically felt:

The systematic denial of the Kurdish identity and the coercive methods employed by the Turkish government had a "backlash effect," resulting in the emergence of Kurdish opposition movements. I conclude that a state's vision of an ideal homogenous entity is the recipe for ethnic conflict in multicultural societies. (Cemiloglu, 2009, p. 74)

Thus, we have to ask: Would Kurdishness be presented as a unified identity if not for a common enemy, assimilationist Turkish policies? The example of Zaza nationalism suggests that the solidarity in question is still a rather weak and unsuccessful one. Vali (2006) notes that the fragmented Kurdish autonomy movements in the region are unable to create a unified "nationalist political culture" and have a "characteristically ambiguous identity, vacillating between nationalism and *ethnicism*, often changing form and direction in pursuit of parochial interests and 'immediate' political objectives" (p. 51).

Juan Cole, who calls Iraqi Kurdistan "the Taiwan of the Middle East" (for being an unrecognized *de facto* state), questions whether the territorial-based nationalism promoted by the Kurdish Democratic Party (KDP) is in the best interests of the Kurdish people:

> My own view is that the KDP's romantic territorial nationalism is anachronistic and inappropriate to a Gulf oil state, and likely to be undermined by economic developments. There is much more petroleum in the Shiite south than in Kurdistan, and pumping and refining it will require a big skilled labor force. Large numbers of Kurds will almost certainly be drawn down to Basra Province to work the Rumaila and other fields (and there is more black gold in Maysan and elsewhere not yet exploited). Just as Kurdish nationalism in Turkey was blunted by the way the Kurds were spread around the country as laborers in construction and light industry (and the way they came to vote just like their Turkish neighbors in Istanbul and elsewhere), Kurdish nationalism in Iraq may well be blunted by the enormous labor migration to the south that is likely to occur over the next two decades. (Cole, 2010, para. 9)

If Cole is right, then the economic future of Iraqi Kurds, like the Kurds of Turkey, lies outside the Kurdish-speaking regions. The resulting dilemma—economic prosperity, or cultural preservation?—resembles the broader one posed by globalization, e.g. in the form of emigration to Europe. Under these circumstances, it is difficult to imagine that Kurdish languages can avoid losing ground to various majority tongues. At the same time, surely such a world would not result in, to use Mufwene's phrase (2008, p. 223, cited above), "all . . . losses and no gains." Elsewhere Cole writes that

> I am not sympathetic to movements coming out of 19th century romantic nationalism, which tend to reify ethnicity in an almost

racist manner and posit essentialist connections between land and people (especially silly in those parts of the Middle East, such as Iraq, where a third to a half of people were pastoralists wandering around until the twentieth century). . . . Kurds would be wiser to forget about trying to control territory in the 19th century way and surrender to the messiness, ethnic mixing and multiple identities, and uprootedness of postmodern life. (Cole, 2009, para. 13)

Conclusion

Languages do not die, at least not without inverted commas. The charge of linguicide, however sincere, is an activist tactic. By invoking Nazism, protests against already serious trespasses may succeed in rallying even more support from the international community, and greater endurance from the resistance. Alternatively, they may be suspected of violating Godwin's law.[8] By constantly resorting to language like "kill" and "genocide," writers like Skutnabb-Kangas and Hassanpour reify languages into entities distinct from the very real human rights problems of their speakers. The logical ramifications of the ecolinguistic metaphor are troubling: the same egalitarian sentiments that decry the colonization of English[9] as well as various nationalistic chauvinisms inadvertently conceal the concept of linguistic purity, with its fearful parallel of cultural purity.

The Enlightenment principles of nationalism were reactions to feudal or imperial authoritarianism. Democratic or representational political paradigms, along with the emergence of the middle class(es), were rightly regarded as secessionist, revolutionary, and disintegrative in character. The rhetoric of linguicide seems to recapitulate this pattern, but with the ethnic group replacing the nation-state (which in turn substitutes for the former empires). One might object that what eco-linguists advocate is not the dissolution of the nation-state but simply its conformity to international law, and the observance of the human rights of its minorities. Unfortunately, while the sentiment sounds just, it may not with logical consistency be made by eco-linguists, given their theory's unavoidable ramifications of language purity and, most importantly, of an essential aspect of language that provides the (rather deterministic, in keeping with the biological metaphor) ability to view the world in a certain unique and non-negotiable manner (i.e. without external influences altering, diluting, and eventually destroying the uniqueness of the language). The researcher searching for a "pure" Kurdish language or culture swiftly falls into confusion. What exactly constitutes Kurdish? How can we decide which elements are internal, and which external?

The notion of linguistic imperialism erroneously assumes a passive role for the societies that use English. Yet weak mother-tongue speakers are not passive victims of language absorption by the *lingua franca*. They also alter it. Joseph (2006, p. 53) points out that until recently linguistic minorities usually found themselves in one of two possible situations: integration into the dominant social context in which they found themselves, thus spurring them to pursue competence in the official language or *lingua franca*; or else political autonomy/accession to a bordering state dominated by that minority. Today the role of a minority as an interest group of tax payers and citizens separates the issues of justice and utility or security, both dialectically and politically. In a modern democracy, a minority will be able to voice its concern over the state's language policy. National security concerns often bypass international democratic sentiment calling for freedom from governmental restrictions; however, anxiety over national cohesion usually does not, since the nation-state, though it may be one's home, no longer goes unquestioned. This calls to mind Joseph's (2006) comments on political philosopher Will Kymlicka, who writes that "justice is the goal of any rational society [;] [thus giving] equal language rights for all groups within a nation-state in every sphere" (as cited in Joseph, 2006, p. 56). As Joseph explains, although Kymlicka's view of a just society privileges linguistic and cultural diversity, he is nevertheless not oblivious to considerations of security and national unity. Kymlicka views language purification laws as harmless if their aim is merely to safeguard against national disintegration. However, it has been historically shown time and again that the aim of such types of purification is never merely that, but is invariably accompanied by authoritarian and racist ideologies and policies, as witnessed by Turkish policies toward minority languages.

As a Kurdish politician put it: "Being a nation or a minority are sociological facts. It is impossible to create or destroy these facts by laws" (Cemiloglu, 2009, p. 73). Nevertheless, notwithstanding linguistic or historical explorations into a group's purported origins and identity, the most important criterion for group definition, according to Jwaideh (2006), "is the concept universally held among members of the group" (p. 290). In the case of the Kurds, their intensity and focus changes depending on who the common enemy is. Skutnabb-Kangas' and Phillipson's approach fails exactly because of this principle. Languages cannot be considered in isolation as if they held some sort of *a priori* existence. Rather, as forms of human behavior, they are tools connected to histories of the people who use them, and exist in interaction with that people's environment, including other tribal or ethnic groups. Whatever human rights violations may be committed against individual speakers, the deterioration and eventual extinction of a language through neglect is not a crime. Neither the language nor its speakers are compromised by contact with the dominant language, or its economic and social utility. To call for the preservation of a language and its protection from extinction is to advocate linguistic purity. A dominant language not only makes a mother tongue obsolete through the former's economic advantage, but also through the latter's absorption into the former, with the dominant language's mannerisms, idioms, vocabulary, and phraseology infiltrating the mother tongue and eroding the mother tongue's originality and purity. Beyond that, the concept of linguistic purity is a fantasy. Such purity is never exhibited by any group apart from geographically isolated tribes.

In this light, one can imagine the intricacies of disputed group identity within a contested region—and the role of language in the affirmation of one or another identity—with particular political anxieties for all concerned. If the determination of identity is daunting in its simplest forms, it becomes impossible when attached to issues of self-determination, secession, autonomy, and minority rights. Kurdish language and identity came into existence as the result of complex historical processes. Whatever legal recognition they may ultimately achieve, they cannot actually become unified, living realities with an independent ontological existence. European pressures have provided a stage on which rather vague connections among the different Kurdish groups can present themselves as a single ethnicity petitioning for its rights. While the variations among the Kurdish groups are admitted, and considered as subcategories of the main Kurdish identity, this rhetoric of homogeneity has been in the service of political activism aimed at various desired purposes, whether in the form of all Kurdish groups' appeals for Western sympathy and support, the PKK's demands for autonomy in Turkey, or the diaspora's wish for minority rights abroad. The same rhetoric may be applied to the task of reconciliation with the dominant culture, as hinted by the following pronouncement from the Parliamentary Assembly for the Council of Europe:

> The Assembly *encourages Turkey*, as a Council of Europe member state, but also Iran, Iraq and Syria to acknowledge that the Kurdish language and culture *are part of the heritage of their own country*, that they are a richness that is worth being preserved and *not a threat to be combated* and asks them to take the necessary measures. (Russell-Johnston, 2006, para. 3, italics added)

In the above text, we have an example of well-meaning laws that fail to take into account the socio-political processes that have led to the Kurdish problem and also to past European policies not so dissimilar to those of Turkey today. The failure stems from the starting point, the assumption, of language being a non-negotiable human right whose secure status constitutes the starting point for any subsequent negotiations—an approach doomed to fail in the case of dominant nation-states that feel threatened by armed secessionist groups calling for language rights. The rights themselves are sacred, and the merits or demerits of the groups involved or the political forces associated with them debatable. Whence the predictable consequences:

> Drawing from the Treaty of Lausanne, the Turkish state still refuses to acknowledge the Kurds' minority status, which in turn prevents the Kurds from claiming special rights that the non-Muslim minorities are entitled to. The Turkish state remains reluctant to assign such a status to Kurds as the authorities assume this act would threaten the "unity and indivisibility" of the country. (Cemiloglu, 2009, p. 71)

However, solutions to problems of international and domestic disputes rarely, if ever, present themselves without negotiations and appeasement of fears, guarantees, and mutual shows of good faith. Cemiloglu goes on to acknowledge that "the European Union's recognition of Turkey as an official candidate has most definitely accelerated the pace of the reforms" (p. 71).

Nationalism, like globalism, poses an existential threat to any number of minority languages and cultures. To what extent actual human beings stand to suffer, or benefit, from such abstract changes is difficult to say. How important is it to maintain a particular language (or elements thereof)? Who decides? It is one thing to press for freedom of speech or association, but to the extent that protections for Kurdish languages translate into support for traditional Kurdish society raises questions as to the nature of Kurdish identity, the practicality and reasonableness of such efforts, and what is in the best interests of the peoples concerned. Moreover, languages and cultures are not only characterized by diversity, but evolve and adapt to changing circumstances, making the preservation of idealized, homogenous forms highly problematic. Indeed, our own globalized descendants will one day look back on all our cultures and identities as elements of some evolving fusion which they would hardly recognize. In this light, the survival of Kurdish, or English, or any other language is arguably less important than whether our children's children are happy.

Notes

1. See Skutnabb-Kangas and Phillipson (1999); Hassanpour, Skutnabb-Kangas, and Chyet (1996); and Phillipson and Skutnabb-Kangas (1989).
2. Skutnabb-Kangas' website also stresses her interest in "the links between biodiversity and linguistic diversity," a phrase which appears in even the shortest of her several biographical blurbs (alongside a note of her affiliation with an "ecological farm"). Retrieved 9 September 2009, from http://www. tove-skutnabb-kangas.org.
3. This use of "interlinguistics" was first proposed by Danish linguist Otto Jespersen in a 1931 article, "Interlinguistics" (available at http://interlinguistics. net/IL.html). For a survey of the field as it stands today, see the trilingual (Chinese/English/Esperanto) webpage of Liu Haitao at http://ling.cuc.edu.cn/ hliu/ikindex.htm. Interlinguistics in this sense is not to be confused with the concept of an "interlanguage" (or interim language) found in discussions of second-language learning, where it refers to linguistic systems of L2 speakers that approximate the target language. For an example of Esperanto propaganda calling for language diversity, see the "Prague Manifesto" of the Universala Esperanto-Asocio: http://uea.org/info/angle/an_manifesto_ prago.html (Skutnabb-Kangas and Phillipson have participated in Esperanto events.)
4. As elsewhere in South-East Asia, ethnic Chinese in Indonesia have long enjoyed a disproportionate share of the local economy, a fact that has inspired regular outbursts of resentment. In 1965 and 1966, the failure of an attempted communist coup resulted in a government massacre of several hundred thousand suspected communists, including an uncertain number of Chinese who were either deemed guilty by association with the People's Republic (perversely, in view of their well-established capitalist sympathies) or slain out of opportunism. Restrictions on Chinese-language publications were imposed in 1967, and lifted between 1999 and 2000. Indonesian Chinese were also encouraged to abandon obviously Chinese family names and religious practices (Friend, 2003, p. 170).
5. Since the 1980s Carel Boshoff and other activists, noting the gradual diminution of the status of Afrikaans and Afrikaners in South African society, have pressed for the establishment of a self-governing *Volkstaat* ("people's state," homeland). The 1994 post-apartheid constitution provides for this possibility; however, the African National Congress eventually ruled out support for such a project. At the time of writing some 2000 Afrikaners have moved to the settlements of Orania (in the Northern Cape) and Kleinfontein (near Pretoria), which they hope to establish as nuclei of a future *Volkstaat*.
6. See the comments section (fourth comment, dated 8 March 2010) of http:// thelousylinguist.blogspot.com/2010/03/linguistic-genocide.html.
7. The majority of Kurds are Sunni Muslims, and traditionally follow the Shafi'i school of Islamic jurisprudence (in contrast to the Hanafi school favored by Turkey's *Diyanet* or religious directorate). Kurds form an important minority

among the Alevi (a family of folk Shi'i groups concentrated in eastern Anatolia, many of which simultaneously identify with the Bektashi Sufi *tariqa*), and predominate among the Yazidi (who have a syncretic oral tradition and are based in Lalish, near Mosul, Iraqi Kurdistan) and Ahl-i-Haqq ("People of Truth," an Iranian *ghulat* sect also known as Yârsân or Kaka'i). Perhaps 2 million Iranian Kurds (mostly around Kermanshah) are mainstream Ithna 'ashariyyah ("Twelver") Shi'a.

8. "Godwin's law" (named for its creator, Mike Godwin) is an Internet meme associated with Usenet. Its original version observes that "As an online discussion grows longer, the probability of a comparison involving Hitler or the Nazis approaches one." Subsequent iterations transform Godwin's adage into a protest against gratuitous comparisons with Nazism, and the debate-ending *reductio ad Hitlerum* argument form.

9. The concept of linguicide is related to the view of English as a so-called "killer language" which displaces other mother-tongues in a colonialist, imperialist manner. The theory has been criticized (e.g. by Mufwene, n.d. and Joseph, 2006) on the grounds that it assumes a passive role on the part of non-English speaking societies, while overstating the linguistic goals of English-speaking governments (which have not always encouraged "native" populations to learn the language). Reliance on English as the global *lingua franca* has inspired fear of worldwide cultural unification, or "McDonaldization." Such Jeremiads unfairly reduce an entire culture to one of its economic aspects; and overlook the fact that no language ever remains unaltered or undifferentiated and without regional variations (see Kibbee, 2003).

References

"Askalon" (26 February 2010). 10 modern cases of linguistic genocide. Listverse. Retrieved 10 May 2010, from http://listverse.com/2010/02/10-modern-cases-of-linguistic-genocide.

Cemiloglu, D. (2009). Language policy and national unity: The dilemma of the Kurdish language in Turkey. A case study on language policy between 1924–2009. *College Undergraduate Research Electronic Journal*. Retrieved 15 February 2010, from http://repository.upenn.edu/cgi/viewcontent.cgi?article=1115& context=curej.

Cole, Juan R.I. (2009, July 1). Death toll in Kirkuk rises to 33, Growing Arab-Kurdish violence threatens stability of Iraq; 4 US troops killed. *Informed Comment*. Retrieved 2 November 2010 from http://www. juancole.com/2009/07/death-toll-in-kirkuk-rises-to-33.html.

Cole, Juan R.I. (2010, August 13). Kurdish general again insubordinate, angles for US to remain in Iraq. *Informed Comment*. Retrieved 2 November 2010 from http://www.juancole.com/2010/08/kurdish-general-again-insubordinate-angles-for-us-to-remain-in-iraq.html.

Dwyer, A. M. (2005). The Xinjiang conflict: Uyghur identity, policy, and political discourse. *Policy Studies, 15*. Washington, DC: East-West Center.

Fraser, S. (1 August 2005). Turkey's Kurdish language schools to shut down over lack of interest, bureaucratic Hurdles. *Associated Press*. Retrieved 1 December 2009 from http://www.encyclopedia.com/doc/1P1-111714977.html.

Friend, T. (2003). *Indonesian destinies*. Cambridge, MA and London: Harvard University Press.

Gozke, O. (22 April 2002). Keeping Kurdish language alive. *Bianet News Center*. Retrieved 1 December 2009, from http://bianet.org/english/women/9425-keeping-kurdish-language-alive.

Hassanpour, A. (2000). The politics of a-political linguistics: Linguists and linguicide. In R. Phillipson (ed.), *Rights to language, equity, power, and education, celebrating the 60th birthday of Tove Skutnabb-Kangas* (pp. 33–39). New Jersey: Lawrence Erlbaum Associates.

Hassanpour, A., Skutnabb-Kangas, T., and Chyet, M. (1996). The non-education of Kurds: A Kurdish perspective. *International Review of Education, 42*(4), 367–379.

Human Rights Watch Report (1996, October). *Syria: The silenced Kurds, 8* (4). Retrieved 1 December 2009, from http://www.hrw.org/en/reports/1996/10/03/syria-silenced-kurds.htm.

Joseph, J. E. (2006). *Language and politics*. Edinburgh: Edinburgh University Press.

Jwaideh, W. (2006). *Kurdish national movement: Its origins and development*. Syracuse, NY: Syracuse University Press.

Kibbee, D. A. (2003). Language policy and linguistic theory. In J. Maurais and M. A. Morris (eds.), *Languages in a globalizing world* (pp. 47–57). Cambridge: Cambridge University Press.

Kreyenbroeck, P. G. (1992). On the Kurdish language. In P. G. Kreyenbroeck and S. Sperl (eds.), *The Kurds: A contemporary review* (pp. 68–83). London: Routledge.

McDowall, D. (1996). *A modern history of the Kurds*. London: I. B. Tauris & Co. Ltd.

Miller, J. J. (8 March 2002). How do you say "extinct"? Languages die; The United Nations is upset about this. *Wall Street Journal*, W13. Retrieved 1 December 2009, from http://www.heymiller.com/2010/08/language-extinction.

Mufwene, S. S. (2008). Globalization and the myth of killer languages. Retrieved 15 February 2009, from http://humanities.uchicago.edu/faculty/mufwene/publications/globalization-killerLanguages.pdf.

Phillipson, R., and Skutnabb-Kangas, T. (1989). Linguistic human rights and the Kurdish language. *Human rights in Kurdistan. Documentation of the international conference on human rights in Kurdistan* (pp. 60–68). Bremen: The Initiative for Human Rights in Kurdistan.

Phillipson, R., and Skutnabb-Kangas, T. (eds.) (1994). *Linguistic human rights overcoming linguistic discrimination*. Berlin: de Gruyter Mouton.

Rudelson, J. J. (1997). *Oasis identities: Uyghur nationalism along China's Silk Road*. New York: Columbia University Press.

Russell-Johnston, D. (7 July 2006). The cultural situation of the Kurds: A report submitted to the European Parliamentary Assembly, Committee on Culture, Science and Education. United Kingdom Alliance of Liberals and Democrats for Europe, Doc. 11006.

Schleifer, Y. (5 October 2005). Opened with a flourish, Turkey's Kurdish-language schools fold. *Christian Science monitor*. Retrieved 15 February 2009, from http://www.csmonitor/2005/1005/p07s02-woeu.html.

Skutnabb-Kangas, T. (2000). *Linguistic genocide in education—or worldwide diversity and human rights?* London, UK: Lawrence Erlbaum Associates.

Skutnabb-Kangas, T. (2002). When languages disappear, are bilingual education or human rights a cure? Two scenarios. In L. Wei, J. Dewaele, and A. Hausen (eds.), *Opportunities and challenges of bilingualism* (pp. 45–68). Berlin: Walter de Gruyter.

Skutnabb-Kangas, T. (2006). *Tove Skutnabb-Kangas speaking at UC Berkeley.* Retrieved 17 March 2009, from http://www.youtube.com/watch?v= SugkhNnRKGg.

Skutnabb-Kangas, T. (19–21 January 2009). The stakes: Linguistic diversity, linguistic human rights and mother tongue based multi-lingual education or linguistic genocide, crimes against humanity and an even faster destruction of biodiversity and our planet. Keynote presentation at Bamako International Forum on Multilingualism, Bamako, Mali. Retrieved 7 April 2009, from http://www.tove-skutnabb-kangas.org/pdf/Tove_Skutnabb_Kangas_Keynote_ presentation_at_Bamako_International_Forum_on_Multilingualism_Bamako_ Mali_19_21_Jan_2009.pdf.

Skutnabb-Kangas, T., and Bucak, S. (1995). Killing a mother tongue – How the Kurds are deprived of linguistic human rights. In T. Skutnabb-Kangas and R. Phillipson (eds.), *Linguistic human rights: overcoming linguistic discrimination* (pp. 347–370). Berlin: Mouton de Gruyter.

Skutnabb-Kangas, T., and Phillipson, R. (1999). Linguistic genocide and human rights: Kurdish considerations. In P. Sundqvist (ed.), *The Kurds. Perspectives on a unique culture* (pp. 25–48). Helsinki: Suomen Rauhanliitto YK-Yhdistys.

Vali, A. (2006). The Kurds and their "others": Fragmented identity and fragmented politics. In F. A. Jabar and H. Dawod (eds.), *The Kurds: Nationalism and politics* (pp. 49–78). London, Berkeley, Beirut: Saqi.

Van Bruinessen, M. (2006). Kurdish paths to nation. In F. A. Jabar and H. Dawod (eds.), *The Kurds: Nationalism and politics* (pp. 21–48). London, Berkeley, Beirut: Saqi.

Wood, G. (12 June 2006). Iran bombs Iran: Meet the Kurdish guerrillas who want to topple the Tehran regime. *Slate.* Retrieved 15 February 2009, from http:// www.slate.com/id/2143492/?nav= fo.

Zhou, M. (2003). *Multilingualism in China: The politics of writing reforms for minority languages 1949–2002.* Berlin and New York: De Gruyter Mouton.

Zubaida, S. (2006). Religion and ethnicity as politicized boundaries. In F. A. Jabar and H. Dawod (eds.), *The Kurds: Nationalism and politics* (pp. 93–102). London, Berkeley, Beirut: Saqi.

Index